BALTIC LINGUISTICS

BALTIC LINGUISTICS

Edited by
THOMAS F. MAGNER
and
WILLIAM R. SCHMALSTIEG

THE PENNSYLVANIA STATE
UNIVERSITY PRESS
University Park and London

Copyright ©1970 by The Pennsylvania State University

All rights reserved
Library of Congress Catalog Card Number 71-79842
Standard Book Number 271-00094-5
Printed in the United States of America

To
ALFRED SENN
teacher, scholar, colleague

CONTENTS

PREFACE

In the fall of 1967 we conceived the idea of holding a symposium devoted to scholarly papers on subjects in the field of Baltic linguistics. The idea of a symposium or conference is not in itself novel or exciting, but it was with some trepidation that we approached the planning of this symposium, not knowing how many of the few Balticists in America would travel to central Pennsylvania to attend one. The meeting was held on April 5-6, 1968, and to our considerable delight a surprisingly large number of specialists and interested scholars participated in what is probably the first such conference held outside the Baltic republics.

This volume contains all the papers then presented with the exception of two. In addition, we have included papers by three scholars not able to be present: "On the Balto-Slavic Dative Plural and Dual," by J. Kazlauskas, Dean of the Faculty of Humanities at the University of Vilnius in the Soviet Socialist Republic of Lithuania, "Accent in the Lithuanian Noun Declension," by Bill J. Darden of the University of Colorado, and "Stress Placement and Accent Classes in the Lithuanian Noun," by David Robinson of Ohio State University. The paper, "Concerning the Relationships of the Prussian Language with Congeners," by the great Balticist, Jānis Endzelīns (1873–1961) was included because of its relevance; the paper, "The Old Prussian Verb," is by William R. Schmalstieg who, in his role as director, was obviously present at the conference but did not complete this work until later. One paper, "Old Prussian Adverbs in -n," by Olga C. Shopay appeared in the Fall 1967 issue of the *Slavic and East European Journal* and it is here reprinted with the permission of the University of Wisconsin Press; Miss Shopay completed her work for this paper while a graduate student at The Pennsylvania State University. The papers are arranged alphabetically according to the name of the author; arrangement by language category was considered, but it was felt that such groupings would be quite disproportionate and not particularly useful.

We would like to express our appreciation to the Department of Slavic

Languages and to the Slavic and Soviet Language and Area Center, both of The Pennsylvania State University, for generous aid and encouragement in setting up the Baltic conference; it is a tribute to the farsightedness and flexibility of our colleagues in the "Slavic" organizations that they recognized the value of Baltic linguistics both for its own sake and for its meaning for Slavic studies.

We are happy to dedicate this volume to Professor Alfred Senn, the Nestor of Baltic studies in the United States. These papers are a living testimonial to the scholarship and teaching of Professor Senn who will celebrate his 70th birthday this year.

T. F. Magner

W. R. Schmalstieg

THE DATIVE OF SUBORDINATION IN BALTIC AND SLAVIC

HENNING ANDERSEN

The nature, origin, and development of the Baltic and Slavic dative absolute constructions are problems which have long attracted the interest of students of Baltic and Slavic linguistics, but, as recent publications show, they are still far from being settled. With respect to the Slavic dative absolute, some scholars boldly maintain that it is a syntactic calque from the Greek, entirely bookish in its origin. But even if it is granted that these investigators are wrong, and that the dative absolute was as much an integral part of the syntax of Common Slavic as it must have been of Common Baltic, the question of how these constructions arose is still controversial. Are the Baltic and Slavic datives absolute dialectal variants, developed from a Proto-Indo-European absolute construction (one can call this the monogenetic view) or did absolute constructions develop independently in the various Indo-European dialects? (This is the polygenetic view.) Regardless of which of these possibilities one chooses, it is still possible to attach particular importance to the fact that Baltic, Slavic, and Germanic, unlike other Indo-European language families, all use the dative in their absolute constructions. Or again, one may prefer to consider this a mere coincidence. And it must be recognized that these and other issues concerning primarily the question of when the dative absolute arose are distinct from the problem of how it arose, that is, by what syntactic changes it came into being.

While the issues relating to the origin of the dative absolute have been much discussed, the question of the development of the dative absolute, i.e., its attested decline and gradual replacement with equivalent syntactic constructions, has received scant attention. Even the crucial questions concerning the nature of the dative absolute, its relation to other constructions to which it was opposed, and the motivation for the choice of case, have barely been explored. It is the last-mentioned question which is the subject of the following discussion. First, however, I should like to say a few words about the origin of the dative absolute. This seems necessary for two reasons. In the first place, it is important to understand the relation of this question to the other problems concerning the dative absolute. In the second place, the decision to discuss the Slavic dative absolute on equal terms with that of Baltic needs to be justified.

The arguments that can be advanced in favor of the view that the Slavic dative absolute is an inherited rather than a borrowed syntactic construction are not new, though in recent years the substance of one of them has changed significantly. Two of the traditional arguments concern the dative absolute as attested in Old Church Slavonic.

The first of these argues that since the Slavic absolute construction uses the dative case, it cannot be a calque from Greek, which has a genitive absolute. This is not a strong argument, for it assumes that the Old Church Slavonic and the Greek case systems were commensurate so that a syntactic calque from Greek necessarily would employ the "same" case in Old Church Slavonic. There is no basis for this assumption.[1]

The second argument in favor of the indigenous origin of the Old Church Slavonic dative absolute is based on the fact that it is relatively independent of the corresponding Greek construction and translates not only the Greek genitive absolute, but a variety of constructions like the *en tǭ* plus infinitive, the accusative plus infinitive, appositive participial phrases, subordinate temporal clauses, and even coordinate sentences.[2] This point has often been emphasized and has so far not been invalidated. In a recent study, the Czech scholar Ladislav Nečásek has investigated the relation between the dative absolute in the Old Church Slavonic gospel texts and the Greek constructions they translate with the evident aim of showing that the dative absolute was not an indigenous construction, but was introduced into Old Church Slavonic thanks to the "will power and authority of the personalities of the Greeks Constantine and Methodius."[3] Nečásek's study does not accomplish this aim, however, for, as he is forced to concede, the problem of the native or foreign origin of the Slavic dative absolute cannot be solved on the basis of the Gospel translations. And even if it could be made to look likely that the datives absolute of the Gospel texts were 100 percent dependent on the genitives absolute of the Greek original, it would still be highly implausible, and of course impossible to demonstrate, that the attested productivity of the dative absolute was due simply to pious respect for SS. Cyril and Methodius.

The use of the dative absolute in medieval Slavic texts, both translated and original, is not the only evidence that this construction is an inherited feature of Slavic syntax. Examples of participial constructions reminiscent of datives absolute have long been known from various contemporary Slavic dialects, specifically Bulgarian and Ukrainian dialects. Many scholars have been skeptical toward these examples, and perhaps justly so.[4] But in recent years indisputable examples of dative plus gerund constructions have been recorded in various East Slavic dialects. If sentences like *stojačy jamu u vadz'e p'jauka up'ilas'a u naɣu* 'while he was standing in the water a leech attached itself to his leg' or *d'on p'at' prašlo jamu rad'iušys'* 'five days went by after he had been born,' can be produced by dialect speakers today, we have no right to set aside medieval evidence.[5] Indeed, if we did not have the medieval attestation of the dative absolute, the existence of this dative plus gerund construction would by itself suggest that Slavic at one time had constructions analogous to the absolute constructions of Baltic, Greek, Latin, etc.

The assumption that the Old Church Slavonic dative absolute is a syntactic calque from the Greek introduces an unwarranted complication into the historical syntax of the Slavic languages. On the one hand, it leaves the South Russian dative plus gerund without historical antecedent. And on the other hand, it makes the rest of early Slavic participial syntax hard to reconcile with the comparative evidence of the other Indo-European languages. A comparative analysis of the participial syntax of the earliest Indo-European languages shows, as Meillet and Vendryes point out, that "l'usage des constructions absolues remonte à l'indo-européen."[6] It is fundamentally wrong to disregard this fact in discussing the Slavic dative absolute.

The comparative evidence and the evidence of the modern dialects permit us to conclude that some time in the past Slavic had an absolute construction which used the dative. On this background it seems absurd to hold Greek influence responsible for the productivity of the dative absolute which is attested in the medieval Slavic literature.

In reconstructing absolute constructions as part of Proto-Indo-European syntax, one has to abstract from two sets of facts concerning the attested languages.

In the first place, it is clear that the development of participial systems belongs to the history of the individual Indo-European dialects.[7] But it is essential to recognize that the development of these morphological cate-

gories is distinct from the existence of a syntactic pattern, a set of transformational rules which produced absolute constructions, i.e., sentences
containing a participle instead of a finite verb form. The fact that these
transformational rules in the various languages where they are found
operate with different participles is a function of the diversity of the
participial systems and has no direct bearing on the reconstruction of the
Proto-Indo-European absolute construction. This latter problem in comparative Indo-European syntax must be solved on the basis of a comparison
of syntactic rules, not of systems of participles.

The second set of facts that has to be abstracted from is the use of different cases in the absolute constructions of the different languages, the
ablative in Latin, the genitive in Greek, the locative and genitive in
Sanskrit, the dative in Baltic, Slavic, and Germanic. This diversity has by
many scholars been taken as evidence that absolute constructions arose
independently in the various Indo-European languages, but this inference
is unwarranted.[8] It is perfectly possible to suppose that case usage in the
absolute construction can have changed in the individual Indo-European
dialects as their respective case systems evolved. Indeed, one must allow
for this possibility if one assumes that a case system is not a mere inventory
of forms, but a coherent system of grammatical meanings. What this means
is that although there are sufficient grounds for positing for Proto-Indo-
European a set of syntactic rules which produced absolute constructions,
we should not try to determine which case was originally used in these
constructions.

It is clear, then, that the question of the nature of the Baltic and Slavic
dative absolute can be dissociated into two distinct problems. The first is
that of the form of the syntactic rules which produced the absolute constructions. This is first of all a synchronic problem pertaining to the
earliest attested stages of Baltic (Old Lithuanian) and Slavic (Old Church
Slavonic and Old Russian), but it has a diachronic dimension in the question of how these rules are related to the Indo-European prototype. The
second problem is purely synchronic: what is the motivation for the choice
of the dative in the absolute constructions? How is the case selection consistent with the meaning of the dative case in these languages and the
function of the absolute construction?

I should like to suggest an answer to these questions.

In a recent paper I have shown that in Russian the use of the dative with
a number of verbs and adjectives that are said to govern the dative is
determined by an abstract feature of meaning that these lexical items have
in common.[9] The semantic feature in question is very general and is found

also in syntactic constructions in which the dative is used without it being possible to say that it is "governed" by some specific word. What these lexical items and constructions have in common is that they denote what I shall call implicating relations. This special use of the dative is not limited to Russian, but is also found in other Slavic languages, including Old Church Slavonic. It seems to be characteristic of the Baltic languages as well.[10]

We have to distinguish two kinds of implicating relations, symmetrical relations and transitive relations. Let us begin by considering some verbs.

If one contrasts a simple transitive verb like *myléti* 'love' with a verb like *prieštaráuti* 'contradict,' which governs the dative, it is easy to see that while each of these verbs denotes a relation between two entities represented by substantives, the relations are logically very different. A sentence like *Jonas myli Mariją* 'John loves Mary' speaks only of John's love, but says nothing about Mary's feelings. By contrast, the meaning of a verb like *prieštaráuti* 'contradict' is necessarily relevant both to the subject and to the dative object. If it is true that *Pavyzdžiai prieštarauja mano taisyklėms* 'The examples contradict my rules,' then it is true also that *Mano taisyklės prieštarauja pavyzdžiams*. This is because the notion of contradiction involves a symmetrical relation between the participants of the message. Love, on the other hand, involves a nonsymmetrical relation: the fact that John loves Mary does not imply that his love is requited.

There are several verbs whose meaning involves symmetrical relations which govern the dative in Lithuanian: *prilygti* 'equal, be equal to,' *atitikti* 'correspond to, agree with.' From Russian one can mention, besides *protivorečit'* 'contradict,' *ravnjat'sja* 'equal,' *sootvetstvovat'* 'correspond to,' *soputstvovat'* 'be concomitant with.'

The other kind of implicating relations we have to consider are logically transitive relations.[11] These are relations of the type that if the relation holds between two terms *a* and *b* and between *b* and a third term *c*, then it holds also between *a* and *c*. The verb *prilygti* 'be equal to,' which denotes a symmetrical relation, can also be used to exemplify transitive relations, for if $a = b$ and $b = c$, it is necessarily the case that $a = c$. As a verb denoting an asymmetrical transitive relation, one can mention *priklausyti* 'belong to': from the sentences *Laukas priklauso ūkiui* 'the field belongs to the farm' and *Ūkis priklauso valstybei* 'the farm belongs to the state,' we may infer that *Laukas priklauso valstybei*.

Russian verbs denoting transitive relations are *prinadležat'* 'belong to,' *predšestvovat'* 'precede,' and, in its figurative meaning, *sledovat'* 'follow, conform to.'

Besides the verbs we have mentioned so far, there are transitive verbs which denote, not the existence of an implicating relation, but the establishment of such a relation between the accusative object and the dative object. Thus, for instance, the causative verb *prilyginti* 'to liken to' posits the symmetrical relation of similarity between the two substantives of a verb phrase. And in the sentence *Liublino unija pajungė Lietuvą Lenkijai* 'the Lublin Union subordinated Lithuania to Poland,' the verb *pajungti* establishes the transitive relation of subordination between the two countries.

Other verbs that denote the establishment of implicating relations are *priešpastatyti* 'contrast to' and *pasipriešinti* 'oppose, resist.' From Russian one can mention *upodobit'* 'liken to,' *podčinjat'* 'subordinate to,' *protivopostavljat'* 'contrast with,' *podvergat'* 'subject to,' *predpočitat'* 'prefer to.'

Finally, a few adjectives can be mentioned, which are constructed with the dative and denote implicating relations: *artimas* 'near,' *lygus* 'equal to,' *priešingas* 'contrary to,' *proporcionalus* 'proportional to'; and from Russian, *ravnyj* 'equal to,' *podobnyj* 'similar to,' *protivopoložnyj* 'opposite to,' *proporcional'nyj* 'proportional to,' *parallel'nyj* 'parallel to.'

The last few examples are significant, for they show that the use of the dative with these categories of words denoting implicating relations is not a dead syntactic convention, but is synchronically motivated. The existence of neologisms among these words, whether loan words (like *proporcionalus*) or loan translations (like *priešpastatyti,* which translates the Russian *protivopostavljat'*) permits us to infer that if the meaning of a new lexical item is interpreted as denoting an implicating relation, it can be constructed with the dative.

It has to be mentioned that although the use of the dative with lexical items denoting implicating relations is very similar in the Baltic and Slavic languages, a comparison between any two of these languages will reveal a number of words which are constructed differently in spite of their identical meaning. To take an example, the Russian adjective *podobnyj* 'similar to' governs the dative. The etymologically identical Polish adjective *podobny*, on the other hand, is constructed analytically with the preposition *do* 'to.' Similarly in Lithuanian, the synonymous adjective *panašus* is constructed analytically with the preposition *į*. The Latvian synonym, *līdzigs*, again, governs the dative.

There is reason to believe that most such contrasts of synthetic and analytic constructions are products of a general tendency toward analytic expression of syntactic relations. There are a number of examples of words being constructed with the dative in Old Lithuanian which require a preposition in Contemporary Lithuanian. Thus Fraenkel cites from Daukša *"sudêrinus mumus Diewą Tewą"* 'having conciliated God Our Father with us' where today one would say *su mumis* rather than *mums.*[12]

In order to interpret the use of the dative with these lexical items, one has to consider not only *their* meaning, but also the meaning of the dative case. I think we can assume for early Slavic and for Baltic the general meaning that Roman Jakobson has defined for the dative of Contemporary Standard Russian.[13] According to Jakobson, the dative and the accusative are defined as directional cases. The use of a directional case to mark the second term of an implicating relation seems well motivated, for whether the relation is transitive or symmetrical, the need to single out one of the terms as subject imposes a hierarchy on the terms of the relation. The difference between the dative and the accusative Jakobson defines with reference to their relative prominence in the sentence. The dative is defined as marginal, for it marks an entity as not directly affected by the action of the verb, as existing independently of the event expressed by the verb. This is evidently applicable to the second term of an implicating relation.

If the choice of the dative with the lexical items we have looked at is determined by the semantic feature that they share, by the fact that they denote implicating relations, it seems likely that it is this same semantic feature that explains the use of the dative in the Baltic and Slavic absolute constructions.

Let us briefly look at the meaning of the dative absolute.[14]

The dative absolute can be equivalent to an adverb of time. As such it presents an event either as simultaneous with the event of the main clause or as anterior to it. Both simultaneity and anteriority are transitive relations.

The dative absolute can state the cause of the event narrated in the main clause. Causality is a transitive relation.

The dative absolute can be equivalent to a concessive clause, i.e., it can state a cause that has failed to affect the event narrated in the main clause. Causality—even when thwarted—is a transitive relation.

The dative absolute can state a condition on which the event of the main clause is contingent. The conditional is yet another modality of the cause–effect relation.

Finally, the dative absolute can state a circumstance which accompanies the event narrated in the main clause. It seems that accompanying circumstances have to be concurrent with the events they accompany. That is to say, they involve a transitive relation.

All these different meanings of the dative absolute are contextual meanings, meanings that are not part of the construction as such, but derive from the content of the message in which it occurs. They are all consistent with the invariant function of the absolute construction, which is to present a narrated event as subordinate to another narrated event. And, not surprisingly, they all involve the same kind of implicating relation as subordination: subordination is a transitive relation.

Since the absolute construction presents a subordinate narrated event which is not directly affected by the narrated event of the main clause, the use of the dative to mark this subordinate narrated event is fully consistent with the general meaning of the dative. It seems not inappropriate to call this special use of the dative case the dative of subordination.

Harvard University

NOTES

1. R. Růžička insists correctly that there is no identity between the Greek genitive and that of Old Church Slavonic except in name; cf. his "Struktur und Echtheit des altslavischen dativus absolutus," *Zeitschrift für Slavistik* 6 (1961), p. 594.
2. Cf. Ján Stanislav, "Datív absolutný v starej cirkevnej slovančine," *Byzantino-slavica* 5 (1933-34), p. 29 ff.
3. "Staroslověnské dativní vazby participiální a jejích předlohy v řeckém textu evangelií," *Slavia* 26 (1957), p. 30.
4. Cf. Stanislav, *op. cit.*, p. 40 ff.
5. These and other examples can be found in V. I. Borkovskij, P. S. Kuznecov, *Istoričeskaja grammatika russkogo jazyka*[2] (Moscow, 1965), p. 486 f. Cf. also O. S. Mel'nyčuk, *Rozvytok struktury slov'jans'koho rečennja* (Kiev, 1966), p. 183.
6. A. Meillet, J. Vendryes, *Traité de grammaire comparée des langues classiques*[2] (Paris, 1953), p. 617.
7. Cf. A. Meillet, *Introduction à l'étude comparative des langues indo-européennes* (University, Alabama, 1964), p. 277.
8. The polygenetic view of the origin of the Indo-European absolute constructions is closely linked with the theory that absolute constructions arose through mis-interpretation of appositive participial phrases. This theory was originally pro-posed in slightly different versions by Potebnja (*Iz zapisok po russkoj gramma-tike*, 2 [Xar'kov, 1888], pp. 340–342), Delbrück (*Grundriss der vergleichenden Grammatik der indogermanischen Sprachen*, 4 [Strassburg, 1897], p. 493 f.), and Brugmann (*Griechische Grammatik* [Munich, 1900], p. 523). Since it is still being repeated in textbooks and monographs as *the* explanation of the origin of the absolute constructions, it seems appropriate to insist that this theory explains nothing. It does not explain how the supposed misinterpretation was possible, for the theory assumes that absolute constructions were ungrammatical when they arose. It does not explain the choice of case for the absolute constructions.

And it does not explain why absolute constructions, when they were lost, were not continually renewed in the languages which preserved participial constructions. Since this theory contributes nothing to our knowledge, it can safely be abandoned.

9. The paper was read before the annual meeting of the Modern Language Association in Chicago, Dec. 28, 1967. I am grateful to Professor Dean S. Worth for his valuable comments at that time.

10. In the following, I shall take my examples only from Lithuanian and Russian. Dative government in Old Church Slavonic and Old Russian has been surveyed by A. B. Pravdin ("Datel'nyj priglagol'nyj v staroslavjanskom i drevnerusskom jazykax," *Učenye zapiski Instituta slavjanovedenija* 13 [1956], pp. 3–120) and R. Mrazek ("Datel'nyj padež v staroslavjanskom jazyke," in *Issledovanija po sintaksisu staroslavjanskogo jazyka* [Prague, 1963], pp. 225–261].

11. It is possible that some of the verbs defined here as denoting transitive relations should be viewed rather as denoting asymmetrical relations. To decide this question, all the syntactic properties of the verbs in question have to be considered. I hope to return to this question elsewhere.

12. For further examples, see E. Fraenkel, "Syntax der litauischen Kasus," *Tauta ir Žodis* 5 (1928), p. 45.

13. See his "Beitrag zur allgemeinen Kasuslehre," *Travaux du cercle linguistique de Prague* 6 (1936), p. 264 f.

14. For a survey of the meanings of the dative absolute in Lithuanian, see V. Ambrazas, "Absoliutinis naudininkas 16–17 a. lietuvių kalbos paminkluose," *Lietuvių kalbotyros klausimai* 5 (1962), pp. 56–80. The Slavic dative absolute is discussed by J. Stanislav, *op. cit.*, pp. 43–85.

THE VOCALIC PHONEMES OF THE OLD PRUSSIAN ELBING VOCABULARY

MICHAEL L. BURWELL

From a phonological standpoint the Old Prussian (OP) Elbing Vocabulary (EV) is an extremely enigmatic document, both in itself and in relation to the other Old Prussian monuments.[1] Since this text is representative of a language long extinct (ca. 1700), heavy reliance must be made on the two extant Baltic languages for determining the sound value of the Old Prussian orthography. While this is methodologically correct, it is sometimes as hazardous as reconstructing forms for Proto-Indo-European. For many words there are, of course, no apparent cognates, even outside the Baltic sphere. And even where cognates are available for scrutiny, there is no definite assurance that Old Prussian has not deviated from this or that expected form, particularly with respect to vowel quantity and rounding. This situation is further complicated by the fact that apparently all the Old Prussian monuments were compiled by Germans and not native speakers of Old Prussian, thereby increasing the potential for gross spelling misinterpretations. Moreover, when one compares the Elbing Vocabulary to the Vocabulary of Simon Grunau and to the three catechisms, contradictions arise which cause one to wonder whether any sense at all can be made out of its orthography.

Since the middle of the last century several concerted attempts have been made to uncover the Elbing Vocabulary vowel system. The most notable researchers on this problem have been Berneker, Trautmann, Endzelīns, and, more recently, Kazlauskas and Mažiulis. Although the latter two are structurally oriented, their approaches to this task have had much in common with those of their predecessors. In the first place, all of them have relied quite heavily on the orthography as representing a true phonemic interpretation of the language. Moreover, all have introduced accentual conditions as an explanation for some alleged vocalic developments and have given them validity not only for Old Prussian but for Common Baltic (CB) as well. Furthermore, Kazlauskas and Mažiulis have formulated some very innovatory vocalic patterns. It is my belief that much more critical attention must be paid to the aforementioned considerations of orthography, accentual conditions, and vocalic patterning if a tenable solution is to be reached regarding the vocalic phonemes of the Elbing Vocabulary.

To set this problem in its proper perspective, it is necessary to begin at the Common Baltic stage. There has been some difference of opinion as to just what sort of vocalic system comprises Common Baltic. In the first place, although Berneker, Trautmann, and Endzelīns discuss vowels singly and do not assemble them into a pattern, they are generally agreed that IE $*/\bar{a}, \bar{o}/ > $ CB $*/\bar{a}/$.[2] The only explanation for this merger is offered by Trautmann, who states that it occurred on analogy with the coalescence of IE $*/\breve{a}/$ and $*/\breve{o}/$ to CB $*/\breve{a}/$.[3] Hence, analyzing long vowels and diphthongs as combinations of two short vowels, we can reproduce their conception of a Common Baltic system as follows:

$$i \qquad u$$

$$e \qquad a$$

This quadrangular arrangement is a realistic one in terms of its structure; but it is inadequate because it necessitates extra steps in order to account for the presence of the diphthong /ua/ in the two extant Baltic languages. Lithuanian (Li.) and Latvian (Latv.) /ua/ occurs in words reflecting IE $*/\bar{o}/$. Thus, rather than posit an /ō/ from CB $*/\bar{a}/$ ($<$ IE $*/\bar{a}, \bar{o}/$), it seems more reasonable merely to retain an $*/\bar{o}/$ in Common Baltic.

The contemporary scholars Kazlauskas and Mažiulis, however, have proposed Common Baltic systems which involve a larger number of vowels:

Kazlauskas[4]		Mažiulis[5]	
$\breve{\imath}$	$\breve{\bar{u}}$	$\breve{\imath}$	$\breve{\bar{u}}$
	$\bar{o}_1$		$\bar{\underset{.}{o}}$
$\breve{\bar{e}}$	$\breve{\bar{o}}_2$	$\breve{\bar{e}}$	$\breve{\bar{o}}$

These two systems are symbolically slightly different, but they appear to represent one and the same theoretical point of view, namely that IE

*/ă/ merged with */ŏ/, and that IE */ā/, while becoming somewhat rounded, did not coalesce with IE */ō/. A short */o/ (but not a short */a/!) is posited here solely on the basis of orthographic evidence in the Elbing Vocabulary, the oldest Baltic text. Here there are several words containing *o* where *a* is expected (e.g., *bordus* 'beard,' cf. Li. *barzdà*; *smorde* 'foul odor,' cf. Li. *smardìnti* 'to produce a foul odor'). It is theorized, following Endzelīns,[6] that they were influenced by some rather more archaic Pomesanian dialects, where an */ŏ/ still existed.[7] In so concluding, these men take seriously the principle that IE */ă/ and */ŏ/ fell together early in the development of the various IE language subgroups. But their view nevertheless complicates unduly the history of Baltic vocalic development, since they are assuming that IE */ă, ŏ/ > CB and early OP */ŏ/ > later OP /ă/. It seems that this crucial occurrence of orthographic *o* in the Elbing Vocabulary can be explained in a more plausible manner, namely as a simple misinterpretation of nondistinctive consonant labialization (a phenomenon particularly evident in languages showing a phonemic opposition of palatalized and nonpalatalized consonants). This means that any nonpalatalized consonant (and especially a labial or velar) before a nonfront vowel was phonetically heavily rounded, and that this feature was mistakenly ascribed to the following vowel instead.[8] Thus, for example, when the German scribe was given the word /bardus/, he, being a speaker of a language not having phonemic palatalization of consonants, interpreted the heavy labialization of the /b/ as belonging to the /ă/ instead. Such an explanation seems valid not only on the basis of the Elbing Vocabulary, but, more significantly, because of orthographic vacillations in one and the same word in the catechisms (e.g., *grīkan* 'sins (g.pl.)' in Catechism III; but *grecon* 'id.' in Catechism I).

As for the representatives of IE */ā/ and */ō/ in Kazlauskas' and Mažiulis' systems, they are plausible in light of the almost consistent orthographic evidence for rounding in the Elbing Vocabulary, and later; but their inclusion renders the above vocalic phoneme patterns highly improbable, since they contain more back than front vowels in a nontriangular arrangement. Those scholars who reject such a system do so on the basis of statistical data on the one hand, and physiological-psychological evidence on the other. (Of course, the first consideration is but a reflection of the validity of the latter.) For example, in his examination of many various vocalic patterns, N. S. Trubetzkoy gives evidence of no nontriangular system possessing more back than front vowels. He comments:

In jedem Vokalsystem enthalten die maximal-dunkle und maximal-helle Eigentonklasse immer die gleiche Zahl von Schallfüllestufen. Dies gilt

ohne Vorbehalt für die Vierecksysteme, während in den Dreiecksys-
temen noch der ausserhalb der Eigentonklassen stehende Vokal der
maximalen Schallfüllestufe dazukommt. So muss z. B. ein vierstufiges
Vierecksystem vier Vokale der maximal-dunklen und vier Vokale der
maximal-hellen Eigentonklasse enthalten, während ein vierstufiges Drei-
ecksystem nur drei dunkle und drei helle Vokale und ausserdem noch
den maximal offenen Vokal enthält.[9]

There is another stipulation as to what constitutes a possible vowel
pattern—a condition which the above systems also fail to meet. In order
to make this principle clear, it is necessary to remind the reader that
vowel systems contain at least two dimensions of contrast: that of tongue
height (which is the more crucial one); and that of frontness–backness
(sometimes correlated with unroundedness–roundedness). According to
Charles Hockett, the second dimension may apply at all tongue heights,
but except in rare cases, "the number of contrasts along the second
dimension is never greater for a lower tongue height than for a higher
one."[10] Kazlauskas' and Mažiulis' systems violate this rule; the former's
$\bar{o}_1$ and the latter's $\bar{\varrho}$ have no front correlates, whereas a correlation supposedly obtains between the lower vowels.

The above principles of vowel arrangement are based on two considerations. One is the ability of the human oral cavity to produce various
vocalic sounds. It seems reasonable to concur with André Martinet, who
has stated that, due to the asymmetrical shape of the vocal organs, less
room is provided for the formation of back vowels than of front vowels.[11]
Consequently, to propose that a language has more distinctive back vowels
than front seems to sharply contradict oral physiological evidence.

The other consideration, which is actually the converse of the first,
deals with the ability of the human ear to distinguish various vowels from
each other. Here the principles of the formant theory come into play. It
is generally accepted that differences in the positions of the first two
formants are related to the more significant differences in vowel quality.
Furthermore, a correlation can be made between the first formant and
vowel height on the one hand, and between the second formant and vowel
frontness on the other.[12] Experiments using spectrographs have shown
that the difference in frequency between these two formants is less for
back vowels than for front vowels. For example, the first two formants for
the English front vowel [e] (spoken in isolation) are 400 and 2100, whereas for the back vowel [o] they are only 550 and 900.[13] This reveals that it
would be more difficult to distinguish back vowels from each other than it
would be for front vowels. Thus, not only from the standpoint of generation, but also from that of recognition, it is unlikely that a pattern of

vocalic phonemes would display more contrasts among its back members than among its front members.

In opposition to the Common Baltic patterns proposed above, I support Christian Stang's system, which is the same as that of a late stage of Indo-European except that *ŏ/ has merged with */ā/:[14]

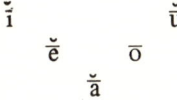

Next, it is necessary to deal specifically with the orthographic evidence in the Elbing Vocabulary. Here the orthographic reflexes of IE (or CB) */ā/ and */ō/ deserve primary consideration. Each is represented in the Elbing Vocabulary by the following symbols:

IE */ā/

1. *o* (predominantly): e.g., *menso* 'meat'; *sliwaytos* 'plums'; *brote* 'brother' (cf. Li. *broterelis*); *woble* 'apple' (cf. Li. *obuolỹs*).
2. *oa*: e.g., *doacke* 'starling' (cf. OHG *dâha* 'jackdaw'); *noatis* 'nettle' (cf. Li. *nōterės* 'small nettles'); *soakis* 'warbler' (cf. Li. *šókti* 'to spring').
3. *a* (rarely): *ponasse* 'upper lip' (lit.: 'under the nose,' cf. Li. *pō* 'under' and *nósis* 'nose'); *pomatre* 'stepmother'; *passons* 'stepson' (cf. Li. *pósūnis*); *wosigrabis* 'spindle-tree' (cf. Russ. *grab* 'hornbeam').

IE */ō/

1. *o*: e.g., *podalis* 'worthless pot' (cf. Li. *puodėlis* 'small pot'); *glossis* 'willow' (cf. Li. *glúosnis*).
2. *oa*: e.g., *woasis* 'ash tree' (cf. Li. *úosis*); *poadamynan* 'sweet milk' (< IE */pō-/ 'to drink').

Berneker,[15] Trautmann,[16] and Endzelīns[17] believe that CB */ā/ and */ō/ fell together as EV /ō/ in most cases. However, they also believe that, under certain accentual conditions, some variations arose. For example, according to Berneker, /oa/ resulted if the vowel occurred under a falling accent (e.g., *noatis* 'nettle'; *ploaste* 'bedsheet').[18] Moreover, Trautmann comments that the occurrence of *a* as a reflex of IE */ā/ is a result of its being in an unstressed syllable and that it is short rather than long.[19] The others have provided no justification for these deviations.

Of the two aforementioned Lithuanian Balticists, only Kazlauskas has proposed an Old Prussian vowel pattern. It differs from his Common Baltic system only in the respect that $*/\ocaron/$ has been transformed into $/\acaron/$:[20]

$$
\begin{array}{ccc}
\icaron & \ucaron & \\
 & & \bar{o}_1 \\
\ecaron & \acaron & \bar{o}_2
\end{array}
$$

In it we see that he does not believe that $*/\bar{a}/$ and $*/\bar{o}/$ merged in Old Prussian although both are rounded. Furthermore, he agrees with Trautmann that the sporadic occurrence of *a* as a representative of IE $*/\bar{a}/$ is due to accentual conditions and that the vowel has been shortened.[21]

The above explanations for the development of CB $*/\bar{a}/$ and $*/\bar{o}/$ into Old Prussian display some inadequacies. First, contrary to Kazlauskas and in agreement with the others, it is highly likely that $*/\bar{a}/$ and $*/\bar{o}/$ fell together since, with a handful of exceptions, both show the same orthographic reflexes (*o, oa*). However, the assertion that they reveal more than one *phonemic* reflex in the Elbing Vocabulary is doubtful. In the first place, the mere shortening of $*/\bar{a}/$ in an unstressed syllable would imply that in order for it to become $/\bar{o}/$ (or /oa/), it would have to fall under stress. However, in the $\bar{a}$-stem inflectional endings, where both the singular and plural are *consistently* represented by *-o* ($< */\bar{a}/$; e.g., *mergo* 'maiden') and *-os* ($< */\bar{a}s/$; e.g., *sliwaytos* 'plums'), respectively, it is quite unlikely that all of them are stressed. The same can be said for the occurrence of the ligature *oa*, which allegedly was found only under a falling (circumflex) accent.

In attempting to formulate my own proposal for an Elbing Vocabulary vocalic system, I have come to the conclusion that no solution can be offered which does not have its particular weaknesses. Therefore, the explanation which follows is by no means intended to be definitive. Nevertheless, I believe that it strains our credulity less than previous analyses. Hence, I propose the following rather simple history of Baltic vocalic development:

(A.) Late Indo-European: $*\icaron$ $\ucaron$

$$
\begin{array}{ccc}
 & \ecaron & \ocaron \\
 & \bar{a} &
\end{array}
$$

(B.) Common Baltic: $*\icaron$ $\ucaron$

$$
\begin{array}{ccc}
 & \ecaron & \bar{o} \\
 & \bar{a} &
\end{array}
$$

(C). Old Prussian (EV):[22]

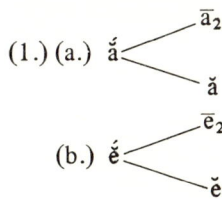

(1.) (a.) å⟨ ā₂ / ă

(b.) é⟨ ē₂ / ĕ

(2.) (a.) $\bar{a}_1$ is raised and merges with $\bar{o}$.

(b.) $\bar{e}_1$ is raised and correlates with $\bar{o}$.

(3.) (a.) $\bar{o} >$ ua

(b.) $\bar{e}_1 >$ ie

ĭ	ŭ
ē₁	ō
ĕ₂	ā
ĭ	ŭ
ĕ	ā

Thus, if chronological considerations are ignored, the elements of this process actually occurred in Common East Baltic and later in Lithuanian.[23] Moreover, the resultant diphthongization of /ō/ to /ua/ fully explains all the orthographic variations which reflect IE */ā/ and */ō/.[24] Since this diphthong was foreign to the German spoken during this period, it is not surprising that the German scribe symbolized it improperly.[25] In the first place, the consistent occurrence of *o* in the inflectional endings of many endings (e.g., *genno* 'housewife'; *wisnaytos* 'cherries'), and elsewhere (e.g., *glossis* 'willow,' cf. Li. *glúosnis*; *medione* 'hunt,' cf. Li. *medžioti*), simply shows what was to the scribe the absorption of the first element of the diphthong by the preceding consonant. Also, that the second element [a] was written as *o* is explainable as a simple misinterpretation of the rounding which in fact preceded this sound. In those few cases where an *a* does appear, it can simply be assumed that the initial component of the diphthong was seen as belonging to the preceding consonant, but that the second element escaped misinterpretation.[26]

Finally, the representation of /ua/ by *oa* is perfectly understandable in view of the phonetic similarity of [u] and [o] in the first place and, in the second place, because of the tendency of a heavily labialized foregoing consonant to obscure the distinction between the two. Indeed, in the Elbing Vocabulary we do possess unambiguous proof of such misinterpretation of the [u] - element as [o], as, for example, in *passons* 'stepson,' cf. Li. *pósūnis.*[27]

Since the change /ō/ > /ua/ has been proposed, it is highly likely that the diphthongization of /ē₁/ to /ie/ accompanied it. Unfortunately, due to the paucity of written discourse in the dialect under consideration, only one suspected instance of this change is found, namely *plieynis* 'ash-powder,' cf. Li. *plénys*. However, as with /ua/, it is entirely possible that /ie/ was misinterpreted (as *e*) because of the strangeness of this sound to Holczwesscher.

The question may be posed as to whether all the reflexes of IE */ā/ and */ō/ cannot be posited as /ā/, with any orthographic deviations merely being the result of misinterpreted consonant labialization. To be sure, this is a legitimate query. After all, such a phonetic feature is almost certainly present in Old Prussian. Moreover, the orthographic reflexes of IE */ā, ō/ are predominantly *o* and *oa*, which are precisely the same letters betraying labialization in words where the vowel in question is very definitely an /a/ (e.g., *bordus* 'beard,' cf. Li. *barzdà*; *doalgis* 'scythe,' cf. Li. *dalgis*). More-over, the merging of /ō/ with /ā/ is what seems to have happened in the language of the catechisms (e.g., *brāti* 'brother,' cf. Li. *broterēlis*; *dātwei* 'to give' (< IE */dō/)–Catechism III).

However, in the final analysis this explanation must be rejected. This is so predominantly because the *ā*-stem inflectional endings (< */-ā/; < */-ās/) contain, without a single exception, an *o*, even after what are suspected to be palatalized consonants (e.g., *sutristio* 'whey'; *crausios* 'pears'). This stands in direct contrast to the consistent occurrence of *a* in the desin-ences of all of the 64 neuter substantives and adjectives (e.g., *assaran* 'lake'; *golimban* 'blue').[28]

A final consideration is that of the status of /ŏ/ in the dialect underly-ing the Elbing Vocabulary. Because of the large number of Slavic borrow-ings in it (e.g., *aboros* 'hay rack,' cf. Pol. *obor* 'barnyard'; *golimban* 'blue,' cf. Pol. *golębi*), it would be unwise to deny its presence. However, as in Lithuanian, it must be emphasized that this vowel is present *only* in borrowings. The question now is whether it had already been assimilated into the established phonemic system or was still a member of a fragmen-tary 'coexistent' phonemic system (to use Fries' and Pike's terminology).[29] Because the Old Prussian system proposed above does not contain a long /o/, thereby making it difficult to include a short /o/ in it, it is most likely that the nonindigenous /ŏ/ still lay in an innovating phonemic pattern.

As stated, this or any attempt to establish a plausible vocalic phoneme system for the dialect underlying the Elbing Vocabulary is by no means in-controvertible. Our very inaccessibility to this language except in the meagerest of documents is reason enough for that. But what this discus-sion has intended to emphasize is this: (1) that it seems better to formulate a vowel pattern of an extinct tongue on the basis of known developments in languages closely related to it rather than develop tenuous vowel arrangements; and (2) that where orthographic vacillations occur, it seems more advisable to account for them, where at all possible, on the basis of a highly probable internal phonetic phenomenon rather than set up elaborate criteria for their distribution.

The Pennsylvania State University

NOTES

1. The five basic Old Prussian documents are *The Elbing Vocabulary* (ca. 1400); *The Vocabulary of Simon Grunau* (between 1517 and 1526); *The First Catechism* (1545); *The Second Catechism* (1545); and *The Third Catechism* or *Enchiridion*, translated by the German Abel Will and published in 1561. The only extant Elbing Vocabulary manuscript is but a copy of an earlier original. The protograph is ascribed to a German monk named Peter Holczwesscher. Cf. G. H. F. Nesselmann, "Kritische Bemerkungen über das deutschpreussische Vokabular des *Codex Neumannianus*," *Altpreussische Monatsschrift*, 6 (1869), pp. 319–20, and V. Mažiulis, *Prūsų kalbos paminklai* (Vilnius, 1966), pp. 27–28.

2. Erich Berneker, *Die preussische Sprache* (Strassburg, 1896), p. 254. Reinhold Trautmann, *Die altpreussischen Sprachdenkmäler* (Göttingen, 1910), p. 124. (Etymological information regarding Old Prussian words is taken from the dictionary found in the back of Trautmann's grammar.) J. Endzelīns, *Altpreussiche Grammatik* (Riga, 1941), pp. 38–39.

3. Trautmann, *op. cit.* p. 122.

4. J. Kazlauskas, "K razvitiju obščebaltijskoj sistemy glasnyx," *Voprosy Jazykoznanija* 9 (1962), iv, p. 24.

5. V. Mažiulis, "Nekotorye fonetičeskie aspekty balto-slavjanskoj fleksii," *Baltistica* 1 (1965), p. 17. It should be noted that in both Mažiulis' and Kazlauskas' systems the short and long vowels are patterned separately. But since it seems structurally wiser to combine both short and long vowels into one system, I have modified their representations accordingly.

6. J. Endzelīns, "Zum *o* für *a* im Elbinger Vokabular," *Studi Baltici* 5 (1935–36), p. 98.

7. Kazlauskas, 21. Mažiulis ("Nekotorye fonetičeskie aspekty . . . ," 17) refers to Kazlauskas rather than Endzelīns when positing a CB */ŏ/.

8. William R. Schmalstieg, "Labialization in Old Prussian," in *Studies in Slavic Linguistics and Poetics in Honor of Boris O. Unbegaun.* (New York, 1968), pp. 189–193.

9. N. S. Trubetzkoy, *Grundzüge der Phonologie* (Travaux du Cercle Linguistique de Prague) 7 (Prague, 1939), p. 102.

10. Charles F. Hockett, *A Manual of Phonology* (Indiana Univ. Publications in Anthropology and Linguistics) 11 (Baltimore, 1955), p. 83. The clear "rare exceptions" include Potawatomi, Oneida, Lifu, and some Portuguese dialects. The

latter show the following system (p. 89):

$$
\begin{array}{ccc}
\text{i} & & \text{u} \\
\text{e} & & \text{o} \\
\text{ε} & \land & \text{ɔ} \\
& \text{a} &
\end{array}
$$

Thus, although Portuguese seems to be the only Indo-European language showing such a vocalic arrangement, Hockett does note that even this system is unstable, since with nasalization the /ɛ a ɔ/ disappear. Moreover, in other dialects there is no contrast between /ʌ/ and /a/. Hence, in view of this rarity and instability, it is very doubtful that Old Prussian possessed such a pattern.

11. A. Martinet, "Équilibre et instabilité des systèmes phonologiques," *Proceedings of the Third International Congress of Phonetic Sciences* (Ghent, 1939), pp. 30–34, as cited by Ferdynand Antkowski in *La Chronologie de la monophtongaison des diphtongues dans les langues indo-européennes* (Poznań, 1956), pp. 14–15.

12. H. A. Gleason, Jr., *An Introduction to Descriptive Linguistics*, rev. ed. (New York, 1961), p. 367.

13. *Ibid.*

14. Chr[istian] S. Stang, *Vergleichende Grammatik der Baltischen Sprachen* (Oslo, Bergen, Tromsö, 1966), p. 22.

15. Berneker, *op. cit.* p. 254.

16. Trautmann, *op. cit.* p. 124.

17. Endzelīns, *Altpreussische Grammatik*, pp. 38–39.

18. Berneker, *op. cit.* p. 255.

19. Trautmann, *op. cit.* p. 125.

20. Kazlauskas, *op. cit.* pp. 21–22.

21. *Ibid.*

22. The lengthening of /ă, ĕ/ probably occurred when under stress and in an open syllable, as in Li. *māno* 'he thinks.' However, this phenomenon is not thoroughgoing, for in Lithuanian we also encounter such a form as *màno* 'my.' It is not clear why such a contrast was still maintained in this environment. The raising of /ā/ to /ō/ and of /ē₁/ to a close /ē/ is, as in Lithuanian, a direct consequence of the lengthening of stressed /ă, ĕ/ in an open syllable, since the original short/long contrast for the original low vowels was thereby being put in jeopardy.

23. */ō/ and */ā/ actually fell together in some Lithuanian dialects, although not in the standard language.

24. In this regard it is worth mentioning that contemporary Latvian uses only an *o* to symbolize /ua/. Moreover, Endzelīns himself (in "Was ist im Altpreussischen aus ide. *ō* [und *a*] geworden?" *Studi Baltici* 5 [1935–36], p. 143) considers it possible for the dialect of the Elbing Vocabulary to have developed a diphthong (presumably /ua/) as a reflex of IE */ā, ō/, although the orthography would not have shown it. This is likely, he states, because in Lithuanian Mažvydas seems to have represented the diphthong arising from */ō/ merely as *o*. Endzelīns' positing such a development in the Elbing Vocabulary would then parallel what he has also theorized for the catechisms, namely that */ō/ has become predominantly /ua/, although the orthography shows only *o*. Although I do not fully agree with Endzelīns' theory, nevertheless that a dichotomy may have existed between sound and symbol is a point well taken.

25. According to several of the Elbing Vocabulary's glosses, the German of this time and region had already experienced the monophthongization of /uo/ to /ū/ (e.g., *muter* 'mother' and *Brud'*[er] 'brother' for MHG *muoter* and *bruoder*,

respectively). Hence, it seems certain that a diphthong like /ua/ was strange indeed to Holczwesscher.

26. The four cases where IE $*/\bar{a}/$ is represented by *a* might also be explained as due to the influence of German (*ponasse* 'upper lip'—Ger. *Nase* 'nose') and Slavic (*pomatre* 'stepmother'—Old Pol. *macierz* 'mother'; *passons* 'stepson'—Russ. *pasynok*; *wosigrabis* 'spindle-tree'—Russ. *grab* 'hornbeam').

27. It should be noted that when an etymological $*/\bar{a}/$ or $*/\bar{o}/$ occurs in initial position, orthographic *w* (most likely representing an excrescent [v]) always begins the word. Unfortunately, this phenomenon cannot be used as a support for the presence of the diphthong /ua/, since there are languages which display this feature but do not possess an /ua/ (e.g., Russ., as in *vosem'* 'eight,' cf. OCS *osmĭ*). Moreover, there are languages which do have an /ua/ but which do not always develop an excrescent [v] (e.g., standard Li., as in *úosis* 'ash tree').

28. Another possibility is that the words in the Elbing Vocabulary were collected from speakers representing two dialects. Thus, it could be proposed that in one dialect $*/\bar{o}/$ and $*/\bar{a}/$ merged to $/\bar{o}/$, whereas in the second dialect the resultant $/\bar{o}/$ further passed to /oa/ (as actually occurred during one stage of Old High German). As suggested earlier, the rare occurrence of *a* ($< */\bar{a}/$) could be explained as a result of German and Slavic contamination. However, such a theory as this would presuppose that all $\bar{a}$-stem nouns (which end exclusively in *-o* or *-os*) were supplied by that informant (or those informants) speaking a dialect (or dialects) showing the merger of $*/\bar{a}/$ with $*/\bar{o}/$. In this respect it is a less tenable argument than the one proposed in the body of this paper.

29. Charles C. Fries and Kenneth L. Pike, "Coexistent Phonemic Systems," *Language* 25 (1949), pp. 29–50.

THE NOMINATIVE PLURAL AND PRETERIT SINGULAR OF THE ACTIVE PARTICIPLES IN BALTIC

WARREN COWGILL

A puzzle in the morphology of Lithuanian which has to this day not received a satisfactory solution is the nominative plural masculine (also feminine) of the active participles, of the type present *vedą* 'leading,' *tùrį* 'having,' future *vèsią* 'going to lead,' preterit *vẽdę* 'having led,' imperfect *vèsdavę* 'having been leading.' The active participles of Lithuanian in general continue Indo-European consonant stems in *-nt-* for the present and future and in *-wos-/-us-* for the preterit and imperfect, with which were associated feminines formed by adding *-ī/-yā-*, and which were largely extended to *-ntja-* and *-usja-* in Balto-Slavic. Compare the accusative singular masculines *vẽdantį, tùrintį, vèsiantį, vẽdusį*, based on the unextended consonant stems, and the genitive singular masculines *vẽdančio, tùrinčio, vèsiančio, vẽdusio*, based on the extended stems.

But the nominative plural forms quoted above fall out of the pattern altogether, whether viewed from the standpoint of Indo-European at large or from the standpoint of normal Lithuanian adjective paradigms. In Proto-Indo-European the nominative plural ending of nonneuter consonant stems was **-es*, which is still preserved as *-es* or *-s* in *r-* and *n*-stem nouns in the more conservative Lithuanian dialects; e.g., *dùkteres, dùkters* 'daughters,' *ākmenes, ākmens* 'stones.'

For the participles compare Hittite *appant-es* 'seized'; Sanskrit *bhárant-as* 'carrying,' *saniṣyánt-as* 'desiring to win,' *vidvā́ṃs-as* 'knowing'; Greek *phéront-es* 'carrying,' *eidót-es* 'knowing'; Gothic *frijonds*, Old English *friend* 'friends' from Proto-Germanic **frijōnd-iz*; Old Irish *carait* 'friends' from Proto-Celtic **karant-es*; Tocharian (both A and B) *kälpoṣ* 'obtained,' where the palatalized final -*ș* points to an earlier ending with a short front vowel, such as **-es*; and Latin *ferent-ēs* 'carrying,' with the regular Latin replacement of **-es* by *-ēs* in the nominative plural of consonant stems. Especially important are the Slavic forms, Old Church Slavonic present *vedǫšte* 'leading,' preterit *vedŭše* 'having led,' of which the former continues PIE **wed(h)ont-es* intact except that **t* has been palatalized (Proto-Slavic **t́* giving OCS *št*) by analogy with the forms extended to *-ntja-*, while *vedŭše* continues Indo-European **-wós-es* unchanged except for generalizing the zero grade **-us-* of the participial formant.

Accordingly, from the combined evidence of an imposing number of Indo-European languages, including Slavic, Baltic's closest relative, we should expect Lithuanian forms ending in *-nt(e)s* and *-us(e)s*, e.g., pres. **vedantes, *vedan(t)s*, pret. **veduses, *vedus(s)*. But of such forms there is no trace.[1]

From the viewpoint of Lithuanian inflectional patterns, we might expect that if the old ending was *not* preserved, it would have been replaced by *-ys* as in modern standard *dùkterys, ākmenys*, or that the adjectival *ja*-stem inflection of most oblique cases would have been pressed into service to furnish a nominative plural masculine. In fact, both these developments have occurred. Plurals of the type *vēdantys, vèsiantys, vēdusys* are typical of Žemaitic dialects, being mentioned already in 1653 as typical of the Memelenses by Daniel Klein (1653: 60); to judge by A. Senn (1966: 175, 177), they have now become accepted as the literary norm in present and future tenses. And adjectival inflection is now regularly found in the compound, "definite" inflection *vēdantieji, vēdusieji*, replacing earlier forms of the type *vedājie, vedējie*; the rarity of uncompounded *vēdanti, vēdusi* was explained already by Johannes Schmidt (1883: 362) as due to the inconvenient identity of these forms with the uncompounded nominative singular feminine.

But the existence of such easily understandable forms as *vēdantys, vēdusys* and *vēdantie-, vēdusie-* only deepens the mystery surrounding *vedā̜* and *vēdę*. If the language had the resources to build these straightforward and obvious replacements for **vedantes, *veduses*, what can have been the circumstances that led to putting such aberrant forms as *vedā̜* and *vēdę* into the participial paradigms of Lithuanian?

If we turn to the other Baltic languages for enlightenment, we find that Old Prussian has only forms comparable to Lithuanian *vēdantie-* and *vēdusys*: present *skellāntei, skellāntai* 'obligated,' pret. *immusis* 'having taken,' etc. Standard Latvian uses forms of the *vēdantie-, vēdusie-* type (but with the nominal ending **ai* rather than the pronominal **ie*): pres.

vẹdoši, pret. *veduši*. Dialectal pres. *gribuets* evidently corresponds to the Lithuanian type in *-antys*, and dialectal pret. *-ušš* is evidently from **-ušis*, a contamination of *-uši* with an **-usis* corresponding to Li. *-usys* (Endzelīns, 1923: 719, 729). But there is a relic *ẹsu* 'being' (: Li. *ēsą*) given as nominative plural masculine in Adolphi's grammar of 1685, and used also in nineteenth-century dialects as nominative singular of all genders (Endzelīns, 1923: 720). This relic (plus, as will be seen, the regular Latvian nominative singular masculine of the preterit participle in *-is*) establishes that the type of Lithuanian *vedą, vēdę* goes back at least to the Common East Baltic ancestor of Lithuanian and Latvian, but contributes nothing to an elucidation of its origin.

Most attempts that I know of to explain these enigmatic nominative plurals start from the fact that they look exactly like the nominative-accusative neuter forms of their paradigms. Present *vedą* and future *vèsią* are easily derived from Proto-Indo-European neuter singular prototypes.[2] Skt. *bhárat* and Lat. *ferēns* make it likely that the Indo-European nominative-accusative singular neuter of present active participles ended in zero-grade **-n̥t* even when associated with thematic indicatives, but analogic replacement by **-ont* is very easy—cf. Gk. *phéron*—and would lead regularly to Baltic **vedan*, whence East Baltic **vedą*, remaining in conservative forms of Old Lithuanian and elsewhere being denasalized to *vedā, vedŭ*. Athematic forms like *ēsą*, stem *(e)sant-* 'being,' *dúodą*, stem *dúodant-* 'giving' show a similar generalization or (in the reduplicated presents) introduction of **-ont-* in the suffix syllable. And, whatever the prehistory of the Baltic *-i-* and *-ā-* presents, forms like *tùrį* 'having' and *mãtą* 'seeing' are derived regularly from the participial stems *turint-* and *matant-* (shortened from **matānt-* by Osthoff's Law as it applies to Baltic), as if PIE ***turint, **motānt*.

But in the preterit the use of *vēdę* as neuter singular is just as unexpected as is its use as nominative plural masculine. It does not share a single sound with the Indo-European suffix *-wos-/-us-* or with the Baltic suffix *-us(ja)-* of most of the remaining cases. What it does resemble is the nominative singular masculine *vēdęs*, to which Latvian *vedis* corresponds exactly.

In Proto-Indo-European it is fairly clear that the nominative singular masculine and the nominative-accusative singular neuter of the *-wos-* participle ended in **-wṓs* and **-wós* respectively. Compare for the masculine Gk. *eidṓs* and Avestan *vīduuå*, and for the neuter Gk. *eidós* (the nominative-accusative neuter is not attested in Avestan). Sanskrit nom. sg. masc. *vidvā́n* and neuter *tatanvát, samvavr̥tvát* are analogic for forms in

*-vā́s, *-vás (cf. vocative cikitvas etc.), probably on the pattern of the -vant-stems, which shared "middle cases" in -vat- with the perfect participles. On this question, and on the development of Indic -vat-, -vad- in place of Indo-Iranian *-uš-, -už-, see Szemerényi (1967: 9–11). Sanskrit -vā́n and -vát are at best innovations parallel to Lithuanian -ęs, -ę, not something attesting an inherited formation with *-ns- or *-nt-.

In Slavic, the Balto-Slavic generalization of zero-grade *-us- has led to identical forms in masculine and neuter, both of which are vedŭ, pointing to Balto-Slavic *vedus. In Prussian the masculine nominative singular ends in -uns (also spelled -ons, -ans), which looks like *-us secondarily affected by the present participles in -an(t)s, while the neuter nominative-accusative singular is not certainly attested.

Johannes Schmidt (1883: 342 ff) explained vēdęs, vedis starting from a PIE nom. sg. *-wēns, a view which has rightly been given up by modern scholars. Christian Stang (1966: 266) still operates with stem forms *-wēs or *-wes-, but is forced to assume complicated and unlikely analogic changes; and an e-grade *-wes- existed in the Proto-Indo-European paradigm at most in the locative singular (*widwés, *widwési?), from which it can hardly have spread to nominative singular case forms without leaving more trace in the oblique cases than Li. dial. pùvesos and the like.[3] Jan Otrębski (1956: 257) and André Vaillant (1958: 555–556) take vēdęs, vēdę as built to the preterit indicative stem ved-ē- in the same manner as a present participle. In this they are basically right, but the exact way in which the East Baltic preterit participle combines forms in -ē-nt- with forms in -us(ja)- can be clarified when we understand the plurals vedą̃, vēdę better.

In the article already referred to, Schmidt thought that the plurals of the present participles were originally neuter singulars, inherited from a time when Indo-European neuter consonant stems were not marked for number (1883: 363–364), and that the double use of pret. vēdę as neuter singular and masculine plural was modeled on the double usage of present vedą̃ (1883: 362). Spread of neuter (singular and) plural vedą̃ to masculine use is contrary to the general Baltic pattern, in which the near merger of masculine and neuter genders was mostly accomplished by generalizing masculine forms at the expense of neuter forms (type tiẽ dēbesys vs. OCS ta nebesa). But Schmidt believed he had support for an occasional generalization of neuter at the expense of masculine in the ending -ai of the nominative plural of masculine a-stem nouns, which he thought was originally a neuter ending; this is another of his views which has since been generally given up.

In *Die Pluralbildungen der indogermanischen Neutra* (1889: 162–165)
Schmidt modified his explanation slightly, now deriving *vedą* from PIE
neut. pl. **-ōnt*, an archaic formation in which number was marked by
lengthened grade ablaut alone, as attested in Avestan *rauuascarą*[4] and
implied by Vedic *sā́nti*.

Endzelīns (1918: 189) objected that an Indo-European **-ōnt* would have
developed to Lithuanian **-ų*, not *-ą*, and that a neuter plural in **-ont*, as
originally posited by Schmidt, is not attested in other Indo-European
languages, and even if it did exist, would in all probability have been replaced in Baltic prior to the remodeling of the nominative plural masculine
by forms of the type **vēdančia*, corresponding to OCS *vedǫšta* from
*-antjā (1918: 190). Endzelīns was thus forced to suppose that the Baltic
plurals in *-ą* come from the Indo-European neuter *singular* (1918: 195),
whose use as masculine (and feminine) plural he rather lamely supposed
(1918: 198–199) could have started with use of neuter singular forms as
predicates to subjects of any gender or number.

Stang (1966: 264–265) accepts Schmidt's derivation of *-ą* from **-ōnt* as
far as the phonology is concerned, but objects that the type of Avestan
mīždauuą is very archaic, being found only in Avestan,[5] so that an
internal Baltic solution is preferable. Therefore he hesitantly adopts
Endzelīns' view that *vedą* is neuter singular in origin, its use as masculine
(and feminine) plural having started in predicative construction. He points
out that the use of *vedą* beside *vēdančios* as nominative plural feminine
supports the hypothesis that it originated as a neuter, and mentions that
the use of participles in reported speech could have contributed to the reevaluation of neuter singular as plural, suggesting that an expression like
girdė́jau (*kad*) *ateĩsią* could have first meant 'ich habe gehört, dass jemand
kommen wird,' and only later come to mean 'dass sie kommen werden.'
For preterit *vḗdę*, in both its usages, Stang repeats unchanged Schmidt's
explanation that it is analogic to present *vedą* (1966: 267).

Otrębski (1956: 250, 258) similarly accepts Endzelīns' explanation of
the present plurals as old neuter singulars and Schmidt's explanation of
the preterit *-ę* as formed on the analogy pres. *-ąs* : *-ą* = pret. *-ęs* : X.[6]

But it is manifestly unsatisfactory to have to explain the plural present
and future participle forms as originally neuter, in contrast to the otherwise total disappearance of neuter forms from plural paradigms in East
Baltic, and even more difficult to suppose that we have here either a very
archaic form of neuter plural, of which Slavic preserves no trace, or else
the outcome of a syntactic transformation rather weirder than supposing
that the use of uninflected *jung* in Modern German sentences like *Die*

Männer sind jung would lead to *junge Männer* being replaced by *jung Männer* while *junger Mann, junge Dame, junges Tier*, and, at least optionally, *junge Damen* and *junge Tiere* remained. And the explanation of preterit *vēdę* as based on nominative singular masculine *vēdęs* would be secure only if the source and motivation for *vēdęs* were securely established.

A much more natural and simple explanation is possible if we widen our vision to consider two features of Baltic grammar in addition to the inflectional paradigms of the participles themselves. To paraphrase something I said in *Symbolae . . . Kuryłowicz* (1965: 50), a problem baffling by itself may become simpler in the context of the whole grammar of the language, and one of the ways in which there is most hope for historical linguistics to advance, in technique if not in theory, is in applying wider fields of data to unsolved problems.

The first special feature of Baltic grammar is the use of etymologically third singular finite verbs with third person subjects of any number. This is a feature common to all the Baltic languages, attested already in the earliest sixteenth century texts, e.g., Li. *Maksla schito tewai iusu trakszdawa tureti* 'Your fathers thirsted to have this teaching,' from Mosvid's Catechism of 1547; OP *kai tennei polijnku bhe segge ka tennei skellāntei ast* 'das sie bleiben, vnd thun, was sie schuldig sind,' from Will's Enchiridion of 1561; Latv. *Sche gir te schwete dessmitte Dewe boussle* 'These are the holy ten commandments of God,' from Canisius' Catechism of 1585 (page 258 of August Günther's facsimile edition of 1929).

This neutralization of the category of number in the third person of verbs is one of the most striking and characteristic innovations of Baltic grammar as compared with the other Indo-European languages. Its uniform occurrence in all the Baltic languages indicates that it developed while the ancestors of Prussian, Lithuanian, and Latvian were still very little divergent from one another, very likely well before A. D. 1000. Inquiry into the reasons for it is outside the scope of this paper, except to say that homonymy of third plural verb forms with already existing participial plurals in *-nt* is in no way a necessary condition for the replacement of third plural by third singular forms in finite verb paradigms.

Thus in British Celtic third singular verbs are largely used with plural subjects—e.g., Middle Welsh *Pereid y rycheu* 'the furrows last'—but there is no present participle to be in competition. Nor is it obvious that the ambiguity of pre-Baltic **jai vedan* 'they (are) leading' and 'they lead' would have been so inconvenient as to be a major factor in giving acceptability to the construction, at first a solecism, **jai veda* 'they lead(s).'[7]

The second special feature of Baltic grammar is the use of participles in place of finite verbs in indirect discourse, especially when the speaker is reporting something without vouching for its accuracy. We have already seen Stang's example, *girdėjau* (*kad*) *ateĩsią*. In Lithuanian this construction is frequent from the earliest texts, e.g., *anis . . . tikieiose Dwasse regy* 'anie . . . tikėjos dvasią regį, they thought they were seeing a ghost' in Bartholomäus Willent's 1579 translation of Luke 24.36 (as found on page 83 of Bechtel's 1882 edition of Willent's work). In Latvian I have not searched the early texts thoroughly for examples. But the construction is certainly well established in the language now (cf., Endzelīns, 1923: 757–763) and for the nineteenth century I can cite numerous references to it in A. Bielenstein's *Lettische Grammatik* (1863), e.g., (in modernized spelling) *N. N. saimniece katru dienu ar ogām braucot*(*i*) *Lēpajā*? 'Die N. N. Wirthin soll, (wie man sagt), all Tage mit Beeren nach Libau fahren?' (1863: 372). In Prussian we have no examples of participle for finite verb—cf., e.g., *As druwē, kai mien Deiws Teikūuns ast* 'ich gleube, das mich Gott geschaffen hatt'—but its absence may be due only to slavish imitation of German syntax on the part of the translators.

Neither of these innovations—use of third singular verbs with plural subjects and of participles for finite verbs in indirect discourse—can have occurred all at once. There must have been a time when both third singular and third plural verbs occurred with plural subjects, and there must have been a time when, even more than now, finite forms occurred beside participles in indirect discourse. If these times overlapped at all, it was possible for third plural finite forms to be reevaluated as nominative plural participles.

That *vedą* (aside from problems of accent) is what we should expect as third plural present indicative in Lithuanian was recognized already by Schmidt (1883: 362). In the third singular Baltic has generalized the ending -ϕ from PIE secondary *-t* in all stems with two or more syllables and the PIE primary ending *-ti* (often shortened to *-t*) after monosyllabic stems, e.g., OLi. *est*(*i*) 'is,' *bit*(*i*) 'was' (Stang, 1966: 409–410). Accordingly, in third plural we should expect Baltic *-n* from PIE secondary *-nt* everywhere, except that perhaps instead of monosyllabic *san* 'they are' and *jan* 'they go' the forms would have been *santi, *janti.[8]

Let us consider what the situation would have been in prehistoric Baltic with a present like *veda-* 'lead' after the loss of *-t* and before the East Baltic reduction of final *-n* to nasalization. At this time the third person singular was already *veda*, as in conservative Modern Lithuanian, and the third plural present indicative was *vedan*, with *-an* from PIE *-ont*. In the participle the nominative singular was masc. *vedans*, fem. *vedantī*, neut. *vedan*, the regular ancestors of Lithuanian singular *vedąs*, *vedanti*, *vedą*; in the nominative plural the masculine was probably still *vedantes* (cf. OCS *vedǫšte*), the feminine was *vedantjas*, ancestor of Li. *vēdančios*, and the neuter, as far as it still existed, was in all probability *vedantjā*, parallel to OCS *vedǫště*.

So long as the syntactic patterns inherited from Proto-Indo-European were preserved, the nominative plural participles *vedantes*, *vedantjās*, *vedantjā* and the third plural finite *vedan* were clearly distinct in usage. In particular, one said only *jai (esan) vedantes* 'they (masc.) are leading,' *jās (esan) vedantjas* 'they (fem.) are leading' and *vedantes vīrai* 'leading men,' *vedantjās genās* 'leading women' whether the participle was predicative or attributive, and only *jai vedan, jās vedan* 'they lead,' *sakā (kad)*[9] *jai* (or *jās*) *vedan* 'he says (that) they lead' whether the verb was in direct or reported discourse, and regardless of the gender of its subject.

But the use of third singular verbs with plural subjects and of participles as predicates in reported statements opened the way for possible confusion. This would be especially true if we suppose, adopting a principle that has been used repeatedly by Kuryłowicz, that the innovated use of third singular verbs with plural subjects moved faster in grammatically basic principal clauses than in the subordinate clauses that are logically derived from them. The principle is the same as that involved in German *Haupt* being replaced by *Kopf* in its central meaning 'that which is attached to the neck of an animal' while being retained in peripheral meanings like 'chief' and in derivatives like *Hauptstadt, Hauptsache*.

In that case, we would suppose that at a time when *jai/jās vedan* had pretty well given up in favor of *jai/jās veda* in principal clauses, *sakā (kad) jai/jās vedan* was still quite common, being in competition not so much with *sakā (kad) jai/jās veda* as with *sakā (kad) jai (esan) vedantes*, *sakā (kad) jās (esan) vedantjās*. In this situation *vedan*, identical in form with the neuter singular of the participle and largely restricted to constructions in which participles were favored, could well be perceived as an aberrantly inflected (endingless) nominative plural of the participle. As such it would have succeeded in completely replacing the old nominative plural masculine *vedantes*, even from its attributive uses, and in at least partially replacing the nominative plural feminine *vedantjās*, while itself giving up all vestiges of use as a finite verb. 'Dass sie kommen werden' would be the original, etymological meaning in Stang's *girdėjau (kad) ateīsią*, and *vedą* etc. are sometimes used as feminine not because they

were originally neuter, but because they were originally finite verbs unmarked for gender.[10]

There is no need to discuss in detail the various Baltic present stem
formations. In general it is quite automatic that the Indo-European third
plural ending *-(e)nt has undergone exactly the same transformations as
the participial suffix *-(o)nt-, so that e.g., tùri 'habentes' and mãtą
'videntes' offer just the same problems as do tùrįs 'habens' and mãtąs
'videns.' It may be noted that in the athematic reduplicated paradigm,
where Slavic has introduced *-ont- into the participle (OCS dady, dadǫ̆stě)
but not into the indicative (OCS dadętŭ, like Skt. dádati), Li. dúodą, dedą
show the same vocalism as do dúodąs, dedą̃s.

In the future, nom. pl. vèsią agrees with the inherited participial forms
in pointing to an Indo-European thematic suffix *-sye-/-syo- identical with
that of Indo-Iranian.

Why was the regularly formed *vedantes replaced by the anomalous
*vedan, which besides lacking a case-number-gender ending was identical
with the nominative-accusative singular neuter of the participle? The
difficulty implied by the latter point is minor: the neuter may already
have been greatly restricted in its occurrence in East Baltic, the only area
where the incorporation of *vedan into the participial paradigm is certain,
and in any case homonymy of neuter singular and masculine plural would
have been no more inconvenient than the homonymy of nominative
singular feminine and neuter plural in some paradigms which has been
widely tolerated for long periods in many Indo-European languages.

*Vedan of course had the advantage over *vedantes of being shorter.
And Calvert Watkins has called my attention to the possibility of influence
from a Finno-Ugric sub- or adstratum. In Estonian, the closest Finno-
Ugric language that I know anything about, the third plural present indicative is normally identical with the nominative plural of the present active
participle, e.g., kasvavat 'crescunt, crescentes,' and 'any . . . sentence with
the present tense morpheme may be presented as indirectly reported
speech without assuming responsibility for the accuracy of the sentence
. . . by [using] the present participle vAH in the partitive-singular case'
-vatt (Harms, 1962: 136) e.g., maja asuvatt 'the house is said to be located,'
mehet olevatt 'the men are said to be.' No doubt there is a causal connection between this use of a participial form in unvouched-for reports and
the similar usages of East Baltic, although I know too little of Finno-Ugric
to say whether there is reason to believe that the construction originated in
Finnic and spread from there to Baltic. But the identity of third plural
present verb forms and nominative plural participles is clearly inherited in

Finnic; indeed, there seems every reason to think that in these languages the third plural present in -*vat* is etymologically nothing other than the nominative plural of the present participle, used predicatively. Hence the double value of -*vat* in Finnic would have favored syncretism in Baltic of third plural and nominative plural participle among the bilinguals who certainly existed for a long time and in large numbers; in the competition between **vedan* and **vedantes* for the two positions, the shorter form had the advantage.

For the preterit, the ending -*ę* of Lithuanian is clearly the third plural belonging to preterits formed with the Baltic suffix -*ē*-, of the type Li. *vēdė* 'led,' third plural Baltic **veden* from **vedent* from **ved-ē-nt*. As Otrębski and Vaillant saw, the past participles in -*ęs*, -*ę* are based on the preterit indicative in -*ē*-; but it is the masculine and neuter singular that are analogic to the plural, not the other way around.

The syntactic conditions for restructuring third plural finite forms as nominative plural participles would have been the same in the preterit (and imperfect) as in the present and future. Here too we can suppose that **(jai/jās) veden* 'they led' had practically gone out of use except in constructions where it was in competition with **(jai) veduses*, **(jās) vedusjās* 'they (allegedly) led,' and that it then replaced **veduses* and optionally **vedusjās* in all their uses.

Formally there would have been at first no superficial similarity between the third plural preterit **-en* and the past participle in -*us(ja)*- to support reinterpretation of **-en* as a participial form (it is altogether unlikely that the Baltic preterit suffixes in -*ā*- and -*ē*- continue Indo-European formations that had participles or that -*nt*-participles as such were ever created to these stems in the prehistory of Baltic), but such formal support was evidently not necessary, and the present and future did offer indirect support for plural participles in **-n*; we can suppose that the third plural indicatives were reevaluated as a unit.

It is now possible to explain the nominative singular masculine and neuter *vēdęs* (Latv. *vedis*), *vēdę* without recourse to ill-founded Indo-European prototypes or to complex and unlikely analogic remodelings. **Vedens*, **veden* have simply replaced the inherited forms on the model of the present (and future) participles, where nominative singular neuter was identical with the nominative plural masculine and the nominative singular masculine was the same with the addition of -*s*. Pres. sg. **vedans*, **vedan* : pres. pl. **vedan* = X : pret. pl. **veden*.

Probably the main reason that the old nominative singular masculine and neuter forms of the preterit participle were replaced is that the inherited forms had, by generalization of zero grade in the suffix, fallen together as *vedus–cf. OCS vedŭ. This would have been anomalous in not distinguishing masculine from neuter, and in being the only nominative singular masculine formation in the language that was not marked either by an ending -s or by a distinct stem form (type piemuõ, ménuo).[11] The surface pattern of present nom. sg. masc. *veda-ns, nom. sg. neut. and nom. pl. *veda-n vs. all the other forms with *veda-ntī, *veda-ntjā- was a model for having nominative singular masculine and neuter of the preterit participle agree with the nominative plural in having a form *ved-en(s) radically different from the *ved-usī, ved-usjā- of the rest of the paradigm.

The endings based on the ē-preterit were generalized also to verbs where the preterit indicative was formed with the suffix -ā-, e.g., Li. lìko 'remained,' Latv. lika 'put,' with past participles Li. lìkęs, lìkę, Latv. licis. Likewise the Lithuanian imperfect, type vèsdavo, has participles vèsdavęs, vèsdavę. The reason for this generalization of ē-forms has been seen by Otrębski (1956: 257) and Vaillant (1958: 555). In Common East Baltic there were no present or future stems in -ē-, so that endings *-ens, *-en were unambiguously preterit. But preterit forms in *-ans and *-an, shortened from *-ānt, would have ended the same way as present participle forms from stems in -ā- (e.g., Li. mãtąs, mãtą 'seeing') and -a- (e.g., Li. vedąs, vedą), as well as the athematic type ēsąs, ēsą 'being.' In the case of verbs with simple a-present and ā-preterit and no root ablaut, like Li. dìrbti 'work' or sésti 'sit down,' there would have been complete coalescence. Hence the generalization of *-ens, *-en, as being more distinctively preterital and avoiding all possibility of confusion with present participles. Generalization of one set of endings was helped by the fact that most forms of the preterit participles had the uniform suffix -us(ja)-, formally independent from the indicative, whether formed with -ē- or with -ā-.

To sum up: the Indo-European third plural indicative, far from disappearing without a trace in Baltic, has been transformed into the East Baltic nominative plural in -ą, -į, -ę of the active participles, as preserved in Lithuanian and reconstructible for Latvian from the relic ęsu in the present and the nominative singular -is of the preterit participles. And the nominative singular masculine and neuter -ęs, -ę of the East Baltic preterit participles, far from requiring a Proto-Indo-European nominative singular *-wēns, a complex and unlikely series of analogic remodelings within the paradigm of the preterit participle itself, or the existence of -nt-participles as such to the preterit indicative in -ē-, are formed by a simple and plausible analogic proportion to the present participles and the new East Baltic nominative plural preterit participles.[12]

Whether a similar reevaluation of third plural finite forms as participles took place in Prussian it is impossible to say for sure, in the absence both of forms directly continuing Balto-Slavic *-ntes, *-uses and of forms in -an, -en used as nominative plural participles. Indirect evidence indicating that the remodeling did occur in Prussian as well as in East Baltic is the nominative singular masculine ending -uns (-ons, -ans) of the Prussian preterit participle, e.g., aulauuns 'having died.' The -n- of this ending is generally explained as analogic to that of the present participles in -an(t)s, e.g., Szemerényi (1967: 17). But if that were the whole explanation, I would expect to find the -n- in other parts of the preterit participle's paradigm, instead of the forms like nom. sg. fem. aulausē and acc. pl. masc. aulausins that actually occur. In other Indo-European languages where the wos-participle has been remodeled after nt-adjectives, the remodeling has not been restricted to the nominative singular masculine; cf. Skt. jāgṛvádbhis (and vidvā́ṃsam?), Gk. eidótos (Szemerényi, 1967: 23–24, on the probable role of the nt-stems in introducing -t- here) and Aeol. katelēlúthontos, Tocharian A obl. sg. masc. and nom. -obl. pl. fem. kälpont. In Prussian, what analogic proportion could cause nom. sg. -ants to make *-us into -uns without acc. pl. -antins making -usins into *-unsins or *-untins?

I suggest rather that -uns is for *-ens, assimilated in vocalism to the inflected forms in -us-, and that *-ens in turn is built on a nominative plural in *-en, of the same type as in East Baltic. If so, the reevaluation of third plural finite forms as participles would belong to the Common Baltic period; and since a crucial factor in that reevaluation is the existence of constructions where there could be uncertainty as to whether a verb form was finite or participial, the use of participles as predicates in reported speech would also belong to the Common Baltic period, despite the lack of examples in Prussian.

It can also be asked whether the inherited nominative plurals in masc. *-ntes, *-uses and fem. *-ntjās, *-usjās survived at all beside *-n, *-en in (East) Baltic. For the feminines it is clear that formally Li. vēdančios, vēdusios and the corresponding forms in Latvian can equally well be inheritances or new creations on the basis of the oblique stems in -ntjā- and -usjā-; but the use of vedą, vēdę as feminine seems easier to explain if there was a time when the inherited forms had been given up altogether and *vedan, *veden were used as nominative plural of both genders. This minimizes the amount of time that competing forms for one niche in the paradigm have to be assumed.

For the masculine it is clear that the type Li. vēdantie-, vēdusie-, Latv. vędoši, veduši, Pruss. skellāntei can have been built on oblique -ntja-,

-usja- without the help of retained **vedantes*, **veduses*. The type Li. *vēdantys*, *vēdusys*, Latv. *gribuets*, Pruss. *immusis* must be based on forms that could be interpreted as belonging to *i*-stems, i.e. (mainly) the accusative singular masculine in Proto-Baltic **-ntin*, **-usin*. I do not think that plurals in **-ntes*, **-uses* beside **-n*, **-en* are required for this analogy to have operated in addition to the analogy that created *vēdantie-* etc. True, in noun paradigms *-ys* is regularly a replacement of *-(e)s*. But the noun paradigms of Baltic offer nothing comparable to nom. pl. **vedan*, **veden* beside acc. sg. **vedantin*, **vedusin*, and within the adjective paradigms the *u*-stem type (Li.) acc. sg. *skaũdų*, nom. pl. *skaũdūs* beside other cases mostly built on **skaudja-* does offer a pattern for remodeling of acc. sg. **vedantin*, **vedusin*, nom. pl. **vedan*, **veden* beside other cases mostly built on **vedantja-*, **vedusja-* to **vedantin, vedantys, *vedantja-* and **vedusin, vedusys, *vedusja-*.

Yale University

NOTES

1. Endzelīns, *Izvěstija* . . . *Akademii Naukŭ* 22.2 (1918), p. 187, suggested that *nórints*, a variant of the indefinite particles *nórs, nórint* (e.g., *kas norints* 'somebody or other') may be a relic of the old nominative plural. But there is nothing plural about its meaning in the sources where Endzelīns found it, and it may well be simply a blend of *nórs* and *nórint*.

2. I cannot consider here the question of accentuation. But nominative singular neuter and nominative plural masculine of these participles have regularly the same accent as nominative singular masculine, and to the extent that the accent of the former has not developed straightforwardly from Proto-Indo-European models, it has evidently followed the same innovations as the latter.

3. Li. *sesuõ*, acc. *sēserį*, in which precisely the nominative singular is the one form not affected, shows what really happened in Baltic when *e*-grade spread from the locative of an *-oC*-stem.

4. Bartholomae, *Grundriss der iranischen Philologie* 1.1 (Strassburg, 1896) p. 221 takes this as not an original *nt*-stem, and substitutes *hạm* for **hā̃n* as a better example. Both authors agree on Gathic *mīždauuạn* as an example of the original neuter plural formation of *nt*-stems.

5. He might have mentioned that the formation is, apparently, found also in Hittite, e.g., *ud-da-a-ar* 'words, affairs' (although not, to my knowledge, in *nt*-stems), and the fossilized numeral Lat. *quattuor*, Gothic *fidwor*. But these only help to establish the formation as Proto-Indo-European, without enhancing the likelihood that it would have survived into Baltic as part of the regular paradigm of participles.

6. Vaillant in *Grammaire comparée des langues slaves* 2, (1958) p. 545, has a quite different explanation, viz, that *vedǫ* started in the definite paradigm, where *vedǫjie* was formed to sg. *vedǫsis* on the analogy of *a*-stem adjectives like sg.

geràs-is, pl. *gerìe-jie*. But the analogy is not perfect, since *gerìe-* is not simply *geràs-* minus *s*; and it is most unlikely that an innovation starting in the fondé and comparatively rare definite paradigm would have spread to the basic and frequent simplex paradigm. (To be sure, Vaillant's analogy would work equally well—or badly—without the intermediary of the definite forms. *Gēras* : *gerì* ≠ *vedą̄s* : *vedą̆*.) Zinkevičius (1966: 378–379, 381–382) calls the forms in *-ą̆*, *-į̆*, and *-ę̆* old neuters, not specifying whether originally singular or plural.

7. Cf. Stang, *Vergleichende Grammatik der baltischen Sprachen* (Oslo, 1966), p. 411.

8. Or rather, monosyllabic forms were probably avoided here by generalizing full grade **esan*, **ejan*. This is suggested by the situation in Old Lithuanian, where inflected participial forms (in modernized spelling) *sañčio*, *eñčio* etc. (beside *ēsančio* etc.) and gerunds *sañt*, *eñt*, with recently lost ending, are attested in Daukša (Senn, *Handbuch der litauischen Sprache* 1 [Heidelberg, 1966] pp. 290, 295) and in Klein's *Grammatica lituanica* (Vilnius, 1957) pp. 123, 125, but the nominative singular and plural masculine are only *ēsąs*, *ēsą* and *ējąs*, *ėją*.

9. Or whatever conjunction(s) the language then used to introduce indirect discourse.

10. The opposite change of participles to finite verb forms—e.g., Russian *byl*, Persian *bud*, Hindi *thā* 'was'—is of course much more common, requiring only the consistent omission of a verbal copula to get started. A distant parallel to the Baltic development is the Old Icelandic preterit infinitive in sentences like *Hvat hyggr þú brúði bendo?* 'Quid putas tu puellam significasse?,' where *bendo* is etymologically a third plural preterit indicative that was reinterpreted as infinitive from use in sentences like *Hvat hyggr þú brúðir bendo?*, originally 'What do you think the girls meant?,' but taken as 'What do you think the girls to have meant?' OIc. *bendo*, however, did not lose its primary value of third plural preterit indicative.

11. *Mēnuo* is the only other masculine *s*-stem inherited by Baltic, and it is significant that here too the nominative was remodeled after a different stem type (for a recent discussion, see Szemerényi, *Studi micenei ed egeo-anatolici* 2, [1967], p. 15).

12. Not surprisingly, the comparatively rare third duals have not led to dual participle forms of the type **vedate(s)*, **vedēte(s)*—for the putative shape of the ending cf. OCS *-te*, Skt. *-tas*—beside masc. *vēdančiu*, *vēdusiu*, *vēduse* and fem. *vēdanti*, *vēdusi*.

REFERENCES

Bielenstein, A. 1863. *Lettische Grammatik.*

Endzelīns, Jānis. 1918. *Izvĕstija Otdĕlenija Russkago Jazyka i Slovesnosti Imperatorskoj Akademii Naukŭ*, 22, 2.

Endzelīns, Jānis. 1923. *Lettische Grammatik.* Heidelberg.

Harms, Robert T. 1962. *Estonian Grammar.* Bloomington, Ind.

Klein, Daniel. 1653. *Grammatica lituanica.* Regiomonti (reprinted Vilnius, 1957).

Otrębski, Jan. 1956. *Gramatyka języka litewskiego*, 3. Warsaw.

Schmidt, Johannes. 1883. *Zeitschrift für vergleichende Sprachforschung*, 26.

Schmidt, Johannes. 1889. *Die Pluralbildungen der indogermanischen Neutra.* Weimar.

Senn, A. 1966. *Handbuch der litauischen Sprache,* 1. Heidelberg.

Stang, Christian. 1966. *Vergleichende Grammatik der baltischen Sprachen.* Oslo.

Szemerényi, Oswald. 1967. The perfect participle active in Mycenaean and Indo-European, *Studi micenei ed egeo-anatolici*, 2. Roma.

Vaillant, André. 1958. *Grammaire comparée des langues slaves*, 2. Lyon-Paris.

Zinkevıčius, Z. 1966. *Lietuvių dialektologija.* Vilnius.

THE STATE OF LINGUISTICS IN SOVIET LITHUANIA

L. DAMBRIŪNAS

During World War II Lithuania lost a considerable part of its intelligentsia, including almost all the linguists from the universities of Vilnius and Kaunas; only the oldest scholar in the field, Professor J. Balčikonis, remained.

Lack of qualified personnel was the first obstacle which delayed linguistic studies in Lithuania during the first decade after World War II. The second important hindrance to serious work was the influence of the linguistic theories which prevailed in the Soviet Union at that time. The inventor of these theories, a Soviet linguist named N. J. Marr, was considered to be the best adapter of Marxist doctrine to the field of linguistics. These obstacles have indeed been recognized by the Lithuanian linguists themselves. Later, one of them wrote these words: "In the first years after the war, the speedy development of Lithuanian linguistics was hindered, on the one hand, by a great shortage of trained personnel, and on the other hand, by the influence of the antiscientific theory of N. Marr."[1] But even after 1950 when, in the words of one linguist, "the pseudo-Marxist idealistic and fantastic teachings of Marr" had been abolished, troubles for Lithuanian linguists did not disappear entirely. One linguist has written as follows: "The personality cult of J. Stalin, which had gained strength at that time, could not help affecting Soviet linguistics. For a certain period of time, people followed the theories expressed in Stalin's work 'Marxism and the Questions of Linguistics' too dogmatically, even literally; creative thought was stifled considerably by dogmatism and a mania for quotations."[2]

It is necessary to note still another obstacle faced by Lithuanian linguists—the fear of structuralism. Having rejected Marrism, Soviet linguists did not want, for a certain period of time, to recognize structuralism as a positive new trend in linguistics. Such well-known Russian linguists as Serebrennikov, A. Chikobava, O. Akhmanova, and others denounced it. It seemed to them that structuralism did not conform to the principles of Marxism because, as one Lithuanian linguist wrote, it is "unreal, idealistic, and fears historicism . . . while a comparative-historical method of linguistic investigation satisfies the basic requirements of Marxist dialectical method: to investigate every phenomenon in its historical movement and in connection with other phenomena."[3]   Not long ago, however, the attitude of Soviet linguists toward structuralism changed. Many books on the subject have been translated into Russian from West European languages.   As a result Lithuanians are also permitted to investigate any linguistic problem from the viewpoint of structuralism, and this influence can be seen in some of their works.

A number of young Lithuanian linguists grew up during the first decade after World War II, and after the death of Stalin the first new linguistic works began appearing. Linguists were organized into teams as the compiling and the publishing of the large *Dictionary of Lithuanian Language* was resumed, material for the atlas of Lithuanian dialects was collected, and a series of monographs was written as preparation for a large grammar of the Lithuanian language.

At the present time the following institutions take part in various linguistic works:

1. The Institute of Language and Literature of the Lithuanian Academy of Sciences in Vilnius.

2. The University of Vilnius.

3. The State Institute for Teachers in Vilnius.

4. The State Institute for Teachers in Šiauliai.

Today there are perhaps about 30 active linguists in Lithuania. The number is fairly high as compared with that of more than two decades ago. This can be explained by two facts: first, academic work is paid considerably better than many other professions; second, linguists are practically free to do as they please in their work.

In order to get a better picture of what is being done in Lithuania presently, let us look at some work in detail.

DICTIONARIES

One of the most important linguistic works being produced in Lithuania is *The Dictionary of the Lithuanian Language*[4] which is being published by The Lithuanian Academy of Sciences in Vilnius. As of this date, six big volumes of approximately 1,000 pages each have appeared, plus a seventh somewhat smaller one. The writing of the eighth volume has been completed, and the ninth one is being prepared. There will be 15 volumes altogether. This dictionary includes all words found not only in literary language but also in living dialects and in the oldest Lithuanian literature as well. It can be compared with the *Oxford English Dictionary* in scope and purpose.

The compiling of this dictionary was begun by the great Lithuanian linguist K. Būga. However, he managed to prepare only the first two parts of the first volume, including an extensive introduction on the accent and intonation of Lithuanian and on the Baltic languages in general.[5] After his death, the work was abandoned for a few years. But in 1930 The Ministry of Education of Lithuania appointed Professor J. Balčikonis to resume it. Balčikonis changed the structure of the vocabulary and organized a team of workers to collect more material and to help in compiling the vocabulary. The first volume was issued during the war in 1941 and the second after the war in 1947. However, the new regime was not pleased with either of the volumes because, in the opinion of its critics, they contained "ideological and factual errors." So a new editorial staff was appointed and was charged with reediting the third volume already completed by chief editor J. Balčikonis. It was reedited according to the instructions prepared "in consultation with the coordinating commission of the Linguistic Institute of USSR Academy of Sciences."[6] The most important innovations in the third and the following volumes are some changes in the arrangement of words and in illustrative phrases or sentences, which are taken primarily from the contemporary literature and press. Since these literary and press items consist mostly of translations from Russian of Lenin's, Stalin's, Marx' and Engels' writings, the illustrative examples from these sources are not quite reliable. The situation is saved, however, by examples taken from other sources, and the vocabulary, generally speaking, is not much harmed. The first two volumes, which are already out of print, have been recently reedited according to the new instructions and are to be published shortly.

Another dictionary worth mentioning is *The Dictionary of the Contemporary Lithuanian Language,* edited by J. Balčikonis and others. This is a dictionary of standard Lithuanian containing some 45,000 entries. Its function is comparable to that of *Webster's Collegiate Dictionary* of American English. The compiling of this dictionary was begun before

World War II, and in 1944 it was nearly completed. It did not, however, satisfy the requirements of the new regime and was reedited according to the "theses of Lenin and Stalin on language matters."[7]

A new edition was reissued in Chicago in 1962. However, this dictionary is not large enough, and the big one is not yet completed. Therefore scholars have to use at the present time the only available comprehensive dictionary. This is a Lithuanian-German dictionary compiled by Professors A. Senn and A. Salys and published by Carl Winter in Heidelberg, Germany.[8]

After World War II some school dictionaries were published in Lithuania—Lithuanian-Russian, Lithuanian-English, Lithuanian-French and others. The largest of these is a Russian-Lithuanian dictionary compiled by V. Baronas and V. Galinis.[9] Published in 1967, it contains about 75,000 words. A series of special terminological dictionaries has also been published, including those in the fields of technology, geology, physics, chemistry, music, sports, and others.

In 1961 a small dictionary of Lithuanian synonyms, the work of A. Lyberis, was issued, and in 1964 there appeared a vocabulary of the writings of Kristijonas Donelaitis, the famous Lithuanian poet in the eighteenth century; it was compiled by J. Kabelka.

GRAMMARS

The Institute of Language and Literature of The Lithuanian Academy of Sciences has been preparing a Lithuanian grammar in three volumes. The first volume, published in 1965, comprises phonology and morphology of nouns, adjectives, pronouns, and numerals. The second volume, which is nearly completed, describes the verb and the inflectional parts of speech. The third part will deal with syntax. This grammar is being prepared by a group of linguists under the direction of Kazys Ulvydas. It is a descriptive and normative grammar. The authors explain its nature in these words: "Its purpose is to give a scientific description of the phonetic and grammatical structure of the contemporary Lithuanian literary language, to disclose the tendencies of developments of its most characteristic phonetic and grammatical structure and to elucidate, as far as it is possible, the phonetic, morphological (inflectional as well as structural) and syntactical norms."[10] Since the seventeenth century, many Lithuanian grammars have been published, but this one seems to be the best ever written. The part on phonetics and phonology is based on experiments made in a phonetic laboratory. It also gives the first precise description of the quality and quantity of Lithuanian vowels and diphthongs as well as consonants. In addition, it deals with accent and intonation, while the morphological part covers inflection and word formation. It also includes historical and dialectal explanations needed for better understanding of contemporary forms. In preparing this collective work, a series of monographs was written on phonetics, morphology, and syntax as well. The work was done by V. Vaitkevičiūtė, A. Valeckienė, A. Laigonaitė, V. Mažiulis, K. Ulvydas and others. When completed, it will undoubtedly be the most comprehensive and best descriptive grammar of the Lithuanian language.

There are also some investigations of Lithuanian historical grammar. Recently (1968) J. Kazlauskas published a *Historical Grammar of the Lithuanian Language (Accent, Noun, Verb);* this work also has relevance for the section following.

HISTORY OF THE LITHUANIAN LANGUAGE

In 1967 there appeared *The History of the Lithuanian Literary Language (16-17 Century)*[11] by J. Palionis. This is the first and most comprehensive description of developments in the literary language during these two centuries. The same author has also written on the development of the literary language at the end of the nineteenth century (1880–1901).

There are some other publications dealing with the history of the Lithuanian language. First of all, the new photographic edition of the *First Lithuanian Grammar*[12] by Danielius Kleinas should be mentioned. It appeared originally in Latin as *Grammatica Litvanica* (1653) and in its shorter German version as *Compendium Litvanico-Germanicum* (1654). Both works have been translated into Lithuanian, and an extensive introduction by T. Buchienė and J. Palionis has been added. This excellent new edition, which appeared in Vilnius in 1957, is very important for those who are interested in the history of Lithuanian grammar. As a matter of fact, its publication marked 300 years since the appearance of the first Lithuanian grammar.

Another important publication for the history of the language is a hymnal by S. M. Sławoczyński.[13] This book was first published in 1646, and presently only one copy is preserved at The National Library in Warsaw. The photographic edition published in Vilnius in 1958 contains adequate commentaries by Jurgis Lebedys. The same scholar is also the editor of another very useful book providing much material on the history of the Lithuanian language. It is a folklore collection called

Minor Lithuanian Folklore of the 17th-18th Centuries (Proverbs, Sayings, Riddles), published in 1956.[14] These folklore items are taken mostly from unpublished manuscripts such as J. Brodowski's dictionary, anonymous collections of minor folklore items, and other sources.

Some other books pertaining to the history of the language are the writings of authors who lived in the first half of the nineteenth century. Among them the following have been published recently: the first book of Lithuanian folksongs collected by Liudvikas Rėza;[15] the selected works of Simonas Daukantas;[16] the complete writings of Dionizas Poška;[17] and the complete works of Simonas Stanevičius.[18]

Here we should also mention the publication of selected works of the two most prominent Lithuanian linguists in the first half of the twentieth century. These are the works of Jonas Jablonskis[19] edited by J. Palionis, and the most important works of Kazys Būga,[20] edited by Z. Zinkevičius. Jablonskis' works, which mostly deal with the problems of standard Lithuanian, are published in two volumes. The first comprises all his textbooks and the second the more important articles and book reviews. K. Būga's works are published in three big volumes, the last of which appeared in 1961. In addition to the three volumes there is a separate 398-page index compiled by Z. Zinkevičius. This new edition is very important for Baltic linguistics, since Būga's writings were out of print. Finally mention should also be made of *Prūsų kalbos paminklai,* (Vilnius, 1966), a new photographic edition of all the monuments of Old Prussian with an introduction by V. Mažiulis.

DIALECTOLOGY

Since World War II Lithuanian dialects have been investigated systematically, and an atlas of Lithuanian dialects is being prepared. For this purpose the whole country was divided into 703 geographical points, and the material was registered in so-called dialectological expeditions. At the present time the collecting of the material has been completed, and the work of cartography is being done.

During the last two decades many monographs describing specific Lithuanian dialects have been written. Some of them were presented as dissertations by candidates for masters degrees. Furthermore, a comprehensive study on Lithuanian dialectology[21] by Z. Zinkevičius has been published recently. This is the newest and most comprehensive work on Lithuanian dialectology. In addition, a large textbook (chrestomathy) of Lithuanian dialects has also been prepared.

Lithuanian toponyms and the names of rivers and lakes are also being registered and investigated. Some hundreds of thousands of them have been recorded in a card index. There is also a card index of personal names containing about 300,000 cards.[22] This material, however, has not yet been published except for one register of Lithuanian rivers and lakes containing about 10,000 names.[23]   A series of articles on the origin of toponyms has been published in periodicals.

PERIODICALS

Six linguistic periodicals founded after World War II are now being published in Lithuania.

1. *Kalbotyra* (Linguistics) published by the University of Vilnius and the Teachers' College has been appearing since 1958. It prints articles not only about Lithuanian but also about other languages studied at these two institutions. Some of the articles have dealt with Russian, English, German, French, Latin, and other languages. In 1967 the eighteenth volume was issued. Until 1958 the two schools published two separate periodicals, in which some articles on language questions appeared; it was called *Mokslo Darbai.*

2. *Lietuvių kalbotyros klausimai* (Questions of Lithuanian Linguistics) has been published since 1957. To date nine volumes have been issued.

3. *Literatūra ir kalba* (Literature and Language) has been published since 1955. The eight volumes issued deal mostly with literature, but some of them contain linguistic works as well.

4. *Lietuvos TSR Mokslų Akademijos Darbai,* Serija A (Works of Academy of Sciences of Lithuanian SSR, Series A) has been published since 1955. A part of this publication is dedicated to linguistic questions.

5. *Baltistica*, first published in 1965, is dedicated to the investigation of all the Baltic languages. The articles are published in Lithuanian, Latvian, Russian, English, German, and French. Among the foreign contributors there are some Americans.

6. *Kalbos kultūra* (Culture of the Language) deals largely with practical problems. It provides explanations of correct usage in phonetics, morphology, symtax, and vocabulary. Two issues have been published annually since 1961.

These are the most important projects being done by Lithuanian linguists in Soviet Lithuania. Some of them, as was mentioned earlier, were not initiated during the postwar period. Rather they are the continuation of works begun before World War II. At the present time, however, there are more Lithuanian linguists than there ever were before. Some of them are still young scholars, and they are working very diligently. Their research in every area of linguistics is well organized. We wish them every success.

As a postscript, I would like to add that everything said about the linguistics in Lithuania can also be said about linguistics in another Baltic country, namely, Latvia. Latvian linguists are working with equal success in almost the same fields as Lithuanians. Some information about their achievements can be found in *Baltistica*, (No. 1/2/ [1965] p. 201).

Washington, D.C.

NOTES

1. J. Palionis, *Kalbotyra* 1 (Vilnius, 1958), p. 6.
2. R. Mironas, "Kalbotyros metodų beieškant," *Kalbotyra* 10 (Vilnius, 1964), p. 246.
3. R. Mironas, *Ibid.* p. 251.
4. *Lietuvių kalbos žodynas*, red. J. Balčikonis, J. Kruopas, K. Ulvydas ir kt., t. 1–7 (Vilnius, 1941–1966).
5.. K. Būga, *Lietuvių kalbos žodynas* (Kaunas, 1924). Reprinted in K. Būgā, *Rinktiniai raštai* 3 (Vilnius, 1961).
6. *Lietuvių kalbos žodynas*/red. J. Kruopas ir kt./, 3, (Vilnius, 1956), p. 3.
7. *Dabartinės lietuvių kalbos žodynas,* red. J. Balčikonis ir kt. (Vilnius, 1954), p. 5.
8. A. Senn and A. Salys, *Wörterbuch der litauischen Schriftsprache Litauisch-Deutsch* (Heidelberg, 1967).
9. V. Baronas, V. Galinis, *Rusų-lietuvių kalbų žodynas* (Vilnius, 1967).
10. K. Ulvydas (Vyr. redaktorius), *Lietuvių kalbos gramatika* (Vilnius, 1965).
11. J. Palionis, *Lietuvių literatūrinė kalba, XVI-XVIIa,* (Vilnius, 1967).
12. *Pirmoji lietuvių kalbos gramatika* (Vilnius, 1957).
13. S. M. Slavočinskis, *Giesmės* (tikėjimui katalickam priderančios), (Vilnius, 1958).
14. J. Lebedys (paruošė), *Smulkioji lietuvių tautosaka,* 17–18 (Priežodžiai, patarlės, mįslės) (Vilnius, 1956).
15. L. Rėza, *Lietuvių liaudies dainos* 1, (Vilnius, 1958), 2, 1964.
16. Simonas Daukantas, *Rinktiniai raštai* (Vilnius, 1955).
17. Dionizas Poška, *Raštai* (Vilnius, 1959).
18. Simonas Stanevičius, *Raštai* (Vilnius, 1967).
19. J. Jablonskis, *Rinktiniai raštai* 1 (Vilnius, 1957), Vol. 2, 1959.
20. K. Būga, *Rinktiniai raštai* 1 (Vilnius, 1958), Vol. 2, 1959, Vol. 3, 1961.
21. Z. Zinkevičius, *Lietuvių dialektologija* (Lyginamoji tarmių fonetika ir morfologija) (Vilnius, 1966).
22. E. Grinaveckienė, J. Senkus, "Toponiminės medžiagos rinkimas ir tyrinėjimas Tarybų Lietuvoje," *Literatūra ir kalba* (Vilnius, 1962).
23. E. Grinaveckienė, J. Senkus, (red.) *Lietuvos TSR upių ir ežerų vardynas* (Vilnius, 1963).

ACCENT IN THE LITHUANIAN NOUN DECLENSION

BILL J. DARDEN

Prior to this volume, the only published treatment of Lithuanian accent from a generative viewpoint is C. Heeschen's "Lithuanian Morphophonemics."[1] This paper is intended primarily as an explanation of Lithuanian accent, but only slightly secondarily as an answer to Mr. Heeschen.

In the surface output, Lithuanian has three possibilities for accented syllables (there is only one accented syllable per word). A long syllable may be either rising (¯) or falling (´). Short syllables are only accented (`). The sonorants *l, m, n,* and *r* count as moras in closed syllables when not preceded by a long vowel. Clearly at some point in the grammar the long syllables can be represented as bimoric, with the ictus on the first (falling tone) or second mora (rising tone). This is the system which Mr. Heeschen adopts.

Lithuanian is traditionally considered to have four accentual classes for nouns, labeled 1, 2, 3, and 4. The examples below are all from declension II. The rules which will account for this declension will also take care of the other declensions, with proper adjustment for different desinences.

Singular

	1	2	3	4
N	várna	rankà	galvà	šakà
G	várnos	rañkos	galvõs	šakõs
D	várnai	rañkai	gálvai	šākai
A	várnā	rañkā	gálvā	šākā
I	várna	rankà	gálva	šakà
L	várnoje	rañkoje	galvojè	šakojè

Plural

N	várnos	rañkos	gálvos	šãkos
G	várnū	rañkū	galvū	šakū
D	várnoms	rañkoms	galvóms	šakóms
A	várnas	rankàs	gálvas	šakàs
I	várnomis	rañkomis	galvomìs	šakomìs
L	várnose	rañkose	galvosè	šakosè

To treat these four classes, Heeschen proposes two morpheme features: [± strong susceptible] and [± post stem]. [Strong susceptible] separates 1 and 2 (−), from 3 and 4 (+).

Classes 1 and 3 are [− post stem], 2 and 4 are [+ post stem]. This provides the proper grouping, since 4 is just like 3 with the pattern of 2 superimposed on it.

According to Heeschen, accent is assigned to the first mora after the stem in those marked [+ post stem], and on the second mora to the left of the word boundary in those marked [− post stem]. The accent is then retracted one mora. For the nominative case this yields:

$$\text{vaȓn-a-a} \longrightarrow \text{vàrn-a-a} \quad \text{(the second } a \text{ is}$$
$$\text{rank-à-a} \longrightarrow \text{rañk-a-a} \quad \text{deleted later)}$$

With accent on the first mora interpreted as falling, and on the second as rising, this yields *várn-*, *rañk-*. If the accent is retracted onto a short syllable, it remains short: *vìzai* (dat. sg.). It is of course true that this is not the correct accent for *rankà*. In the nominative and instrumental singular and accusative plural the accent remains on the desinence. Heeschen solves this problem by marking these cases as exceptions to the retraction rule when used with a stem marked plus post stem.

Heeschen remarks on the as yet unexplained fact that while both long and short syllables appear as roots marked [+ post stem], only long syllables appear in those marked [− post stem]. This is an odd fact, not about Lithuanian, but about his analysis. If we assume that there is not a shift back, with certain cases marked as exceptions, but a shift forward to those case endings, the situation is more clearly analyzable. We have the underlying forms: *vàrn-*, *rañk-* and *viz-*. Certain desinences attract the accent from the last mora of the stem. *Vàrn-*, not having the ictus on the last mora, is not affected by the rule. Note that this removes the necessity of having a morpheme feature [+/− post stem]. The shift forward is determined by the phonological shape of the stem, not its class membership.

That the above analysis is preferable becomes more obvious when we examine polysyllabic stems. Heeschen limited his description to monosyllabic stems. Applied to polysyllabic stems, his rules yield the wrong results. He allows for only one position of accent. For stems marked [− post stem; − strong susceptible] (class 1), that place is on the second mora to the left. In fact, in stems of class 1 the ictus may fall anywhere except on the last mora of the stem. For example: *pāsaka* (paàsak-), *ántis* (ànt-), *išvaizda, mókytojas* (mòokytoj-), *apātija* (apaàtij-). Since the ictus can only fall on the last mora of a class 2 stem, it is clear that there are not two classes 1 and 2, but one class plus a rule. The same rule links class 4 to class 3, but as will be seen below, the position of stress in stems marked [+ strong susceptible] is not free.

To explain the difference between the first two classes and the other two, Heeschen proposes a feature [+/− strong] for desinences. Accent is assigned to the last mora of a [+ strong] desinence which is preceded by a [+ strong susceptible] stem. (This in fact does not work, since the dative plural desinence *-óms* has falling intonation, i.e., accent on the next to last mora.)

Again, because he limited himself to monosyllabic stems, Heeschen can make no generalizations about the place of accent on the stem. In fact, he gives a false impression. Because of the way he assigns stress for stems marked [+ post-stem] —assigning it to the first mora after the stem and then shifting it back to the final mora of the stem—he gives the impression that the alternation is between the last mora of the stem and the last mora of the word. In fact the alternation is between the first and the last syllable of the word.[2] For example: (acc. sg. and dat. pl.) *ážuolą/ažuoláms; drēbulę/drebulėms; áuksakalį/auksakaliáms*. When the stem is monosyllabic and has either a short vowel or rising intonation, the ictus is on the last mora of the stem and thus is subjected to the rule that shifts the accent to a desinence. This creates class 4.

Since the accent, when it falls on the stem of words of classes 3 and 4, is always on the initial syllable, it seems reasonable to consider stems of this class to be stressless, with the stress inserted by a rule. Those endings which Heeschen labels "strong" could be simply stressed desinences. If there were a rule that asserted the primacy of the first stress in the word, these desinences would only be stressed when preceded by stressless stems. Morris Halle[3] has proposed a universal convention whereby when an accent is put on a word all the other accents are lowered. Thus we could simply restress the first stress in the word, thus lowering the stress on the desinence, and later remove all accents lower than the highest. A rule can then stress the first syllable of the word without a stress.

Note, however, that while position of stress is predictable in the above classes, the intonation is not (e.g., *ážuolą, drẽbulę*). This means that syllables must be marked for the intonation that they will receive if stressed. There is a lot of redundancy in the intonational marking. One need not mark single-mora syllables, and, if one decides to solve the technical problem of marking a syllable by marking individual moras as [+/− high], then only one mora per syllable need be marked. Also, since accent is inserted by rule only in initial position, we need the [+/− high] distinction only on the initial mora. (Below I suggest that some of the desinential accents are inserted by rule, so we need the distinction on the initial mora of a stem and the final mora of a desinence.) Nevertheless, this treatment presents intonation as a paradigmatic feature of syllabics in Lithuanian. In gaining a segmental feature, however, we have lost two morpheme features. In this analysis there are no accentual classes. The accentual pattern is completely determined by the position of accent in the underlying form. In the underlying form any syllable or no syllable may be accented.

As an alternative to having intonation as a feature, we could set up two accentual classes by a morpheme feature. (I would prefer the name [+/− mobile] to [+/− strong susceptible].) There would then be a redundancy rule that marked all stems not accented in the first syllable as minus mobile. I prefer the former solution, in particular as it makes Lithuanian very similar to Slavic.[4]

Finally, the distribution of accented desinences is not random. Some of the accents could be inserted by rule. In the plural and dual, for instance, there is a pattern of initial stress in the nominative and accusative, vs desinential stress in the other cases. This pattern also appears in Slavic.[5] Using the features which Jakobson developed for Russian,[6] we can interpret this as an opposition of natural classes. The nominative and accusative are both marked [− peripheral, − quantitative]. He terms the nominative and accusative the "direct" cases, the others the "oblique." We may have a rule that accents the last syllable of the desinences of the oblique cases of the dual and plural. There is also a rule which accents the desinences of nominative, genitive, and locative singular of declensions II through V. The stressed desinences not covered by rule will be listed below.

To recapitulate, we have the following ordered rules (relevant ordering is indicated by numbers):

1. Accent the last high mora of:
   a. The desinences of the oblique plural and dual.
   b. The nominative, genitive, and locative of the singular in declensions II-V.
2. a. Accent the first high mora of an unaccented word.
   b. Accent the first accented mora of a word.
3. In the environment $\acute{m}C_1$ ___ (m stands for mora), accent the first mora of the following desinences: accusative plural; nominative/accusative dual; nominative singular -a (of second declension); the instrumental singular of the first, second, and fifth declension (these are probably the same underlying desinence, while the third and fourth have -mi); the locative singular of the first declension.[7]
4. Remove all accents except the highest in a word.

Classes 1 and 2 are accented stems. If the accent falls anywhere but on the final mora of the stem, it remains fixed. If the accent is on a final mora, i.e., on a final syllable which is either short or has rising intonation, rule 3 operates. This creates class 2. Thus we get (nom. sg.) *rankà, vizà*; (ins. sg.) *rankà, vizà*; (acc. pl.) *rankàs, vizàs*, (nom./acc. dual) *rankì, vizì*, but all the other cases have *rañk-, viz-*.

Classes 3 and 4 are unaccented stems. If the ending is accented, the accent falls on the ending. The oblique nonsingular, and the nominative, genitive, dative singular of declensions II-V are accented by rule 1. The dative plural and dual are marked [− high] on their last mora so as to get falling intonation. The stressed desinences not covered by rule are: the instrumental singular -mi (in declensions III and IV); and, in declension I, the nominative singular, -is, the nominative plural, and the locative singular. There is oscillation as to whether or not the locative singular -e is accented.[8]

If there is no accent in a word, rule 2a inserts one on the first syllable. Initial syllables which take rising intonation have their first mora marked [− high]. If the stem is monosyllabic and has either a short syllable or rising intonation, this puts the accent on the last mora of the stem, and rule 3 can operate, creating class 4.

Rule 2b assures that, in the case of an accented stem and accented ending, the accent on the stem dominates. Rule 4 will remove the lowered accent from the ending.

University of Colorado

NOTES

1. Quarterly Progress Report 85, Research Laboratory in Electronics, MIT, Cambridge, Mass., 1967.

2. This is true of nouns and indefinite adjectives but not true of ordinal or cardinal numbers, cf. *septynì, septynerì* 'seven,' *septynerì, septýnerius* 'seven (with plural nouns)' *septiñtas, septintà* 'seventh.' A. Senn, in *Handbuch der litauischen Sprache* 1 (Heidelberg, 1966), p. 103, discusses a few noun stems which optionally alternate between stem-final and desinential position.

3. R. Paul V. Kiparsky, "Über den deutschen Akzent," *Studia Grammatica* 7 (1966)

4. Bill J. Darden, "The Expression of Morphological Redundancy in Generative Grammar: An Example from Russian Accent," *The Chicago Journal of Linguistics* 1 (1) (Chicago, 1967), pp. 85–102.

5. Edward Stankiewicz, "Unity and Variety in the Morphophonemic Patterns of the Slavic Declensions," *American Contributions to the Fifth International Congress of Slavists* (Sofia, 1963) pp. 263–286.

6. Roman Jakobson, "Beitrag zur allgemeinen Kasuslehre," *Travaux du Cercle Linguistique de Prague* 6 (1936), pp. 240–287.

7. This rule was historically a phonological rule (De Saussure's law), and if one were assiduous in ferreting out the history for recapitulation through generation, it might be possible to reinstate it as a purely phonological rule. In the surface, all the attracting desinences happen to be short monosyllables (they were historically acutes, which were shortened in final position). However, they are not the only short monosyllabic desinences. The short nominative singulars in -*s* and the short vocatives do not attract the accent. One could consider the vocative to be outside the normal inflectional system, and could make the nominative singulars exceptions to a rule that shifts the ictus from stem final position onto a short desinence; (cf. D. F. Robinson's paper in this volume). If Heeschen is correct in his underlying forms, this would have to occur after the final shortening rule.

8. Christian S. Stang, *Vergleichende Grammatik der Baltischen Sprachen* (Oslo, 1966), p. 298.

CONCERNING THE RELATIONSHIPS OF THE PRUSSIAN LANGUAGE WITH CONGENERS

JĀNIS ENDZELĪNS

(translated by B. Jēgers and W. R. Schmalstieg)

When the light of history first reaches the early Prussians we see them living as neighbors to the Slavic and Germanic people from whom they borrowed various words. Linguistic data indicate that such bonds with their neighbors existed also at the time of the proto-language. I have counted 33 Prussian words, for which, from the point of view of form or meaning, the closest or even the only cognates are found in the Slavic languages. For brevity's sake I shall mention here only the Prussian forms, since it is possible to find etymologies for them in Trautmann's *Die altpreussischen Sprachdenkmäler*: *arwis* 'true,' *assanis* 'autumn,' *audāt sien* 'happens,' *amūsnan* 'ablution,' *bleusky* 'reed, rush, sedge,' *dalptan* 'auger, drill,' *eyswo* 'wound,' *insuwis* 'tongue,' *iswinadu* 'exceptionally,' (see *Filologu biedrĭbas raksti*, 10, p. 18) *camnet* 'horse,' *kūnti* 'takes care of,' *curwis* 'ox,' *mais* 'my,' *maldai* 'young (people),' *maldenikis* 'baby,' *naricie* 'skunk,' *pausto* 'wild,' *peisda* 'arse,' *penpalo* 'quail,' *pistwis* 'dog-fly (musca canicularis),' *proglis* 'fire-dogs,' *salowis* 'nightingale,' *seydis* 'wall,' *seilin* 'diligence,' *sompisinis* 'coarse bread,' *strigeno* 'membrane, brain (*ibid*. p. 140),' *swais* 'one's own,' *tisties* 'father-in-law,' *tlāku* 'step, stamp,' (see *Filologu biedrĭbas raksti*, 10, p. 223), *twais* 'your (sg.),' *waitiāt* 'to speak, to say,' *winna* 'out of,' (see *Filologu biedrĭbas raksti*, 10, p. 81), *wutris* 'smith.' Trautmann (1910: 358) thinks that also Prussian *kiosi* 'beaker, cup' is related to Slavic *čaša* 'cup.' But only rarely do Primitive Indo-European nouns begin with *kj-*, so I conclude with Berneker (1908–13:

137) that the Prussians borrowed from the Slavs this word for a cultural artifact; as far as the ending is concerned, compare Prussian *dusi* < Polish *dusza* 'soul' and we find a soft *k* in place of *č* foreign to the Prussians also in the borrowings *garkity* 'mustard' < Polish *gorczyca* and *akiwijsti* 'evidently' < Polish *oczywisty*; in the words *czisix* 'siskin' and *karczemo* 'village inn' as Trautmann points out (1910: 176) the letters *cz* are probably to be read as *c* (ts). More numerous (1910: 91) are those Prussian words for which closest or only cognates are found in both the Slavic and other Baltic languages: *abbai* 'both,' *addle* 'fir-tree,' *alwis* 'lead,' *anglis* 'coal,' *angurgis* 'eel,' *artoys* 'plow-man,' *asy* 'ridge, border,' *asmus* 'eighth,' *assaran* 'lake,' *assegis* 'perch (kind of fish),' *aulāut* 'to die,' *auwerus* 'that which is cooked out,' *awilkis* 'thread,' *awins* 'ram,' *balsinis* 'cushion,' *bhe* 'without,' *brokis* 'blow, 'hit,' (*bucca*) *reisis* 'beech-nut,' (*but*)*sargs* 'householder,' (*danti*)*max* 'gum,' *dongo* 'place for drinking vessels,' *draugi-* 'together with,' *drogis* 'reed,' *dumsle* 'bladder,' *dwigubbus* 'double,' *emelno* 'mistle-toe,' *galwo* 'head,' *gegalis* 'small diving-bird,' *geguse* 'cuckoo,' *gelatynan* 'yellow,' *gelso* 'iron,' *girnoywis* 'quern,' *guntwei* 'to drive,' *iau* 'always,' *īdis* 'food,' *yccroy* 'calf (of the leg),' *īmt* 'to take,' *is* 'out of,' *caune* 'marten,' *kersle* 'kind of axe,' *klantīuns* 'cursed,' *crausy* 'pear-tree,' *creslan* 'chair,' *cugis* 'hammer,' *kupsins* 'fog, mist,' *ladis* 'ice,' *laisken* 'book,' *linis* 'tench (kind of fish),' *līse* 'crawls,' *lopto* 'spade,' *lunkan* 'bast,' *maiggun* 'sleep,' *metis* 'throw, cast,' *mijls* 'dear,' *mynix* 'tanner,' *nage* 'foot,' *nagutis* 'finger-nail,' *panto* 'fetter,' *peisāton* 'written,' *pelwo* 'chaff,' *pentis* 'heel,' *pirsten* 'finger,' *plauti* 'lung,' (*pra*)*lieiton* 'shed, poured out,' *prei* 'to,' *ragis* 'horn,' *rancko* 'hand,' *romestue* 'kind of axe,' *sardis* 'fenced in horse-yard,' *sari* 'glow, glowing coals,' *sarke* 'magpie,' *schuwikis* 'shoemaker,' *seimīns* 'domestic servants,' *sywan* 'gray,' *slanke* 'large snipe,' *smorde* 'bird-cherry tree,' *stalis* 'table,' *suppis* 'dam on a mill-pond,' *suris* 'cheese,' *tatarwis* 'moor-hen,' *teisi* 'honor,' *wargan* 'evil,' *warne* 'crow,' *warnis* 'raven,' *warto* 'door,' *wetro* 'wind,' *weware* 'acorn,' *wirbe* 'rope, string,' *wissa* 'all,' *woapis* 'color,' *wolti* 'ear (of a plant).' Not only in the lexicon, but also in the grammar in a few instances Prussian differs from the other Baltic languages and agrees with Slavic. We find the sequence of sounds *tl* and *dl* both in Prussian and the West Slavic languages. The Prussian genitive plural ending *-an*, it seems, corresponds to the Slavic ending *-ȥ*, exactly like, e.g., the Prussian accusative *rankāns* corresponds perfectly to the Slavic form *rǫky*. In this connection also, mention must be made of Prussian *mien* 'me' *tien* 'you(sg),' *sien* 'oneself' = Slavic *mę, tę, sę;* Prussian *tebbei* '(to)you(sg.),' *sebbei* '(to) oneself': Slavic *tebě, sebě;* Prussian *mans* (dissimilated from **nans*), *wans* = Slavic *ny, vy;* Prussian

waisei 'you (sg.)know' = Slavic *věsi;* Prussian *(po) stanai* = Slavic *stani*
'become'; Prussian *(is)quendau* 'whence' (see *Filologu biedrības raksti*, 10,
p. 18): Slavic *kądu* 'id.' and (in regard to the suffix) Prussian *maldūnin*
'youth': Old Church Slavonic *grьdyni* 'pride.' But sometimes Latvian and
Lithuanian also coincide with the Slavic languages but differ from Prussian:
the Latvian and Samogitian dative *mun* '(to) me,' Slavic *mьně,* but Prussian
mennei; the Lithuanian dative *kamui* < *kam,* Latvian *kam,* Slavic *komu,*
but Prussian *kasmu;* and the Lithuanian genitive *piršto* '(of the) finger,'
Latvian *pir(k)sta,* Slavic **pьrsta,* but Prussian **pirstas.* One should note,
nevertheless, that *o*-stem ablatives with genitive meaning were probably not
entirely foreign to the Prussian language. The form *swinte* (in the phrase
en emmen thawas bha sunos bha swinte naseilis 'in the name of the Father,
the Son and the Holy Ghost'; in the Second Catechism in this place:
swyntas naseylis 'of the Holy Ghost'; in the Third Catechism: *steise*
swintan noseilīs 'of the Holy Ghost') is, according to Trautmann (1910;
242) to be corrected to **swinten* (*-n* missing since, according to him, the
next word begins with *n-*). But elsewhere we find the accusative in place
of the genitive after a preceding genitive; the sole exception is probably
deiwūtiskan 69, 20 'sacred' (possibly a misprint after the preceding accusative *gruntan* 'grounds'), where the accusative *peisālin* 'writings' follows,
whereas after *swinte* the genitive follows. The accusative **swinten* in
place of a genitive would then be here without an incontestable parallel.
And *swinte* could then be just such a genitive (ablative) as the forms *butta*
or *butte* in such sequences as *butta rikians* 'masters of the house' 61, 6,
(beside *buttas waispattin* 'housewife, mistress of the house!'), *butta tawas*
'father of a family' 33,20 or *butte tawas* 29,20. This does not seem to be
an old compound with a stem form in the first part; see also concerning
maiāsmu '[to] my,' *twaiāsmu* '[to] your [sg.]',' *swaiāsmu* '[to] one's own'
(*Filologu biedrības raksti*, 2, p. 13). Noting the linguistic facts mentioned
so far, one must suppose that not only the Prussians were living in direct
contact with the Slavs, but also Lithuanian and Latvian tribes; and that
coincides with the data of history also.

On the other hand, the closest or only cognates are found in the
Germanic languages for the following (19) Prussian words: *ackons* 'beard
[of corn],' *arrien* 'threshing floor,' *ausins* 'ears,' (as a transformation of
an *n*-stem), *blingis* 'bream, kind of fish,' *doacke* 'starling,' *druwīt* 'believe,'
kaāubri 'thorn,' *kalis* 'sheat-fish,' *krūt* 'to fall,' *layso* 'clay,' *menig* 'moon,'
nautei 'need,' *panno* 'fire,' *pippalins* 'birds,' *redo* 'furrow,' *twaxtan* 'bath-
switch,' *warsus* 'lip,' **wims* (written: *winis* 'knotty excrescence on a tree'),
wīrds 'word.' The words *anctan* 'butter,' *sasins* 'hare,' *ains* 'one,' *newīnts*

'nine,' *saddina* 'puts' (with its short *a*), also show a closer relationship with the Germanic languages; and Prussian *kawīds* 'which' is formed just like Germanic **hwalīkas* > Old High German *hwelīh*. The grammatical endings also show a close relationship to those of the Germanic languages: cf. the Prussian genitives *stessei* (fem. *stesses*) *deiwas*, (of the) God,' the datives (masc.) *stesmu*, (fem.) *stessei* and the comparative *tālis* 'farther' etc. There are 17 words with the closest or only cognates in the Germanic and other Baltic languages: *druktai* 'firmly,' *endyrītwei* 'to look upon,' *gerbt* 'to say,' *granstis* 'drill, auger,' *grandis* 'ring,' *gulbis* 'swan,' *caymis* 'village,' *kugis* 'pommel (of a sword's hilt),' *passortis* 'poker,' *pirmas* 'first,' *playnis* 'steel,' *podalis* 'worthless pot,' *poglabū* 'embraced,' *polijgu* 'similarly,' *skellānts* 'guilty, owing,' *strambo* 'stubble,' *wangus* 'poor forest land.' There are only six cases where Old Prussian corresponds especially with Indo-Iranian, viz. *aytegenis* 'small woodpecker,' *ape* 'brook,' *dadan* 'milk,' *din* 'him,' *stallit* 'to stand,' *tīrts* 'third.' With Greek it corresponds especially well in only three cases, viz. *aglo* 'rain,' *ayculo* 'needle,' *wagnis* 'ploughshare, coulter'; with Greek and other Baltic languages in three cases, viz. *aysmis* 'spit (in cooking),' *pelky* 'marshy ground,' *peuse* 'pine-tree, *Pinus silvestris*'; with Latin in one case, viz. *mēntimai* 'we lie'; with Latin and other Baltic languages in two cases, viz. *ausis* 'gold,' *plonis* 'threshing floor.' Also, working on the Latvian dictionary I found cognates for Latvian (and in general, Baltic) words most frequently in the Slavic and then in the Germanic languages. I shall remind the reader here also that only in the Germanic, Baltic, and Slavic languages do the endings of certain plural cases begin with *m-*. In this connection it should also be mentioned that in the Germanic, Slavic, and Baltic languages (see Endzelīns, 1922: 219 about Latvian *vedene*) the suffix *eno* or *ono* is used in past passive participles and that judging, for example, by Gothic *slahs* 'stroke,' Old Low German *slegi* 'blow,' or Gothic *nauþs* 'need,' Old English *nead* 'id.' one must suppose that the *i*-stems had a mobile accent not only in the Baltic and Slavic languages, but in the Germanic as well. All this leads one to the conclusion that in the primitive Indo-European language those dialects from which later the Germanic and Baltic languages developed (and especially must this be said of Old Prussian) were neighbors. Later—when the proto-language was splitting up—these close bonds were probably interrupted early and for a long time, as in phonetics and inflexion there is a great difference between the Baltic and Germanic languages.

But now Sigmund Feist (1928:52) says, "According to our exposition given above all grounds for proto-linguistic contact between the Balto-Slavic group and the Germanic group come to naught . . . In the pre-historical times they were not neighboring." And since the *Indogerman-isches Jahrbuch* (14, pp. 109 and 259) repeats without counterarguments all of the thoughts of this author, the impression may be created that Feist's arguments have indeed some weight. Therefore these should be taken up here. The fact that in the Slavic, Baltic, and Germanic languages the endings of certain cases begin with *m-* Feist (1928:50) considers to have no significance for the problem of relationships. Feist affirms that the well-known *Matronai* inscriptions with the forms *Aflims, Vatvims,* etc., are not Germanic, but Celtic and that there were, therefore, in Celtic case endings beginning with *m.* But as Pokorny points out in *Wörter und Sachen* (12, 304), not only is there no basis for ascribing these inscriptions to the Celts, but also, the forms met there with -*ms* cannot be Celtic, because their phonetic shape cannot be Celtic. And even if the afore-mentioned inscriptions were, however, Celtic, they would not show that there were no ties between the ancestors of the Balts and the Germanic peoples during the epoch of the proto-language. The correspondences between Gothic *þūsundi* 'thousand,' Old Church Slavonic *tysęšta*, Prussian *tūsimtons*, Feist believes to have rendered unimportant by referring to Tocharian. He points to Tocharian *tumāne* '10,000' where the same root is found as in the Germanic, Baltic and Slavic words for 'thousand.' But even in this case the Baltic word for 'thousand' remains, however, most similar to the corresponding Germanic and Slavic form. Concerning Gothic *ainlif* 'eleven' and Lithuanian *vienuolika,* Feist (1928: 51) confesses that, "a certain similarity cannot be denied, there could therefore be some connection." But on page 52 he states, "Perhaps there is here only a fortuitous coincidence." But this "perhaps" should not be there. And if there are in addition other data which bear witness to old bonds, then the aforementioned agreement is significant for this question of relationships. Also, Feist acknowledges (1928: 51), that, "naturally there are a number of word comparisons which could come from an Indo-European common inheritance and that are retained only in Baltic and Germanic. However, similar comparisons are also found between languages which lie spatially far apart from each other; therefore they prove nothing for a closer relationship." But I have already pointed out that there are more Prussian and Germanic (or Slavic) word comparisons than with words of any other non-Baltic Indo-European language. I must then say that Feist's arguments against Germanic and Baltic linguistic bonds, using Feist's own words, "dissolve into nothing." And the arguments of Feist are not supported by the fact that the Germanic languages belong to the *centum*-group, whereas the Baltic languages belong to the *satəm*-group. If concerning the fate of the sound *k* these languages differ among themselves, it does not, however, follow that in other things they could not have traveled the same road. In some places the *centum-* and *satəm-* groups had to be neighbors.

In lexicon the Prussian language coincides with Lithuanian much more than with Latvian (see Trautmann, 1910: x-xii). In phonetics we find that in the Prussian and Lithuanian languages an *a* has passed to *e* in case of a preceding soft consonant, and that in word-initial position to a great degree *e-* has been replaced by *a-*, a phenomenon which in Latvian we observe only in rare Latgalian dialect examples. Prussian *s, z* (instead of Lithuanian *š, ž*) unites it with Latvian (and Curonian). Likewise the passage of *sj* > *š*. Prussian coincides with Curonian first of all in that both these languages have retained *n* before a fricative, cf., e.g., *sansy* 'goose,' *saninsle* 'belt,' with, perhaps, the Curonian noun *censle* or *iegansts*. If Samogitian *n* has not completely disappeared before a fricative, it might be due to the Curonian substratum. Just as for the Samogitians, so also for the Curonians and Prussians *tja* and *dja* at the end of a stem seems to have changed to *t'e* and *d'e* respectively; cf. Prussian *geide* 'they wait' (and *klantemmai* 'we swear,' see *Filologu biedrības raksti* 2, p. 11 and *wertammai* [?] 'we swear') with Curonian *Apriķi* etc. (see *Finnisch-ugrische Forschungen* 12, 65). The Prussian preposition *sen* 'with' corresponds in vocalism with the Curonian **sen* in the place *Sentatze* (compare the place name *Sotecle-Suotekle* with *uo* from *on,* mentioned by a chronicler). For Prussians the *u* sound was open (wide), as it is sometimes written with the letter *o.* Similarly, in the Samogitian dialect (because of the Curonian substratum?) and in Curonian territory we find *o* in place of *u*, (see *Filologu biedrības raksti*, 4, p. 5). Perhaps short *i* gives an analogy to this: Cf. Latvian *kless* 'crooked, bent in,' Lithuanian *klišas* 'bandy-legged'; and Latvian *dvālekts* 'dry-measure for grain' beside *dvālikts*, Lithuanian *dvōlikis*. And in lexicon frequently Prussian corresponds with Curonian: Prussian *kerscha(n)* 'through' or *kirscha(n)* calls to mind the Curonian place names *Cęrsupji* and *Cirspene*, and Prussian *kelan* 'wheel' shows the same stem form as *duceles* 'two-wheeled carriage' in Curonia. In addition Professor Blese has collected in his book about Latvian personal names (1929: 150–152) 1, similarly sounding Prussian and Curonian personal names and place names (Prussian *Butil, Dinge, Jotill, Curwin, Pundico, Stintil, Swayune, waldūns* 'heir,' *Penen, Pynouwe, gudde* 'bush,' *Lauwete, Skalden, Suste, Tune*: Curonian *Butill, Dynge, Jatill, Kurve, Pundicke, Stentile, Swayun, Waldune, Pęni, Pinavi, Gudavalki, Lavieši, Skaldas, Susti, Tuņi* or *Tūnęns*). Correspondences for many of these names perhaps will be found in Lithuania. Thus from Blese's list we must omit the names *Tullnicke, Vārma*,[2]

Aīsiŋi, Vaiŋuoda, Bārta because these also have cognates in Lithuania: the farm of *Tulnikiai*, Liet. apg. v.v. 714, *Varmė* 720, the village of *Aisėnai* 540, the village of *Vainočiai* 718, the estate of *Bartupys* (Bartupis) 560. West Baltic, i.e., Prussian coincides in several respects with the geographically closer East Baltic—Lithuanian and Curonian—languages, and this is not surprising, but rather perfectly understandable if we take into consideration the fact that the Prussians were neighbors not only of the Lithuanians, but also of the Curonians, whose language otherwise was rather an intermediate step between the Lithuanian and Latvian languages.

The Curonians' rapid assimilation with the Lithuanians in the south and the Latvians in the north leads one to the conclusion that this language was quite close to the Lithuanian and the Latvian language.

If we examine what really unites West Baltic, i.e., Old Prussian with the East Baltic languages, then the chief bases of similarity—with the exception of the great similarity in the lexicon—are negative characteristics: all these languages which are known to us from connected texts only beginning in the sixteenth century, compared with other Indo-European languages during the sixteenth century, are very archaic and consequently we find many very characteristic innovations common to the less archaic languages. In every language there are usually dialects but, for example, we can imagine a Primitive Slavic which is much more monolithic than a Primitive Baltic if in general we can even talk about a Primitive Baltic. It is possible to write indeed a grammar of Primitive Slavic, but not one of Primitive Baltic. It would be possible, for example, to imagine purely theoretically, that that dialect of Primitive Indo-European from which Prussian later developed had been approximately just as near to the dialect from which Primitive Germanic developed as to that dialect from which the East Baltic languages developed, but that later, when the ancestors of the Germanic peoples had become separated geographically from the ancestors of the Prussian people, in language these ancestors of the Prussian people moved closer to the ancestors of the East Baltic people with whom they had remained neighbors. By this I do not wish to say that indeed it was this way, but I only wanted to point out how perhaps it would be possible to understand the rather large differences between the West Baltic and East Baltic languages. But if in the Baltic languages we find very characteristic and common innovations then we must come to the conclusion that the Baltic tribes remained in the vicinity of the Indo-European homeland, because following distant paths they would, it seems, have fallen more under foreign influence and as a result would have changed the appearance of their language more.

REFERENCES

Blese, E. 1929 *Latviešu personu vārdu un uzvārdu studijas.*   Riga.

Berneker, Erich. 1908–13. *Slavisches etymologisches Wörterbuch.* Heidelberg.

Endzelīns, J. 1922. *Lettische Grammatik.* Riga.

Endzelīns, J. *Filologu biedrības raksti* 10. Riga. 1930. *Indogermanisches Jahrbuch*
  14. Berlin. *Finnisch-ugrische Forschungen* 12. Helsinki.

Feist, Sigmund. 1928. *Wörter und Sachen* 11. Heidelberg.

Trautmann, Reinhold 1910. *Die altpreussichen Sprachdenkmäler. Göttingen.*

ESTI AND *YRA* IN MARTYNAS MAŽVYDAS' CATECHISM OF 1547

GORDON B. FORD, JR.

As a companion study to Christian S. Stang's article on *esti* and *yra* in the *Punktay Sakimu* of Širvydas in the *Norsk Tidskrift for Sprogvidenskap* (14, 1947, pp. 87-97) and my recent study on *esti* and *yra* in Vilentas' *Enchiridion* in the *Zeitschrift für slavische Philologie* (33, 1967, pp. 353-357) I shall here investigate the function of these two forms of the third person of the verb "to be" in still another text, Martynas Mažvydas' Catechism of 1547, which is the oldest Lithuanian book. It will be my purpose to determine whether there is a difference in meaning between *esti* and *yra* in this text as there is in Širvydas and Vilentas. In the *Universitas linguarum Litvaniae* of 1737 a difference of meaning is given for *ira* and *esti*. *Yra* is translated by Polish *iest* 'is,' whereas *esti* is rendered by Polish *bywa* 'is accustomed to be.' Jānis Endzelīns in his *Lettische Grammatik* (# 597) agrees with the distinction made in the *Universitas*.

Yra and its shortened form *ir* occur 19 times in the text, whereas *esti* and its shortened form *est* occur 64 times. It is interesting to note here that this ratio is in sharp contrast to that found in Vilentas' *Enchiridion*, where *yra* occurs 106 times and *esti* only 44 times. This shows that by the time of Vilentas *yra* had begun to replace *esti* as a copula.

Yra has three functions in Mažvydas' Catechism: it occurs eight times as a copula (11, 19; 32, 2, 4, 6, 9; 36, 17; 38, 9; 79, 24), four times as an auxiliary verb with the preterite passive participle (11, 20; 24, 8; 31, 21; 34, 18), and seven times as a positive verb of existence (13, 3; 17, 6; 25, 17; 31, 2, 20; 53, 11, 12). All references are to Georg Gerullis' facsimile edition of Mažvydas, *Mosvid*.

Yra occurs as a copula in the following eight cases:

11, 19 *Bet kunigu ira vredas žmanes makiti* 'But it is the duty of pastors to teach people'

32, 2 *Ba kunigaistei ne baisumu ira gierai darantimus* 'for princes are not a terror to those acting well'

32, 4 *Kas gier ira daryk* 'Do what is good'

32, 6 *A iei darissi tatai kas pikt ira* 'But if you will do that which is evil'

32, 9 *kursai kas pikt ira dariss* 'who will do what is evil'

36, 17 *kūrie Panai ira iussu pagal kuna* 'who are your masters according to the flesh'

38, 9 *kurias teisei naschles ira* 'who are really widows'

79, 24 *dienagi kaip ant pradzias Knigieliu ijra* 'on the day as is at the beginning of the little book'

Yra occurs as an auxiliary verb with the preterite passive participle in the following four cases:

11, 20 *Bo ant to wisy ira apskyrty* 'For all are appointed for this'

24, 8 *taipo kaipo schwentaie Euangelyaie paraschit ira* 'just as is written in the Holy Gospel'

31, 21 *kurias patam ijra maczes nogi Dewa ijngistatitas ijra* 'Moreover, the powers which exist are ordained by God'

34, 18 *kursai pagulditas ijra pijnimusu plauku* 'which is presented in plaits of the hair'

Yra occurs as a positive verb of existence in the following 7 cases:

13, 3 *Skaititiniv ira 23* 'There are 23 letters'

17, 6 *Penkias ira dalis maksla* 'There are five parts of the doctrine'

25, 17 *Mes turim stipri wera tikieti iag tikras ir teisusis kunas anaie ipatineie donas ira* 'We should believe with a strong faith that the real and true body is in that form of bread'

31, 2 *Klausikiet tu kure wiresny ira* 'Obey those who are in a higher position'

31, 20 *kurias patam ijra maczes* 'Moreover, the powers which exist'

Ir occurs only twice in Mažvydas' Catechism, both times as a verb of existence:

53, 11 *Visur ir gan neteisibiu* 'Everywhere there is enough unrighteousness'

53, 12 *Ant sweta piln ir piktibiu* 'It is full of evils in the world'

Esti and its shortened form *est* occur 64 times in the Catechism, 55 times as a copula, 7 times as an auxiliary verb, and twice as a verb of existence.

Esti occurs 54 times as a copula in the following positive sentences:

17, 8 *kurias kaźnas kriksczianiu źmagus pawinnas yr kaltas esti makieti bei permaniti* 'which every person of the Christians is obliged and bound to know and understand'

18, 3 *tatai esti, kriksstas schwęntassis* 'that is, holy baptism'

18, 6 *tatai esti, ape giwenima kaźna żmagaus* 'that is, concerning the life of every man'

20, 6 *kurssai ia esti* 'which is his'

23, 4 *S. Matheiupi vi. cap. Schita esti* 'this is in St. Matthew, 6th chapter'

25, 3 *tatai esti dągaus karaliste* 'that is, the kingdom of heaven'

25, 10 *Tatai est, ape schwentągi kuna ir kraugi* 'that is, concerning the Holy Body and Blood'

25, 17 *ipatineie ano wina esti tikras kraugis* 'in that form of wine is the real blood'

25, 22 *Tas est teisiausesis liudimas* 'This is the truest testimony'

26, 8 *tatai esti kunas mana* 'this is my body'

27, 2 *Tas kilikas nauies testamentas esti mana Kraugeie* 'This cup is the new testament in my blood'

27, 13 *Tas atpent teisei dastainas esti* 'On the other hand, he is truly worthy'

28, 3 *tatai est piktai prisitaises* 'that is poorly fit'

28, 18 *Tatai esti ape atleidima greku* 'That is, concerning forgiveness of sins'

30, 2 *tatai esti ape Kunigus* 'that is, concerning pastors'

30, 15 *kuri est pateme Jesuse Christuse* 'which is in Jesus Christ himself'

31, 12 *Ir ghadnas esti darbinikas algas saua* 'And the laborer is worthy of his pay'

32, 5 *Diewa abawem tarnas esti tau ant giera* 'For he is the servant of God to you for good'

32, 8 *Tarnas abawem Dewa esti* 'For he is the servant of God'

32, 16 *Jei tarnai Dewa esti* 'if they are servants of God'

34, 4 *Ba wiras esti galwa matriskies* 'For the husband is the head of the wife'

34, 5 *kaipo ijr Christus esti galua Bażniczias* 'as also Christ is the head of the church'

34, 8 *Atadel kurio budu Bażniczie padota esti Christui* 'And thus in the way in which the church is subject to Christ'

35, 1 *kury schirdis pa akimis Pana Diewa didis ijr brągus daiktas esti* 'which heart is a great and precious thing under the eyes of the Lord God'

35, 21 *Ba tatai esti teisu* 'for this is right'

35, 23 *kursai prisakimas pirmas esti žadegimij* 'which is the first commandment with promise'

36, 11 *žinadamij, iagi ijr iussu pacziu Panas esti dąngusu* 'knowing that your Master also is in heaven'

38, 12 *Ba tatai esti patagu ir pamekt panepi Diewepi* 'for this is appropriate and pleasing to the Lord God'

38, 14 *A taip kuri teisei naschle esti* 'And so she who is really a widow'

38, 18 *schita bebudama giwa, nomirusi esti* 'she is dead while being alive'

38, 23 *Ischpildimas tadrin zakana malane esti* 'Therefore, grace is the fulfilling of the law'

40, 7 *Tas est Diewa prisakimas* 'This is a commandment of God'

43, 3 *Schita giesme esti malda* 'This hymn is a prayer'

52, 12 *Ba musu pacziu teisibes Neks est be tawa gieribes* 'For the righteousness of us ourselves is nothing without your goodness'

56, 12 *Tas kraus tawip brąngus esti* 'This blood from you is precious'

56, 22 *Kursai ischganims mums esti* 'Which is salvation for us'.

60, 5 *Est apgintas stiprus duschias* 'He is the strong Protector of your soul'

63, 4 *kurs esti tikrai io baisumij* 'Whoever is truly in fear of him'

63, 6 *Kurie est ia karaliste* 'who are in his kingdom'

65, 10 *Jag žadis tawa est pilns teisibiu* 'that your word is full of righteousness'

65, 15 *Ved teisus est žadis tawa* 'For your word is righteous'

71, 3 *Kurs amžins est su tewu* 'who is eternal with his father'

71, 4 *Macze, garbe, ligus est Diewui* 'He is equal to God in power and glory'

71, 6 *esti žmagus tikras* 'he is a true man'

72, 9 *Bernelis esti diwnas* 'The boy is wondrous'

72, 10 *esti tikras Diewas* 'he is a true God'

73, 1 *Esti žmagus pilnas, Deiwisteie amžinas, Szmagisteie zmertelnas Panas Jesus Christus* 'The Lord Jesus Christ is a complete man, eternal in divinity, mortal in humanity'

73, 4 *Gražus esti Bernelis* 'The boy is handsome'

73, 7 *Roža esti Jesus Christus* 'Jesus Christ is a rose'

73, 8 *lelia esti Maria* 'Mary is a lily'

74, 15 *Malanus esti Jesus* 'Jesus is merciful'

74, 15 *esti malanes pilnas* 'he is full of grace'

75, 2 *tatai esti ape kuna ir kragij musu Pana Jesaus Christaus* 'that is, concerning the body and blood of our Lord Jesus Christ'

76, 15 *Jag tasai penuksslas liganiu esti* 'that he is the nourishment of sick people'

Esti occurs seven times as an auxiliary verb in the following cases:

24, 6 *bet esti prisakimapi Dewa prerakintas* 'but is joined to the commandment of God'

24, 15 *Szadis Dewa ir żadegimas schwentamimpi Markupi, tapagaliausemi paguldime apraschitas esti tais zadeis* 'The word and promise of God is described in St. Mark in the last chapter with these words'

27, 16 *Vž ius dotas esti jr praletas* 'It is given and shed for you'

28, 5 *Vsz ius dotas esti jr praletas* 'It is given and shed for you'

50, 9 *Kurs est nog tawęs pamektas* 'which is liked by you'

71, 9 *Nomires est ant križaus* 'He died on the cross'

76, 17 *Ir silwartu sukiu esti apslektas* 'and is oppressed by heavy fear'

In negative sentences *esti* occurs only three times, once as a copula and twice as a verb of existence. It occurs as a copula in the following sentence:

24, 5 *Kriksstas ne esti tektai prastas wando* 'Baptism is not only simple water'

It occurs as a verb of existence in the following two cases:

31, 19 *Ba ne esti maczys tektai nogi Dewa* 'for there is no power except from God'

77, 3 *Liekariaus sweikims ne est reika* 'There is no need of a doctor for healthy people'

In Mažvydas' Catechism *esti* functions only as a copula in positive sentences, but in negative sentences it functions both as a copula and as a verb of existence. In Vilentas I found that *esti* functions only as a copula in both positive and negative sentences, whereas in Širvydas *esti* occurs as both a copula and a verb of existence in positive sentences, but only as a copula in negative sentences. The fact that *esti* was sometimes used as a verb of existence in negative sentences in Mažvydas is somewhat puzzling inasmuch as we would have expected *yra* here on the basis of the two earlier studies. However, I believe that we can draw a very significant conclusion from this discrepancy, namely that at the time of Mažvydas *yra* had not yet become generalized as a verb of existence in negative sentences.

The general conclusions that can be drawn from this study are comparable to those which I drew from my study of *esti* and *yra* in Vilentas' *Enchiridion:*

1. *Esti* is more archaic than *yra* as a copula in both positive and negative sentences.

2. The original distribution of *esti* and *yra* can be seen from positive

sentences, where *esti* is only a copula and *yra* functions as a verb of existence.

As I pointed out in my article on *esti* and *yra* in Vilentas' *Enchiridion* (1967: 357), *yra* later began to replace *esti* as a copula in positive sentences and finally replaced *esti* as a copula in negative sentences as well. After *yra* had completely replaced *esti* in its function as a copula, then *esti* came to be used in the restricted meaning 'is accustomed to be.' By the time of the *Universitas* of 1737, *yra* was primarily a copula, and *esti* was restricted to the special function of expressing something habitual or durative.

Northwestern University

REFERENCES

Endzelīns, J. 1922. *Lettische Grammatik.* Riga.

Ford, Gordon B., Jr. 1967. "*esti* und *yra* in Vilentas' *Enchiridion*," *Zeitschrift für Slavische Philologie* 33, pp. 353–357.

Gerullis, Georg. 1923. *Mosvid. Die ältesten litauischen Sprachdenkmäler bis zum Jahre 1570.* Heidelberg.

Stang, Christian S. 1947. "*Esti* et *yra* dans les *Punktay Sakimu* de Szyrwid," *Norsk Tidskrift for Sprogvidenskap* 14, pp. 87–97.

Stang, Christian S. 1966. *Vergleichende Grammatik der baltischen Sprachen.* Oslo, pp. 412–416.

SOME REMARKS ABOUT THE WOLFENBÜTTEL LITHUANIAN POSTILĖ MANUSCRIPT OF THE YEAR 1573

GORDON B. FORD, JR.

The Wolfenbüttel Lithuanian Postilė Manuscript of the year 1573 was discovered in 1898 at the Herzog August Bibliothek in Wolfenbüttel, Germany by Professor Schmidt-Wartenburg of Chicago. It consists of two parts and contains 298 leaves or about 596 pages. The title page of the first part, which consists of 150 leaves, indicates that the work is a collection of sermons based on the Gospels and that this collection was taken from many books of sermons, including those of Nicholas Heming, Anton Corvin, Johannes Spangenberg, Martin Luther, Philipp Melanchthon, Johannes Brent, Arsat, Schoper, Leonhard Culmann, and Jodoch Willich. On the reverse of leaf 150 we find the statement that the work was copied in three weeks and two days and that the copy was finished on September 2, 1573. Thus the manuscript is not the original, but only a copy, the first part of which was made in 1573.

It is not known who composed the original of the postilė, but we find the name Johannes Bielauk and the year 1574 written on the front cover of the manuscript and the name Michael Sappun Bartensteinensis written on the title page in another hand. Viktor Falkenhahn in his work, *Der Übersetzer der litauischen Bibel Johannes Bretke und seine Helfer*, compared these signatures with the handwriting of the manuscript and was able to establish that it was Bielauk and Sappun who made the copy.

The postilė is partly a translation from Latin and German and partly an original work. We know that it must have been written some time between 1563 and 1573 because an event of the year 1563 is mentioned on the obverse of the seventh leaf and the copy was made in 1573.

A linguistic study of the Wolfenbüttel Postilė was made by Wilhelm Gaigalat in 1900 in his dissertation, *Die Wolfenbütteler litauische Postillenhandschrift aus dem Jahre 1573*, published in three parts in the *Mitteilungen der litauischen literarischen Gesellschaft* (5, pp. 1-57, 117-165, and 231-247), but this study, written, after all, 68 years ago, did not adequately treat all the linguistic problems which this manuscript raises and in my opinion needs to be replaced by a new study of the document. Gaigalat's conclusions, as they are outlined on p. 247 of his dissertation, are as follows:

1. The language of the postilė is not uniform, but represents a coalescence of several dialects.
2. The original of the extant manuscript was composed either by one man who was quite familiar with both Žemaitic and East Lithuanian and also possessed a good knowledge of the Slavic languages or by several clerics called together from various regions of Lithuania who saw to it that the postilė was understandable to both Low Lithuanians and East Lithuanians.
3. The original was then copied by a man who knew German and North Lithuanian; as a result of this the many linguistic features especially characteristic of North Lithuanian came into the text.

These conclusions need to be thoroughly reexamined in the light of recent work which dialectologists have done on the Lithuanian language and on the development of the common written language. In his review of my facsimile edition of the Wolfenbüttel Postilė, which appeared in *Draugas* (51, No. 200-34, August 26, 1967, p. 1) Professor Peter Jonikas aptly pointed out that the question of the dialect of the postilė has not yet been solved but because dialectologists have made much progress since the time of the publication of Gaigalat's dissertation and also have begun to investigate the development of the common written language, there is a much better basis for solving this problem. Jonikas added that the creation of a common written language must have had some influence on the dialect mixture of the manuscript:

Ir postilės tarmės klausimas tebėra neišspręstas.   Lietuvių kalbos tarmėtyrai padarius gerą pažangą nuo Gaigalaičio disertacijos pasirodymo laiko, o taip pat ėmus tyrinėti ir lietuvių bendrinės rašomosios kalbos raidą, atsiranda daug geresnio pagrindo ir šiam klausimui išspręsti. Sakysim, rankraščio tarminiam mišiniui bus turėjusi įtakos besikurianti lietuvių bendrinė rašomoji kalba . . .

Northwestern University

REFERENCES

Falkenhahn, Viktor. 1941. *Der Übersetzer der litauischen Bibel Johannes Bretke und seine Helfer.* Königsberg.

Ford, Gordon B., Jr., ed. 1965-1966. *The Wolfenbüttel Lithuanian Postilė Manuscript of the Year 1573 with a General Introduction. Facsimile Edition.* 3 vols. Louisville, Kentucky.

Gaigalat, Wilhelm. 1904. *Die Wolfenbütteler litauische Postillenhandschrift aus dem Jahre 1573* in the *Mitteilungen der litauischen literarischen Gesellschaft* 5, pp. 1-57, 117-165, and 231-247.

Gerullis, Jurgis. 1927. *Senieji Lietuvių Skaitymai.* Kaunas, pp. 40-54.

Jonikas, Peter. 1967. Review of Ford's edition. *Draugas* 51 (200-34), p. 1 (Aug. 26).

THE OLD LITHUANIAN THIRD PERSON IMPERATIVE IN -*K*(*I*)

GORDON B. FORD, JR.

In the oldest Lithuanian texts there occur imperative forms of the third person in -*k* or -*ki* alongside of second person singular forms in -*k* or -*ki*. It is very strange indeed that the same formant -*k*(*i*) should serve for both the second person singular and third person singular imperative, and an attempt will be made in this paper to explain this situation. As far back as 1877 Adalbert Bezzenberger in his important work *Beiträge zur Geschichte der litauischen Sprache* (1877: 218) stated that in Old Lithuanian texts the third singular imperative was not always represented by the permissive, but often by a form identical to the second singular imperative and gave the following examples:

Schwęskiese wardas tawa 'May your name be hallowed,' Martynas Mažvydas' Catechism of 1547 (23, 7), Georg Gerullis, *Mosvid* (1923)

Ateik karaliste tawa 'May your kingdom come,' Mažvydas' Catechism of 1547 (23, 8)

Buki tawa walia kaip dągui taip ir žemeie 'May your will be both in heaven and on earth,' Mažvydas' Catechism of 1547 (23, 9)

Kosznas rugok prisch sawa Griekus 'May everyone be angry at his own sins,' Bretkūnas *Biblia* (1590) Lamentations 3.39

Atàik kàràliste tawa . . . Buk wàla tawa, Postilla Lietuwiszka of 1600, 8

Ateik Karalista tawa, Lazarus Sengstock's edition of Baltramiejus Vilentas' *Enchiridion* (1612), p. 17

Garba buki Diewui 'May glory be to God,' *Giesmes Chriksczionischkos* (1612), p. 1

Diewui Tiewui buki garba 'May glory be to God the Father,' *Giesmes Chriksczionischkos* (1612), p. 43

Kosznas buk tòs dumos 'May everyone be of this mind,' Lazarus Sengstock's edition of Baltramiejus Vilentas' *Euangelias bei Epistolas* (1612), p. 60

ateik karalijste tawo, buk walia tawo, Naujas Testamentas (1701), Luke 11.2

Bezzenberger also mentions *schweskisi wardas tawa, atait karalijste tawa* from Bretkūnas *Biblia* Luke 11.2, but the *-t* of *atait* is doubtless a misprint for *-k*.

In addition to the forms cited by Bezzenberger, I have found others in the oldest Lithuanian manuscript text from the first quarter of the sixteenth century and in Baltramiejus Vilentas' *Enchiridion* of 1579. The examples from the oldest Lithuanian manuscript text are the following (references are both to J. Lebedys and J. Palionis, "Seniausias Lietuviškas Rankraštinis Tekstas" in *Bibliotekininkystės ir Bibliografijos Klausimai*, 3 (1964), p. 121 and to Gordon B. Ford, Jr., *Old Lithuanian Texts of the Sixteenth and Seventeenth Centuries with a Glossary* [1969: 11]):

szvÿskisi vardas tava (Lebedys 1 = Ford 1)
athaÿki tava karalistÿa (Lebedys 2 = Ford 1)
buki thava vala kaÿp dvngvÿ theÿp szamÿaÿ (Lebedys 2 = Ford 2)

There are seven examples of the use of the formant *-k* as an indicator of the third person imperative in Vilentas' *Enchiridion*. All references are to my edition of this text in *A Phonological, Morphological, and Syntactical Investigation of the Old Lithuanian Catechism of Baltramiejus Vilentas (1579)*:

kurem buk garbe ir dekawoghimas ant amžu 'to whom be glory and thanks forever' (10, 7)
Schwenskisi wardas tawa 'Hallowed be your name' (20, 17)
Ateik Karalista tawa 'May your kingdom come' (21, 14)
Buk walia tawa kaip Dangui taip ir Szeme 'May your will be both in heaven and on earth' (22, 4)
Prakeikta buk žeme dael tawes 'Cursed be the earth on account of you' (52, 18)
Pakajus buk su tawimi 'Peace be with you' (64, 19)
garbe buk taw Tiewe ant amžu 'Glory be to you, O Father, forever' (76, 17)

It is unlikely that the original function of the *-k(i)* formant was to indicate the second person singular imperative because, as is well known, we find examples of an older type of second person singular imperative in the

oldest Lithuanian texts. This older type of imperative has its origin in the
Indo-European optative. Examples of this archaic imperative in Mažvydas'
Catechism of 1547 are the following:

Dona musu wyssu dienu dodi mumus nu 'Now give us our bread for all
days' (23, 11)

Ir atleid mumus musu kaltibes 'And forgive us our trespasses' (23, 13)

Atleid mums musu kaltibes 'Forgive us our sins' (52, 1)

Newed mus ingi pagundima 'Do not lead us into temptation' (23, 15)
ne wedi also occurs in the *Forma Chrikstima* of 1559 (see Gerullis, 1923:
105). In Vilentas' *Enchiridion* of 1579 there are four examples of
archaic second person singular imperatives. All of them occur in the very
archaic Lord's Prayer:

Duna musu wissu dienu dudi mumus schę diena (22, 20)

Ir atleid mumus musu kaltes (23, 17)

Ir newed mus ing pagundima (24, 9)

Bet gelb mus nug pikta 'But deliver us from evil' (24, 21)
Bezzenberger gives many other examples of archaic second person singular
imperatives (1877: 222).

If, then, the original second person singular imperative in Lithuanian was
a form derived from the Indo-European optative, one may well ask what
the original function of the forms in *-k(i)* was. It seems likely to assume
that the forms in *-k(i)* were originally restricted to expressing only the
third person singular imperative, while the forms derived from the Indo-
European optative were used for the second person singular imperative. In
time, the archaic second person singular imperative forms tended to be replaced, perhaps due to the fact that the distinction between the second
person singular indicative and the second person singular imperative was
maintained only in the athematic verbs, whereas there was no distinction
in the thematic verbs except for the frequent loss of final *-i* in the imperative and the difference in accentuation between the indicative and imperative. For example, *duosi* was the second person singular indicative and
duodi the second person singular imperative of the athematic verb *duoti*
'give'; *gelbsi* was the second person singular indicative and *gelb(i)* the
second person singular imperative of the athematic verb *gelbti* 'deliver.' On
the other hand, the forms of the second person singular indicative and the
second person singular imperative of the thematic verb *vesti* 'lead' must
once have been *vedi* and *vēdi* respectively. It is likely that the *-i* tended to
disappear in the imperative forms of thematic verbs to distinguish them
from the forms of the second person singular indicative before the third

person singular imperative formation in -*k*(*i*) replaced the older optative formation. Thus the formation in -*k*(*i*) had now a secondary function of designating the second person singular imperative. This secondary function then became the primary function of the -*k*(*i*) formant, and the -*k*(*i*) formant was replaced in its original primary function by the permissive formation with *te*-. It is worth noting that the permissive formation with *te*- does not occur in the oldest Lithuanian manuscript text.

In his fundamental work on Mazvydas, *Die Sprache des litauischen Katechismus von Mažvydas*, Christian S. Stang has attempted to explain all the third person singular imperative forms in -*k*(*i*) by ascribing them to Polish influence (1929: 177). He considers, however, only three examples from the Lord's Prayer. An objection to Stang's theory may be found in the fact that both the texts of Vilentas and Bretkūnas mentioned above were translated from the German, and it is hard to see how Polish influence could have played a role in them.

Northwestern University

REFERENCES

Bezzenberger, Adalbert. 1877. *Beiträge zur Geschichte der litauischen Sprache.* Göttingen, pp. 218–222.

Ford, Gordon B., Jr. 1969. *Old Lithuanian Texts of the Sixteenth and Seventeenth Centuries with a Glossary.* The Hague, pp. 11–12.

Ford, Gordon B., Jr. 1969. *A Phonological, Morphological, and Syntactical Investigation of the Old Lithuanian Catechism of Baltramiejus Vilentas (1579).* The Hague.

Gerullis, Georg. 1923. *Mosvid. Die ältesten litauischen Sprachdenkmäler bis zum Jahre 1570.* Heidelberg.

Lebedys, J. and J. Palionis. 1964. "Seniausias Lietuviškas Rankraštinis Tekstas." *Bibliotekininkystės ir Bibliografijos Klausimai* 3, p. 121.

Stang, Christian S. 1929. *Die Sprache des litauischen Katechismus von Mažvydas.* Oslo, pp. 177–178.

LITHUANIAN *UGNÌS*,
SLAVIC *OGNЬ*

ERIC P. HAMP

It seems strange that at this late date, and with a word so well known to scholarship, there should still be such conflict in the literature on the exact form of these nouns and their cognates. Fraenkel (1963: 1158-1159) gives a full review of the Baltic forms and evidence; there is no need to recapitulate matters here, and the Latvian and Lithuanian are in fundamental agreement. Russian *ogóń* gen. *ognjá*, Ukr. *ohóń* gen. *ohňú*, SCr. *òganj* gen. *ògnja*, Slovene *ôgenj -gnja*, Mak. *ogan ognot*, Bulg. *ògъn*, (adj. formation *ògnen*), Cz. *oheň* gen. *ohně,* Pol. *ogień* leave no doubt of the proto-form: **ogn(j)ь'*.

Fraenkel traces the Slavic form to **ognis,* citing Trautmann and Vasmer, and mentions also, without specifying the exact relationship, Skt. *agni-* and Hitt. *agniš*; he continues "abltd. mit lat. *ignis.*" Ernout-Meillet (1951:549) had already reported the Hitt. *Agniš* as a borrowing from Indic (although Mayrhofer, (1953: 18) implausibly also allows the possibility that it is ultimately cognate), and Laroche has further claimed it as a Hurrian transmission. Trautmann observes (1925: 335; under his headword *ugni-*!): "Ich beurteile das Verhältnis von li. *ugnìs* zu slav. **ognь* wie das von li. *ùpè* zu pr. *ape*: im Ablaut ai. *agni-* m., la. *ignis* m." If one wished to maximize the economy of this solution, it would be better to consider the Sanskrit perhaps not in ablaut. But still we are left with three reflexes, **o* (Slavic), **e* (Latin), and a "reduced" vocalism (Baltic). The motivation for this alternation is hard to discover. Moreover, Trautmann laudably takes account of "das ablautende Slav. **vygnь* in skr. *vìganj* (gen. *vìgnja*) m. 'Schmiede,' č. *výheň* (*výhně*) f. 'Feueresse; Glühofen, Schmiede'." But, as we shall see below, if we include this, we are then committed to an "ablaut" (Dehnstufe) in Slavic of the "reduced" form found in Baltic!

While Trautmann's use of forms is more reasoned than that of others, it leads to a wasteful proliferation and fragmentation.

Vasmer takes essentially the opposite course (1953: 252). He accepts Trautmann's *o- (and "reduced" u-), allows for Latin *e-, and summarily rejects *ngnis (including an impressive list of scholars). This simplicity is bought at the price of declaring "nicht sicher ist Verwandtschaft von *ognъ mit skr. vĭganj . . . čech. výheň . . . " By excluding enough one can solve a lot. Ernout and Meillet (1951: 549) give the most balanced picture: "Le slave paraît avoir le degré o du vocalisme radical, et le lituanien le degré zéro (sous forme u-); l'a sanskrit est ambigu; ignis suppose *egnis ou *ngnis." A perfect statement of the facts in isolation.

Walde and Pokorny (1928, 1: 323) under the entry "ngnis (besser egni-s?)," have a balanced, but less crisp and lucid, discussion of the possibilities advanced. But this account crucially remains inconclusive because Slavic ognъ is declared flatly, on the authority "Vasmer mündlich," to be from IE *ognis and not possibly from *ngnis. It would seem that the insistence of Vasmer (and others) on this derivation of ognъ leads only to the observed fragmented result.

Pokorny (1949: 293) has a list, more than a discussion, but the result is the same: His heading is "egnis: ognis," and no room is left for *ngnis. He gives up entirely on Cz. výheň, SCr. vĭganj. Machek (1957) s.v. výheň has little additional to offer.

On the other hand, it seems to me that Cz. výhěn etc. cannot properly be ignored; and, moreover, when we search for a solution that encompasses this group of words, we see a clear way for a simple unified solution. The set of words in question is well attested in South and West Slavic. SCr. vĭganj gen.'vĭgnja, Slovene vigenj vignja, Mak. vigna, Bulg. vĭgnja (~ vìdnja), Cz. výheň výhně, Slovak výhňa. The proto-form is clearly *výgnjъ.[1] The Bъlgarski etimologicen rečnik (1963: 143) has an informative account of the distribution of the word and borrowings in other Balkan dialects. It concludes with a hypothesis of "Dacian" (= pre-Albanian) ancestry for this word, associated with ore-smelting areas; Slavic would have borrowed *v-ygnjā from Dacian *ōgnyā, in turn a derived form of *ogni-s 'fire.' Thus we return again to the perennial and resistant *O-! Moreover, we accumulate the further complication of a loan from an unattested prehistoric language.

Lehr-Spławiński, (1957: 204-b) insists rightly that we must relate *ognъ and Cz. výhěn etc., and he derives *vygnjъ from *ɝgnjъ, drawing the relevant analogy of wydra from a pre stage *udrá. This is, again, all very well, but of course the u- in *udr- is original and uncontested.

Nevertheless, the only way to derive this clear neo-vṛddhi formation *výgnjъ < *(v)ūgnjo- from *ogn(j)ъ is to assume that *ogn(j)ъ once contained a vocalism in *u. Now, if the initial had once been *un- it might be supposed to have later yielded *ǫ-. Indeed, it might be that Li. ungurỹs 'eel' (: SCr. ùgor, Cz. úhor, Pol. węgorz) is not from an earlier *angurys, as Fraenkel (1963: 1163), following Otrębski (1955: 26) would have it. Further, the vrddhi of *un- would have been *ūn-, which would not yield *ǫ-.[2]

It would seem most probable, then, that the earlier preform was *ungnìs, and the vṛddhi derivative *ūngnio-. Perhaps *ūngnio- early lost the first nasal automatically in such a syllable, and not simply by dissimilation. In any event, in Baltic *ungnìs dissimilated to *ugnìs prehistorically. In Slavic, *ungnìs first gave *ǫgnъ, which later dissimilated to yield *ognъ.

Thus, Balto-Slavic goes back to a simple unitary form *ungnìs, which in turn may be traced to IE *ngni-. This then matches Skt. agní-[3] and Lat. ignis < *engnis perfectly. Instead of various ablaut grades and borrowings, we have a single zero-grade form, two quite natural dissimilations of nasals, and a well-understood Slavic neo-vṛddhi derivative.

It has been insisted that Slavic *ognъ < IE *o-, is supported by Li. agnà 'Energie,' agnùs 'energisch,' Latv. agns 'feurig, brünstig, energisch'; (see Fraenkel, 1963: 2). It is of course possible that these words are not at all related to ugnìs. But assuming they are, we can account for them at the same time by the same phenomenon: *angnùs > *agnùs. The ablaut grade here would then be *ong-nu (or ang-nu-), and the zero-grade seen in *ngni- would not then be isolated.

This brings us then to Balto-Slavic angli-, Skt. áṅgāra-, which Walde and Pokorny (1928, 1: 181) assemble under *ong- 'Kohle,' a root which in the past has been thought to be related to what I now suggest can only be *ngni- 'fire.'[4] In Baltic we find Li. anglìs, Latv. ùogle, OP anglis; Li. acc. sg. añglį points to a falling or "short" diphthong in the first syllable. Therefore *añglís, áñglin.

The Slavic forms are somewhat more complicated in detail. OCS ǫglъ m., and the plural or collective ǫglъje, and Pol. węgiel gen. węgla are clear for the segmental features. Russ. úgol' gen. úglá and SCr. ùgalj ùglja are clear for the place of the accent. Slovene (collective) óglje could agree with these, and with the Serbo-Croatian intonation, which somewhat surprisingly appears to indicate an old acute (rising). However, SCr. ùgalj 'coal' and ùgao 'corner,' both matched by a homophonous Slovene ógel, are ambiguous. On the other hand, Cz. úhel 'angle' points to an old acute (with length preserved), while uhel 'coal' seems to reflect an old circumflex (i.e., shortened). Thus, where we find a clear distinction, the circum-flex, or falling, or "short" diphthong belongs to 'coal.' Hence we re-construct *ǫ̂glъ, and this leads us again to *ańgli-.

It was suggested early (see Walde and Pokorny: 1928, 1: 181) and again uncritically by Pisani (see Fraenkel 1963: 10) that Albanian thëngjill also is to be related, but with some sort of prefix. This is quite unnecessary. Within Albanian dialects, forms in th- and in f- are both found. The f- must be considered the prior, and fëngjill must be borrowed from a Slavic form on the order of *vǫgl-, where the palatalization was heard by the Albanian recipients as being in the g, and the lateral was either treated as being intervocalic or elsē back-formed as if from a palatalized plural (collective). Thus the source of the Albanian would be a Bulgarian-type dialect, pre-cursor of forms related to vъ̂glen. For further detail on this Albanian word see my contribution to the 1967 Second Salzburg Congress of Slavic History.[5]

Skr. áṅgāra- (misaccented by Fraenkel 1963: 10) also has cognates in the Dardic languages which show an interesting interplay with the reflexes of agní-; on this, see my remarks in Acta Orientalia, to appear. The Dardic cognates do not, however, help to clarify any of the ambiguities in the Indic form in relation to *ańgli-. All we can say is that there seems to be a lexeme for 'coal' *ong- or *ang- plus a liquid suffix.

Formally, it is further possible that the initial once comprised a laryngeal, either o- or a- coloring. Then we would have *Heng-(li) 'coal,' *Heng-nú-'fiery,' and *Hng-ni- 'fire.' This might help to explain why the syllabic nasal in Balto-Slavic here gave *un, and not *in as a reflex in the word for 'fire,' although, as I shall argue elsewhere, such an assumption is not necessary to yield an outcome *un.

University of Chicago

NOTES

1. My colleague Zbigniew Gołąb reminds me that for such a vṛddhi formation a jo-stem is much more likely (and the attested reflex!) than Trautmann's schematic i-stem.

2. One may object that bòdǫ apparently developed from *b (h) ūnd(h) ō. A possible resolution would be to suppose that initial ūn- developed differently from medial; but that is a weak refuge that I prefer not to take. One may better claim that the chronology of this late nasal present is different from that of an earlier neo-vṛddhi. Finally, despite the accent of SCr. bùdêm, we may really have a vocalism in *-un- from forms like Li. bùvo etc.

3. For my views on the survival of this word in the Nuristani languages Waigali and Prasun, see the *Shahidullah Presentation Volume* (Lahore, 1966, pp. 95–96); and *Acta Orientalia*, Copenhagen (to appear).

   Most recently on *agní-* see Mayrhofer (Kurzgefasstes etymologisches Wörterbuch des Altindischen; 1, [1953] p. 18), where the usual cognates are compared. Incidentally, Mayrhofer treats OLi. *ungnis* seriously as it is spelt, instead of regarding it as the miswriting that it must be. Regarding the Slavic form Mayrhofer remarks: "Der Anlaut läszt sich nicht vereinigen (wohl aus Tabu-Gründen entstellt . . .) ." I think we may now reject both parts of this statement.

   For Iranian (*-aγni-* in a name?) and Ugaritic guesses, see *Kurzgefasstes etymologisches Wörterbuch des Altindischen*, addenda 1.544.

4. Note, however, Mayrhofer *op. cit.* 1, p. 18: "weiter zu *áṅgāraḥ, aṅgirāḥ, aṅgatiḥ*. Unsicher."

5. To appear in *Linguistique balkanique*.

REFERENCES

Ernout, A. and A. Meillet. 1951. *Dictionnaire Étymologique de la langue latine* 3. Paris.

Fraenkel, Ernst. 1963. *Litauisches etymologishes Wörterbuch*. Heidelberg.

Georgiev, V. 1963. *Bŏlgarski etimologičen rečnik.* Sofija.

Lehr-Spławiński, T. 1957. *Studia i szkice wybrane z językoznawstwa słowiańskiego.* Warsaw.

Machek, V. 1957. Etymologický Slovník jazyka českého a slovenského. Prague.

Mayrhofer, Manfred. 1953.*Kurzgefasstes etymologisches Wörterbuch des Altindischen*, 1.

Otrębski, Jan. 1955. "Aus der Geschichte der litauischen Sprache." *Lingua Posnaniensis* 5 pp. 23–40.

Pokorny, Julius. 1949. *Indogermanisches etymologisches Wörterbuch.* Bern.

Trautmann, Reinhold. 1923. *Baltisch-slavisches Wörterbuch*. Göttingen.

Vasmer, Max. 1953. *Russisches etymologisches Wörterbuch* 2. Heidelberg.

Walde, A. and J. Pokorny. 1928. *Vergleichendes Wörterbuch der indogermanischen Sprachen.* Berlin.

REMARKS ON SOME BALTIC NAMES OF TOOLS OF THE TYPE LITHUANIAN *KÁLTAS* 'CHISEL'

B. JĒGERS

There are quite a few names of tools in the Baltic languages ending in Lithuanian in -*tas*[1] and in Latvian in -*ts*, e.g., Li. *káltas* and Latv. *kal̄ts* 'chisel.' This type of nomina instrumenti is found also in Old Prussian, e.g., *dalptan* 'durchslag' which is interpreted as 'spitzes Werkzeug von Eisen und Stahl, um damit Löcher zu schlagen' 'a pointed instrument of iron and steel for making holes.'[2] It also has cognates in Slavic languages, e.g., Russ. *doloto*, Polish *dłuto*, Czech *dláto*, etc.[3] Another example from the Slavic languages is OCS *mlat̃* , Russ. *mólot*, Polish *młot*, Czech *mlat* 'hammer,' etc.[4]

As the formation of this type of Baltic nomina instrumenti is very simple in comparison to such Lithuanian formants of nouns of similar meaning as -*tuvas, -iklis, -tukas, -alas, -yklė, -ynė*,[5] one is inclined to think that this type of word formation is rather old. One should also remember that the primitive tools themselves also were very simple, as we know from archaeological excavations. If it were possible to find the original meaning of the nomina instrumenti of the type treated here, one would not only be able to imagine the way these tools were made, but one would also have some inkling of the kind of thinking the early Balts did in naming their tools.

If one consults an etymological dictionary and tries to find the original meaning of a name of our type, it can be seen that only in a few cases is this original meaning indicated. Thus Russ. *doloto* 'chisel' is explained by Šanskij[6] as 'to, čem dolbjat' 'that with which one chisels.' Similarly, Šanskij[7] explains Russ. *mólot* 'hammer' as 'to, čem izmel'čevajut' 'that

with which one crushes' whereas Vasmer[8] uses as explanation the word
'Zermalmer' 'that which crushes.' But usually no indication of the possible
original meaning is given. Thus Li. *káltas* and Latv. *kaĩts* 'chisel' are
listed by Fraenkel[9] under Li. *kálti* 'to forge, hammer, beat' (cf. Latv. *kaĩt*)
without any further explanation.

The present paper therefore attempts to show how the Baltic nomina
instrumenti of the type indicated might have acquired their present meaning or, in other words, what was their original meaning, as far as can be
determined.

In order to be able to do so, some well-known facts have to be recapit-
ulated briefly.

The suffix *-to-* is used in Indo-European languages in the formation of
verbal adjectives, especially in the Italic, Germanic, and Baltic languages.[10]
These originally implied that by an action something acquired a certain
state. Later they came to be used as past passive participles, especially in the Baltic languages. Examples: Li. *siũtas,* Latv. *šũts,* OCS
šitъ, Sanskrit *syūtá-* 'sewn'; Li. *júostas,* Gk. *dzōstós,* Avestan *yāsta-* 'girt';
Li. *pìntas,* Latv. *pĩts* 'plaited, braided,' OCS *pętъ* 'stretched,' etc.

Later these forms in quite a few cases lost their verbal character and
became either adjectives or nouns.

As adjectives are used, e.g., Old Prussian *skijstan* 'pure,' Li. *skýstas,*
Latv. *šķĩsts* 'liquid, thin' (:Li. *skýsti* 'to become liquid, melt,' Latv. *šķĩst*
'to dissolve'); Li. *báltas,* Latv. *balts* 'white'[11] (:Li. *bálti* 'to become white');
OP. *salta,* Li. *šáltas,* Latv. *saĩts* 'cold' (:Li. *šálti,* Latv. *salt* 'freeze,
get cold'), etc.[12]

Among the many nouns belonging here[13] there are some which clearly
show that they originally have been past passive participles. Examples:
Li. *dõtas* 'kas duodama, dovana' 'that which is given, gift'; *maĩstas*
((* *mait-tas*) or *maĩtas* 'valgis' 'meal' (originally 'that which was eaten')
(:Li. *maitìnti* 'to feed'); *plúoštas* 'kas atplēšiama, plēša' 'that which
is torn off, bast, bark'; *sviltas -ai* 'kas prisvilę, apsvilęs daiktas' 'that
which has got burned a little,' etc.

Also other nouns belonging here can be explained the same way.

Some time ago I tried to show that Li. *tìltas* and Latv. *tilts* 'bridge'
might originally have been verbal adjectives with the meaning 'auf
den Boden Ausgebreitetes' '(that which was) spread' (:Latv. *talêt* 'to
spread on the ground (for bleaching)',[14] an explanation which has been
accepted by others.[15]

At the same time I also indicated that Li. *mìltai* and Latv. *milti* 'flour' (cf. also OP. *meltan* 'flour') might originally have meant 'Gemahlenes' '(that which was) ground.'[16]

The same explanation has been used by me in treating Latv. *pañts* 'row' and its cognates as '(in die Länge) Gestrecktes' '(that which was) stretched' (cf. OCS *pętъ* 'stretched').[17]

Turning now to the nomina instrumenti under review, it seems possible to say that they originally have been past passive participles to a much greater degree than usually is assumed.

Thus Li. *káltas* and Latv. *kal̃ts* 'chisel' was originally the same as Li. *káltas* and Latv. *kal̃ts* 'forged, hammered.' In other words, this Baltic name for 'chisel' originally might have meant '(that which was) hewn (off),'[18] e.g., a chip of flint or bone later used as a chisel because of its form. This explanation is in conformity with archaeological finds where chips of flint or bone are often called 'chisels.'[19] In this connection it should be recalled that Li. *kálti* and Latv. *kal̃t* are used not only in speaking about working in metals but also working in stone, especially in the making (sharpening) of millstones, e.g., Li. *jis pats mokėjo girnas kálti, nereikėjo jam nè girnakalio* 'he himself was able to make (sharpen) mill-stones, he did not even need a mill-stone hewer'[20] or Latv. *dzirnas kalt* 'Mühlsteine schärfen' 'to sharpen mill-stones.'[21] This latter usage seems to be rather old. Later when metal (bronze, iron, or steel) became available, it replaced in chisels and other tools flint, bone, or stone. And because metal is more or less malleable, Li. *kálti* and Latv. *kal̃t* changed their meaning to 'to forge, hammer' whereas originally they must have meant something like 'to chip, hew (off).'

Similarly also Russ. *mólot* 'hammer' and its cognates acquired their present meaning, having originally meant '(that which was) ground (crushed).' If a piece, e.g., of stone, thus obtained was ground still more (made smooth by grinding) it could be used as a hammer. In other words, the nearest cognates of the Russian word are Li. *máltas* and Latv. *mal̃ts* 'ground' together with the already mentioned OP. *meltan*, Li. *miltai*, and Latv. *milti* 'flour.'

The same will be true of Russian *doloto* 'chisel' and OP. *dalptan* 'durchslag' which originally might have meant '(that which was) beaten, chipped (off)' (:Russ. *dolbítъ* 'to chisel').

Looking at some other representatives of our nomina instrumenti one easily sees that the same explanation can be used. Thus Li. *aũtas* and Latv. *àuts* 'cloth (for wrapping) round the foot' originally was '(that which was) wrapped (around the foot)' (:Li. *aũti*, Latv. *àut* 'to wrap around, to pull on or off foot-wear'); Li. (old) *graĩžtas* 'saw' was '(that which was) cut off (and later used for cutting off, sawing)' (:*gríežti* 'to cut'); *grą̃žtas* 'borer, drill' was '(that which was) turned (in order to drill)' (:*grę̃žti* 'to turn, bore, drill'); *plàktas* 'a big hammer' was '(that which was) made by forging (beating)' (:*plàkti* 'to beat'); *saitas*, *siẽtas*, Latv. *saite* 'band, strap, rope,' OP. *-saytan* in *largasaytan* 'leather strap' was originally '(that which was) bound (together)' (:Li. *siẽti*, Latv. *sìet* 'to bind,' cf. also OCS *sětь*'net'); Li. *spą́stai*, Latv. *spuôsts* 'trap' was '(that which was) set up by stretching, stretched (e.g., a piece of string)' (:Li. *spę́sti* 'to stretch; to set up a trap,' Latv. *spiêst* 'to press'); OP. *warto* 'house door,' Li. *var̃tai*, Latv. *vãrti*, OCS *vrata*, Russ. *vorotá* 'gate,' etc. was '(that which was) opened and shut' (:Li. *vérti*, Latv. *vẽrt* 'to open and shut'), etc.

Otrębski[22] considers also words like Li. *kéltas* or *pláustas* to be nomina instrumenti because they indicate some means (instrument) of transportation. They also can be explained the same way, i.e., Li. *kéltas* originally might have meant '(that which was) taken across (the river)' (:Li. *kélti* in the meaning 'to take across') and then 'that which takes across (the river) = ferry.' Similarly also Lithuanian *pláustas* 'ferry' (cf. Li. *pláusti* 'to rinse, wash,' actually 'to let something float').

Naturally, not all words belonging here can be explained the same way. Some might have been formed by analogy without ever having functioned as participles, others might have gone through a somewhat different change of meaning from the one imagined here.

A good example to illustrate the latter are OP. *deicton, deictan* 'Stätte' 'place,' *deicton* 'etwas' 'something,' Li. *dáiktas* 'thing, object; place' and Latv. *daikts* 'thing; tool' which show a rather interesting combination of meanings. These words are usually considered to be related with Li. *diegti* 'to prick, pierce' and Latv. *diêgt* 'to prick, to sew.'[23]

It seems to me that the oldest meaning in this case is 'dot, spot, place' which once might have meant 'that which is pricked, a prick, a dot.' As a parallel I would like to mention Latin *pūnctum* 'a prick, dot' in relation to *pungere* 'to prick, injure.' The Latin word developed into French *point* which is the basis of the English *point* in the meaning 'a dot, prick, spot, separable or single article, item' whereas the English *point* in the meaning 'a sharp end to which anything tapers, used for pricking; an object or instrument consisting of or characterized by a point which pricks or pierces; a dagger, a pointed sword, or the like; a bodkin' is traced back through French *pointe* to late Latin *puncta* 'the action of piercing; the piercing part of anything; a sharp or pointed extremity.'[24] One should also remember that German *Ort* 'place' originally meant '(sharp) point (of a spear),' a meaning still to be discerned in German *Ort* in the meaning 'awl, bodkin.'[25] Thus one can assume that the Baltic words have gone through a similar change of meaning. The original meaning 'that which is pricked, a prick, a dot'—OP. *deicton* 'etwas' comes closest to this meaning[26]—developed into 'spot, place' (OP. *deicton, deictan,* Li. *dáiktas*) whereas Li. *dáiktas* and Latv. *daikts* in the meaning 'thing, object' might be a later development of 'a pointed (sharp) tool (for pricking)' (Latv. *daikts* 'tool').   In Latv. *daikti* 'insects; snakes'[27]—if this is not a particular usage of Latv. *daikti* 'things'—some remnant of this meaning seems to be found.

Space limitation does not permit discussion in detail of all the names for tools of the type under review.[28]

To sum up: the explanation suggested here seems to open up a new approach for understanding the Baltic nomina instrumenti under review. Their formation has become much clearer by explaining them more consistently than before as old past passive participles. It seems possible to say that we have here before us a typical Baltic formant for names of tools (although scattered remains of this formant can be found also in Slavic and other languages in names for tools). At the same time also, their original meaning starts to emerge. Quite a few of the names of the tools under review turn out to be witnesses of an era in the development of Baltic civilization when tools were much more primitive and were made of materials available at that time, i.e., chips of flint, bone, or stone.

NOTES

1. According to *Lietuvių kalbos gramatika* 1 (Vilnius, 1965), p. 383, there are about 50 of them in Lithuanian.
2. J. Endzelīns, *Senprūsu valoda* (Riga, 1943), p. 156.
3. M. Vasmer, *Russisches etym. Wörterbuch* 1 (Heidelberg, 1950), p. 360.
4. *Ibid.* 2, p. 152.
5. See about them and others *Lietuvių kalbos gramatika* 1, pp. 381–394. For some of the Latvian correspondences see J. Endzelīns, *Lettische Grammatik* (Riga, 1922), §219.
6. *Kratkij ètimologičeskij slovar' russkogo jazyka* (Moskva, 1961), p. 95.
7. *Ibid.* p. 204.
8. *Op. cit.,* 2, p. 152.
9. *Litauisches etymologisches Wörterbuch* (1955–65), p. 211.

10. K. Brugmann, *Kurze vergleichende Grammatik der indogermanischen Sprachen* (Strassburg, 1904), pp. 317–318; W. Vondrak, 1, pp. 576–579.

11. Cognate with Russ. *bolóto* 'swamp, bog,' etc., see M. Vasmer, *op. cit.*, 1, p. 104.

12. More examples are listed by P. Skardžius, *Lietuvių kalbos zodžių daryba* (Vilnius 1941), p. 319.

13. P. Skardžius, *op. cit.*, pp. 320–322; J. Otrębski, *Gramatyka języka litewskiego* 2 (Warsaw, 1956), pp. 235–239.

14. *Språkliga Bidrag* 3 (1958), p. 83, n. 32.

15. E.g., by Fraenkel, *op. cit.*, p. 1094.

16. *Språkliga Bidrag* 3 (11) (1958), p. 83, n. 32.

17. *Ibid.*, p. 85, n. 57. Another possible explanation is mentioned *ibid.*, p. 84, n. 46.

18. Cf. also OP. *calte* 'ein margk' 'a mark (name of money)' which is explained by J. Pokorny, *Idg. etymologisches Wörterbuch* (Bern, 1949), p. 546, similarly, i.e., as 'geschlagenes=geprägtes Geld', 'beaten=coined money' and is listed as a cognate of our words Li. *káltas* and Latv. *kaĺts*.

19. For pictures of such chisels see, e.g., O. Schrader, *Reallexikon der idg. Altertumskunde*, 2. Aufl. 2 (Berlin-Leipzig, 1929), p. 57. It might be noted here that a primitive chisel is called by archaeologists a *celt* (German *Celt*, etc.) on the basis of a late Latin word *celtis* 'chisel' the existence of which is very doubtful, though (see, e.g., A. Walde, *Lateinisches etym. Wörterbuch*, 3. Aufl., von J. B. Hofmann* 1 (Heidelberg, 1938), p. 198). But maybe there is some connection between the Latin word and Li. *káltas* and Latv. *kaĺts*?

20. Balčikonis, *Lietuvių kalbos žodynas* 5 (Vilnius, 1959), p. 154.

21. K. Mühlenbach, *Lettisch-deutsches Wörterbuch, redigiert, ergänzt und fortgesetzt von J. Endzelīns*, 2 (Riga, 1925-27), p. 145.

22. Otrębski, *op. cit.*, 2, p. 236.

23. Fraenkel, *op. cit.*, p. 79. It has to be mentioned, though, that against this etymology such Latvian words as *daiks* 'thing, instrument,' *daiceklis* 'small objects,' *daikari* 'rubbish, odd things' seem to speak. But as Endzelīns, *op. cit.*, p. 158, points out, these forms might have got their *k* from the Latv. synonym *rīks*.

24. See *NED* s.v. *point*.

25. See *Trübners Deutsches Wörterbuch* s.v. *Ort*.

26. Thus already A. Walde, *Vergleichendes Wörterbuch der indogermanischen Sprachen* 1 (Berlin-Leipzig, 1930), p. 833, determines '*Punkt, Stich*' 'point, prick' as the original meaning of the Old Prussian word.

27. Endzelīns, Mühlenbach, *op. cit.*, 1, p. 431, considers it as a probable cognate (*wohl zu*) of Latv. *diêgt* 'to prick' whereas Latv. *daikts* he leaves without an etymology. The etymology of the latter is indicated by Endzelīns, *Senprūsu valoda* (Riga, 1943), p. 158, by referring to A. Walde, *Vergleichendes Wörterbuch der indogermanischen Sprachen*, 1, p. 832 f., where it is considered to be a cognate of Li. *díegti* 'to prick,' etc.

28. Because of the same reason no consideration is given here, e.g., to the often-found parallel forms in *-ta*, cf. P. Skardžius, *op. cit.*, pp. 323–324.

ON THE BALTO-SLAVIC
DATIVE PLURAL AND DUAL

J. KAZLAUSKAS

The problem of the identity of the dative plural formants in Baltic and Slavic is very intricate. As for the Lithuanian dative plural formant *-mus*, its identity with Slavic *-mъ* might seem perfectly obvious, but the Prussian language has the formants *-mas* and *-mans* the vowels of which differ from the Lithuanian counterpart. Not without reason did J. Endzelīns write almost 70 years ago: "Thus in the Baltic languages we find the dative plural ending Lith. *-mus* side by side with Pruss. *-mas* (it is impossible to determine what kind of vowel there might be between *m* and *s* in Old Latvian *-ms*), and Lith. *-mus* is probably identical with Common Slavic **-mъ*."[1] And further: "Tracing the dative plural *-ъ* to *-mos* for the sake of relating it to Pruss. *-mas* and (in respect to the vocalism) to Sanskrit *-bhyas*, Old Latin *-bos* and Old Celtic *-bo* is not profitable, since we do not have any evidence that *u* in Lith. *-mus* must be traced back to IE *u*."[2] A. Meillet discussed this problem in a slightly different way: "La caractéristique du datif est *-mu*, ou l'*u* final est ambigu: la desinence *-mus* du datif pluriel du vieux lituanien fait penser à un ancien **-mus*, tandis que skr. *-bhyah* (cf. Lat. *-bus*) ferait plutôt penser à un ancien **-mos* . . ."[3] The difference in vowels in the dative plural formant of Li. *-mus*, Slavic *-mъ* on the one hand and Pruss. *-mas, -mans*, Celtic-Latin-Venetian-Messapian-Indo-Iranian *-bhos* on the other hand was acknowledged by many other linguists.[4] At the same time desperate attempts were made to prove that the Baltic and Slavic formants in question have their origins in a common archetype. We shall mention here only some of them, those which reflect the diversity of approaches which attempt to derive these formants from the same origin. Thus E. Berneker offered the groundless assumption that *-mas* passed to *-mus* under the influence of the accusative plural *-us*.[5] At one time this kind of explanation was shared by K. Brugmann and A. Meillet.[6]

A. Vaillant considers Prussian *-mus* to be a new formation which originated from a blend of the dative plural ending *-mus* with the dative dual *-ma*.[7] Ignoring for some reason this very simple explanation given by A. Vaillant, V. Mažiulis[8] recently put forward an interesting, but rather intricate hypothesis according to which Pruss. *-mans,* Li. *-mus* were derived from **-mōns,* Slavic *-mъ* from **-mōn,* and Pruss. *-mas* from the dative dual *-ma* (< **-mō*) expanded by the plural *-s*.[9]

It seems to us that the correct solution to the problem of the vocalism of the Balto-Slavic dative plural formants is impeded by the static view of Li. *-mus* on the one hand and a firm belief in the regularity of the phonetic laws without exceptions on the other hand. In dealing with this problem the investigators up to now have undervalued the fact that the dative plural form in Lithuanian was reduced (*-mus -ms*), and that the reduction had started relatively early. The process of reduction is attested already in sixteenth century writings, though not in all of them had it reached the same level of development. For example, in the works of B. Vilentas, J. Bretkūnas, in Margarita Theologica,[10] i.e., in the works of the representatives of the Western Lithuanian dialects, the full form of the dative plural *-mus* is scarcely preserved. The reduced form *-ms* is attested in all the sixteenth century writings, though in many of them the full form *-mus* is still rather frequent. Taking into consideration the fact that the development of Lithuanian proceeded at a very slow pace, the starting point of this reduction must be moved to a much earlier prehistoric time. This reduction was a phonetic-morphological phenomenon. When in the dative plural form stress had been shifted from the last to the preceding syllable,[11] the final syllable was always unstressed. Consequently, under conditions of dynamic stress the unstressed vowel *u* in the final position of the form, which was mostly polysyllabic /i.e., more than two syllables/ and which possessed one syllable more than many other case forms, was reduced to zero.[12] But the loss of a vowel usually occurs not suddenly, but fairly gradually: at first a vowel is weakened and reduced, and only then is it completely lost. Obviously those old Lithuanian writings in which the dative plural *-mus* still prevails, though the form *-ms* exists side by side with the latter, attest just the situation when the final element *-mus* was pronounced with the reduced *u,* which sometimes might have been dropped altogether. Such a reduced *u* might well have been derived from the vowel *o* or *å,* since the latter, when reduced, may easily pass to *-u* (*-ъ*), cf. the Lithuanian dialectal nominative singular *vilkъs vilkas,* Old Slavic *vlъkъ* (*-ъ* < *-os*), etc. Therefore the Lithuanian dative plural formant *-mus* may be derived from *-mås.* This will be even more credible if one takes into consideration the fact that in the Baltic languages instead of modern *a* at one time there used to be *ǎ* (*o*), and this fact has already been proved.[13] Even if we start with the traditionally postulated *a* (not *ǎ*) for the earlier period of the Baltic languages, the labialization of the unstressed short vowel *a* after the labial consonant *m* in the process of reduction is also quite comprehensible. The expansion of labialization to following un-rounded sounds in certain cases in Lithuanian occurs even when it is not attended by vowel reduction, cf. dialectal *nuovė* < *nùavė*, etc. And so there is nothing to prevent us from deriving the vowel *u* in the Lithuanian formant *-mus* from *ǎ* or *a*, and the formant itself from the prehistoric *-mas* (< *-mos*). If we may assume *-mas* (< *-mos*) for a definite period of the same time in the Prussian language we attest the dative plural *-mas* (< *-mos*), then Latvian *-ms* in the dative plural form whose vowel is at-tested neither in the old writings, nor Latvian dialects, must also derive from *-mos*. In this case Slavic *-mъ* also derives not from *-mus*, but from *-mos* (the development of *-ъ* from *-os* in the Slavic languages is perfectly obvious[14]). Consequently, for the Balto-Slavic dialectal region we may assume the dative plural form *-mos*.

A note should be added on the relation of the Prussian formants *-mas* and *-mans*, though what was said above indicates already which of the two is considered an archaism and which is considered a new formation. In the written records of Prussian, which reflect the language very insufficiently, the formant *-mas* side by side with *-mans* is attested only in the personal pronouns (*noūmas* 'for us,' *ioūmas* 'for you'); in other parts of speech the formant *-mans* is used. If this kind of distribution of the formants under review really existed in the Prussian language, then the preservation of the old form *-mas* only in personal pronouns might well be explained by the assumption that because of the peculiar declension of personal pronouns (suppletion, etc.) they may have preserved certain archaisms and their declension may differ from that of other parts of speech (cf. the declen-sion of personal pronouns in Lithuanian dialects which differs greatly from that of other parts of speech). To explain how the formant *-mans* was developed in Prussian is rather a vexing problem. Some linguists have suggested that it derived from *-mas* under the influence of the accusative plural *-ans*,[15] for in the Prussian writings there are cases when the accusa-tive was used instead of the dative and genitive. But it would be more reasonable to attribute these cases to the translator, rather than to the Prussian language.[16] That is why we think that the formant *-mans* must have been developed in a different way. It seems to us that for Prussian we may assume the dative dual formant *-man* (< *-mān*, cf. Old Indic

-bhyām). Surprising as it is, Prussian in this case may be more closely related to Old Indic than to the Baltic and Slavic languages (cf. Pruss. gen. sg. *deiwas* < **deiwasja*, Old Indic *devasya* and East Baltic **deivā*, Old Slavic *vlъka*; Pruss. *stesmu*, Old Indic *tasmāi*, Baltic *tam-*, Old Slavic *tomъ*, etc.). Under the influence of the dative dual **-man* the dative plural *-mas* could well have passed to *-mans*. Identical influence of the dual forms on the plural forms otherwise is not alien to the Baltic languages, cf. at least the Lithuanian dialect. acc. pl. *kárvis* (acc. dual *kárvi+s*), etc.[17]

To derive Li. *-mus* from *-mas* (< *-mos*) at first sight seems to contradict the reliquary dative dual *-ma* (cf. *akima*), where we find *-ma* instead of *-mu*.[18] However, the Slavic languages, possessing the dative-instrumental dual *-ma*, prove that the form *-ma* derives not from *-mo*, but most probably from *-mā*,[19] cf. Old Indic *-bhyām*, as *-mà* in the instrumental case of Lithuanian may derive only from **-mā*. Besides, in the instrumental dual form *-ma* is stressed and this also helped to preserve the vowel *a* in it.

Thus the Balto-Slavic region with the vowel *o* in the dative plural formant is not an exception in the family of Indo-European languages. One and the same vowel must have existed in the dative dual of Baltic, Slavic, and Indo-Iranian, only it must have been *ā*.

All that has been said allows us to draw the further conclusion that the Germanic form *-mz* (cf. the forms attested in the oldest Icelandic and Norwegian manuscripts *tueimR, þrimr, þremr*) most likely derive from *-maz* (-mos), not from *-miz*. This seems to be even more obvious since R. Loewe has proved that in the Germanic dative dual there was an ending which had an initial *-m* and a final nonfront vowel (without *s*).[20]

University of Vilnius

NOTES

1. J. Endzelīns, *Slavjano-baltijskie ètjudy* (Kharkov, 1911), p. 155.
2. *Ibid.*, p. 157.
3. A. Meillet, *Le slave commun* (Paris, 1934), p. 395.
4. Cf. at least W. Porzig, *Die Gliederung des indogermanischen Sprachgebiets* (Heidelberg, 1954), p. 90.
5. E. Berneker, *Die preussische Sprache* (Strassburg, 1896), p. 196.
6. For this see J. Endzelīns, *op. cit.*, p. 154. See also footnote 3.
7. A. Vaillant, *Grammaire comparée des langues slaves* 2 (Lyon-Paris, 1958), pp. 37–38.
8. V. Mažiulis, "K balto-slavjanskoj forme dativa," *Baltistica* 2(1) (1966), pp. 43–53.

9. This explanation is somewhat similar to the above-mentioned assumption made by A. Vaillant.

10. The same in "Psalter" by J. Réza.

11. J. Kazlauskas, *Lietuvių kalbos istorinė gramatika* (Vilnius, 1968), p. 167.

12. On the development of dynamic stress see my article "Fonologinė baltų kalbų kirčio raidos interpretacija," *Baltistica* 2(2), 3(1). I have written about the loss of *e* in a similar position in the article "O nekotoryx arxaizmax v im. pad. mn. č. osnov na *-u* i *-i* baltijskix jazykov," *Lingua Posnaniensis* 14 (1969), pp. 7–17.

13. See my article "K razvitiju obščebaltijskoj sistemy glasnyx," *Voprosy jazykoznanija* No. 4 (1962). It is scarcely credible that the starting point of reduction in the dative plural ending might be moved to the period when in the Baltic languages the two short vowels could have been distinguished. Obviously, this would be incorrect from the chronological point of view. However, see the papers of M. L. Burwell and J. W. Marchand elsewhere in this volume.

14. See at least P. S. Kuznecov, *Očerki po morfologii praslavjanskogo jazyka* (Moscow, 1961), p. 64; G. Y. Shevelov, *A Prehistory of Slavic* (New York, 1965), p. 156.

15. See J. Endzelīns, *op. cit.*, p. 154. Later Endzelīns raised an objection against this unfounded assumption.

16. See R. Trautmann, *Die altpreussischen Sprachdenkmäler* (Göttingen, 1910), p. 210; J. Endzelīns, *Altpreussische Grammatik* (Riga, 1944), p. 81.

17. See J. Kazlauskas, *Lietuvių kalbos istorinė gramatika*, p. 129.

18. *-mu* instead of *-ma* appeared under the influence of the plural formant *-mus*; see P. Arumaa, *Untersuchungen zur Geschichte der litauischen Personal-pronomina* (Tartu, 1933), p. 78.

19. From among the latest works see A. Vaillant, *op. cit.,* p. 39.

20. R. Loewe, *Zeitschrift für vergleichende Sprachforschung* 48, p. 96; V. Pisani, *Geolinguistica e Indoeuropeo* (Roma, 1940), p. 206.

SOME ATTEMPTS TO INVENTORY LITHUANIAN PHONEMES

ANTANAS KLIMAS

In this paper we shall limit our discussion as follows:

(a) only some of the principal attempts to inventory phonemes of literary Lithuanian (Standard Literary Lithuanian) will be considered; (b) the discussion will be limited to the segmental phonemes.

One of the early and important efforts was performed in England by the late W. K. Matthews.[1] (See Table I.)

One can easily see that Matthews followed the Russian system, positing only five vowels for Lithuanian, though remarking that vocalic length is phonemic. Although he does not exactly say so, he seems to consider vocalic length as a suprasegmental feature, thus permitting him to establish a system of only five vowels.

Matthews, however, is very "generous" in inventorying the diphthongal phonemes of Lithuanian; he lists eight of them. He even considers orthographic *ae* as a separate diphthongal phoneme (as in *aeroplanas* 'airplane'), perhaps not having observed the syllable boundary which always intervenes.

He is much more careful in counting the consonantal phonemes. Although he lists the (f'), (c'), (x'), (h'), etc., in subsequent paragraphs, he does not include them in the total number of phonemes.

Schmalstieg (see Table II) rejects the idea of counting any diphthongs as separate phonemes. He considers them as simply consisting of two vocalic phonemes (i.e., /au/ = /a/ + /u/, etc.). Since Schmalstieg considers vocalic length as a segmental feature and finds six "basic" vowels, he lists a total of eleven vowel phonemes in Lithuanian. He does not accept the existence of the short /e/ as the short opposition of /ė:/.

TABLE I[a]

Nonpalatalized Consonants:						
p/b	t/d	k/g				
m	n	(η)				
f/v	s/z	š/ž	x	h		
	c/ʒ	č/ǯ				
	1					
	r		. . . .			22

Palatalized Consonants:						
p'/b'	t'/d'	k'/g'				
m'	n'	(η')				
(f')/v'	s'/z'	š'/ž'	j	(x')	(h')	
	(c')/ʒ'	č'/ǯ'				
	1'					
	r'		. . . .			19

Vowels: i e a o u	. . . .	5

Diphthongs:		ui				
	ei	ie	uo	eu		
	ai	ae	au	. . . .		8
					Total	54

[a]From W. K. Matthews, "Phonemes and Phoneme-Patterns in Contemporary Russian and Lithuanian," *The Slavonic and East European Review* 36 (87) (London, 1958), pp. 317–339.

Although Schmalstieg does mention that /f/, /x/, and /h/ occur only in foreign words, he accepts them as a fact in literary Lithuanian. Thus, by his system, one would calculate the total number of segmental phonemes at 56.

Quite a different interpretation is presented by Miss Augustaitis in her Munich dissertation published in 1964 (see Table III). Approaching the system from the tradition of Trubetzkoy and Jespersen, she does not admit /f/, /f'/, /x/, /x'/, /h/, /h'/, /c/, /c'/, /dž/, /dz'/, /z'/ and /č/ into the consonantal system. In the vocalic system, she does not admit the phonemes /e/ (as in *esù* 'I am') and /o/ (as in *jòtas* 'j'). She lists only the traditional six diphthongal phonemes. My own calculation (never expressed in numbers by Miss Augustaitis) of the number of phonemic elements in her system would be 48.

No one has done more work in this area than Miss Vaitkevičiūtė (see

TABLE II[a]

The Consonants:

		labial	dental	(alveo-palatal) retracted	velar	glottal
stops	voiceless	p	t		k	
	voiced	b	d		g	
	voiceless	f	s	š	x	h
continuants	voiced	v	z	ž		
	nasal	m	n			
affricates	voiced		d̨	d̆		
	voiceless		c	č		

apical trill r
lateral l   palatal glide j

The Vowels: i i: u u:
               ė: o o:
           e e: a a:

My calculation would be: consonantal phonemes . . . 45
                         vowel phonemes   . . . 11
                              Total   56

[a]From William R. Schmalstieg, "A Descriptive Study of the Lithuanian Verbal System," *General Linguistics* 3 (3) (1958), Supplement.

Table IV). Both in her earlier articles and in the Academy grammar, she firmly argues for the largest number of phonemes yet encountered by us: 65.

In vocalism, Vaitkevičiūtė has six basic vowels, plus six long vowels. In diphthongs, to the traditional six (ai, au, ei, ui, ie, uo), she adds /eu/ and /ɔi/.

Kazlauskas (see Table V) argues against two points in Vaitkevičiūtė's interpretation: he considers the /ē/ of Vaitkevičiūtė (as in *poetas* 'poet') simply an invention of linguists. To him the short /e/ in *poètas* 'poet' and in *jis mès* 'he will throw' show little or no phonetic difference, definitely no phonemic difference. He also rejects the idea of considering the diphthongs as separate phonemes. His solution in this regard is the same as that of Schmalstieg (1958). Kazlauskas also considers all 22 consonants as having the phonemic opposition nonpalatalized versus palatalized, except, of course, /j/. Thus, we would count 56 phonemes in Kazlauskas' system.

TABLE III[a]

g	g′	u	ie
k	k′	i	æi
r	r′	i:	ai
b	b′	æ:	ui
p	p′	é:	au
—	j	a:	uo
l	l′	u:	
n	n′	a	
t	t′	o:	
d	d′		
s	s′		
ž	ž′		
m	m′		
v	v′		
—	dž′		
š	š′		
dz	—		
z	—		
—	č′		

Consonants: 33
Vowels: 9
Diphthongs: 6
    Total: 48
(NB. This calculation is mine. AK.)

[a]From Daine Augustaitis, *Das litauische Phonationssystem* (München, 1964).

Pavel Trost (see Table VI) adds something new to the discussion. He admits the existence of /ä/ since, as Klimas and Schmalstieg had already shown,[2] it occurs initially and, thus, cannot be considered as predictable after the preceding palatalized consonant. What is really new is the fact that Trost considers the orthographic diphthongs *ie* and *uo* as long vowels rather than as true diphthongs.

The latest attempt to reach us is by A. Girdenis. Unfortunately, only abstracts of his two papers have so far been published. As one can see in Table VII, Girdenis, similar to Schmalstieg (1958) and Kazlauskas (1966),[3] considers, in the main, all the Lithuanian diphthongs biphonemic.

TABLE IV[a]

Vowels:	ī	i	ė	e	<u>e</u>	ē	ū	u	ō	ɔ	a	ā . . . . 12 [b]

Diphthongs:	ai	au	ei	eu	ɔi	ui	ie	uo . . . . 8 [c]

Consonants:

p:p′	b:b′	t:t′	d:d′	k:k′
g:g′	c:c′	dz:dz′	č:č′	dž:dž′
m:m′	n:n′	s:s′	š:š′	z:z′
ž:ž′	f:f′	v:v′	ch:ch′	h:h′
l:l′	r:r′	-:j	 45

Total   65

[a]From V. Vaitkevičiūtė, "Lietuvių literatūrinės kalbos priebalsinių fonemų sudėtis," *Lietuvių kalbotyros klausimai* 1 (1957), pp. 5–66.

V. Vaitkevičiūtė, "Lietuvių literatūrinės kalbos balsinės ir dvibalsinės fonemos," *Lietuvių kalbotyros klausimai* 4 (1961), pp. 19–46.

V. Vaitkevičiūtė, et al., *Lietuvių kalbos gramatika* 1 tomas (Vilnius, 1965), pp. 43–92.

[b]ė as in *ėmė* 'he took'; e as in *poetas* 'poet'; <u>e</u> as in *jis mes* 'he will throw'; ē as in *mes* 'we.'

[c]In 1961, she listed the diphthong *ōi*, but did not count it as a separate phoneme: it occurs, according to her, only in one word: *ōi* 'ouch.'

TABLE V[a]

11 vowel phonemes:	e	ē	ẽ	i	ī	a	ā	ŏ	ō	u	ũ[b]

45 consonantal phonemes:										
		j	r	r̂		l	l̂	p	p̂	b	b̂
m	m̂	f	f̂		v	v̂	t	t̂	d	d̂
n	n̂	c	ĉ		dz	d̂z	č	ĉ̃	dz	d̂ž
s	ŝ	z	ẑ	š		ŝ̃	ž	ẑ̃	k	k̂
g	ĝ	ch	c̃h	h		h̃̂	[c]			

(Total: 56 phonemes)

[a]From Jonas Kazlauskas, "Lietuvių literatūrinės kalbos fonemų diferencinių elementų sistema," *Kalbotyra* 14 (1966), pp. 73–81.

[b]e: *mèsti* 'to throw,' ē : *kėdė̃* 'chair,' ē: *ẽsti* 'is.'

[c]Instead of the signs l' m' etc., used by Vaitkeviciūtė (1965) for the palatalized consonants, Kazlauskas uses ˆ. He explains in his article that palatalization here is phonemic, not allophonic.

Girdenis also questions the phonemic status of the short [ė] (as in *prioritètas,* see Table VII).[4]   Very interesting to me, however, is his interpretation of the [ie] and [uo] as monophonemic, treating them as long vowels.

TABLE VI[a]

i u (e) (o) ä a	ī ū [b] ē ō ie uo ǟ ā

[a]From Pavel Trost, "Two Remarks on Lithuanian Vocalism," *Acta Baltico-Slavica* 3 (1966), pp. 183–185.

[b](e) and (o) occur only in foreign words. In Eastern Lithuanian, ä > a.

TABLE VII[a]

Vowels:	i:	u:	i	u
	ė:	o:	ė (?)[b]	o
	ie	uo	e	a
	e:	a:		

[a]From A. Girdenis, "Fonologinės pastabos apie lietuvių literatūrinės kalbos vokalizmą," *Dėstytojų mokslinė-metodinė konferencija. Pranešimų tezės* (Šiauliai, 1966), pp. 26–27.

A. Girdenis, "Keturios lietuvių kalbos priebalsių minkštumo fonologinės interpretacijos," *Spalio revoliucija ir visuomeniniai mokslai Lietuvoje.* Mokslinės konferencijos medžiaga (1967 m. gruodžio 6-8 d.) (Vilnius, 1967), pp. 613–615.

[b]The question mark is Girdenis'. In a footnote he explains, that "generally speaking, the existence of this phoneme in Lithuanian is very doubtful."

For the consonantal phonemes, Girdenis, without going into the enumeration of the consonantal phonemes themselves (at least not in the abstract which has reached us), proposes four phonological interpretations for the phonemic opposition, palatalized versus nonpalatalized. These are as follows:

1. To treat this opposition traditionally by marking the palatalization of the consonant:

        sakaū: sakiaū /sakaū/ : /sak'aū/, etc.

2. One may indicate only the fronting of the vowels following a palatalized consonant:

        sakaū: sakiaū /sakaū/ : /sakäū/, etc.

3. One may consider the feature of the palatalization as affecting both

the consonant and the vowel together, thus, considering the palatalization as a suprasegmental feature:

sakaū: sakiaū /sakaū/ : /sakaū̑/, etc.

4. And, finally, one may indicate palatalization simply by marking the "presence" of 'j':

sakaū: sakiaū /sakaū/ : /sakjaū/, etc.

As we have just seen from this brief discussion, there seem to exist a few unresolved problems, considering that one presumably wants to aim for the most economical system of phonemic notation. These problems are:

1. Do we count the short /e/ of foreign words, as in *poètas*, *tèkstas*, *universitètas* as a separate phoneme, or as an occasional allophonic variation of the /e/ (*jis mès*) in the speech of some educated people?[5]

2. Do the consonant phonemes /f/, /x/ and /h/ participate in the phonemic opposition of palatalization? Do the /dž/ and the /dz'/ phonemes really exist as separate entities?

3. How do we interpret the diphthongs?

4. Which of Girdenis' four ways of notating the phonemic opposition in consonants is the best? Or, perhaps, is there an even better way? Is there one best solution?

5. What is the best graphemic way to portray the Lithuanian segmental inventory, once we agree on what to include in it?

In answer to question 1, I agree entirely with Kazlauskas: this "foreign" /e/ occurs only in the learned (and affected) speech of some educated Lithuanians, primarily in the cities. For most Lithuanians, the /e/ in *tekèti* 'to flow' and the /e/ in *tekstas* 'text' are exactly the same.

To answer question 2, the following observations should be mentioned: although it is very difficult to find true minimal pairs to indicate the opposition /f/ : /f'/, etc., the contrast is there, nevertheless, viz.:

furðras: fiūreris
Chur̃ginas: chirurgas
humanìstas: Hiugō
Žùro: su-žiùro
džāzas: Džiānis
dzūkas: dziùkinti

Eventually, if more words with these phonemes come into the language, the opposition may become parallel to that for all the other consonants.

The most difficult problem is question 3, the diphthongs. Vaitkevičiūtè (1961) considers the diphthongs as separate phonemes because:

a. both components belong to the same morpheme;
b. both components occur in the same syllable;
c. the length of the diphthong is approximately the same as that of a long vowel;
d. the lengths of the two components, taken separately, are different from either the length of a short vowel, or that of a long vowel;
e. when in ablaut series, both components change like *one* unit, not separately.[6]

In the Academy grammar (1965), Vaitkevičiūtė brings forth only the first three arguments, (a), (b), and (c).

In opposing Vaitkevičiūtė, Kazlauskas argues as follows: Since Vaitkevičiūtė herself has definitely proven that the so-called mixed diphthongs in Lithuanian are truly biphonemic (i.e., *ul* = /u/ + /l/, etc.), then the so-called pure diphthongs should be treated equally. Kazlauskas argues that *any one* component of these pure diphthongs can carry not only morphemic but even semantic difference: *kálti: kélti, kar̃kti: ker̃kti* (orthographic *ker̃gti*), etc. He also points out the quasihomonyms: *reĩkti: reñkti, kaitrà: kantrà*, etc., in which the difference in the second component of the diphthong obviously has semantic import.

Girdenis brings the following arguments for considering the diphthongs biphonemic:

a. If Vaitkevičiūtė counts eight diphthongal phonemes (see Table IV), then, to be consistent, she should also count at least three more: /oːj/, /èːj/, /iːj/ as in *galvõj, žẽmėj, pilỹj*.

b. In the pure diphthongs, their two components are not fused any closer together than they are in the mixed diphthongs, in other words: *au* = *am* (*a* + *u* = *a* + *m*).

c. Diphthongs *au ai ei ui oi eu* are biphonemic because, among other things, one may interpret them as follows; their first component is a vowel, their second is an allophonic variation of the semivowels /v/ and /j/, although close to the vocalic phonemes /u/ and /i/.

However, Girdenis, like Trost, but in opposition to Kazlauskas, would prefer to interpret the two diphthongs (in Lithuanian grammars they are called 'sutaptiniai dvibalsiai,' fused diphthongs) as specific long vowels. Especially, since in the case of /ie/ and /uo/ no special lengthening occurs

TABLE VIII

Vowels:	i:	u:	i	u		
	ė:	o:		o		
	ie	uo				
	e:	a:	e	a	. . . . (13)	

Consonants:	b : b′	c : c′	č : č′	d: d′
	f : f′	g : g′	h : h′	– : j
	k : k′	l : l′	m: m′	n: n′
	p : p′	r : r′	s : s′	š : š′
	t : t′	v : v′	z : z′	ž: ž′
	dz: dz′	dž: dž′	x : x′	. . . .(45)
			Total	58

in the one or the other component when under different intonations, which is always the case with the rest of the diphthongs, both the "pure" ones and the mixed ones. Thus, in *áu* or *ám*, the *a* is considerably longer than the second component, whereas, in *aū* and *am̃*, it is the opposite. But no one can hear lengthening of *i* versus *e* in either *ie*, or *iė̃*.

I am inclined to agree with Girdenis, especially since in the large part of Lithuania there is no phonemic distinction between *ie* and *iė̃*, between *úo* and *uõ*, just as there is no longer a phonemic distinction between *á* and *ã*, between *ó* and *õ*. That is, /ie/ and /uo/ are treated exactly like all the other long vowels! However, no one will mistake or confuse the *áu* with *aū*, the *ái* with *aī̃*, etc. My suggested system is given in Table VIII.

Concerning the answer to question 4, ("Which is the best way to interpret the palatalized versus nonpalatalized opposition in consonants?"), I will opt the traditional notation: k : k′, m : m′, etc. I think it is the clearest and the least confusing, and is convenient on the typewriter.

Finally, the graphemic notation. I would prefer a notation as close to the normal Lithuanian orthography as possible. I would use the : as the sign of length. I would use the orthographic ⟨ė⟩ as /ė/, but would add the sign of length, /ė:/, to be consistent. I would propose to do the same for the ⟨o⟩, /o:/. Thus, I would, at this time, recommend the system presented in Table VIII as the clearest and most practical system I can devise consonant with current knowledge of the sound system of Lithuanian.

University of Rochester

NOTES

1. There was an earlier attempt. Cf. J. Dambrauskaitė, "Lietuvių kalbos foneminės balsių sistemos nustatymas," *Vilniaus Valstybinio Pedagoginio Instituto Mokslo darbai* 3 (1957), pp. 221–240. It was, however, unavailable to me.
2. Antanas Klimas and W. R. Schmalstieg, "A Note on the Vocalic Phonemes of Lithuanian," *The Slavonic and East European Review* 41 (96) (December 1962), pp. 245–246.
3. Kazlauskas repeats the same assertion concerning the inventory of Lithuanian phonemes in *Baltistica* 3 (2) (1967).
4. Kazlauskas, *op. cit.*, p. 243, asserts that this /e/ as in *prioritètas* is simply an invention of the linguists.
5. There *is* a minimal pair for /o/: /o:/: *jótas*, past participle passive of *jóti* 'to ride': *jòtas*/j/. It is mentioned for the first time in the *Lietuvių kalbos gramatika* (Vilnius, 1965), p. 45.
6. Here, Vaitkevičiūtė follows (so indicated in her footnote) Zinder, *Obščaja fonetika* (Leningrad, 1960), pp. 217–222.

NOUN DECLENSIONS IN THE KŌRSOVAN SUBDIALECT OF LATVIAN

JOSEPH LELIS

Latgalian (East or High Latvian) has developed a three-way—nonpalatal (C), palatalized (C′), and palatal (Č)—phonemic opposition,[1] which is fully functional in dental stop and spirant series.[2] In the *\/ř/ and labials the Č-grade has been depalatalized.[3] In two isolated instances, /ļ/ and /ņ/, the C′ and Č grades are indistinguishable,[4] hence it is useful to indicate these two sounds by a different diacritical mark (which, by a happy coincidence, they already have in the Standard Latgalian orthography). All these features, along with some subsequent morphophonemic readjustments, have induced the Kōrsovan subdialect to revise—in places quite drastically —the noun declension system, which in Latgalian has been much more generalized than it is in Standard Low Latvian.

The Kōrsovan trend at further generalization of the system has practically obliterated the declensions inherited from East Baltic. In their stead a new and more simplified system is emerging that provides only two declensions for each gender: a nonpalatal and a palatalized declension. The latter uses both grades, C′ and Č, to make oppositions to C at the stem ends and in suffixes, especially where the same vowels are used in the endings of both declensions. Where the suffix vowels are different, the new system utilizes the grave:acute vocalic opposition to the same effect.

The process of building this new declensional system is by no means already finished. Adjustments are still being sought, as it can be seen by two alternatives permitted in various instances (the variants still reflecting the old system are mostly heard in the southern part of the District of Kōrsova). However, the trend is already unmistakably clear, and the new declensional system can be described in the above-mentioned terms without any difficulties.

The subsequent tables showing patterns list only five cases, because in the whole Latvian language only these are fully functional. The s. c. Latvian "instrumental" has no distinctive endings and—for any purpose— is better explained in terms of a set of prepositions which take the accusative in the singular and dative in plural (and most of these prepositions have no instrumental meaning at all). In the actual use the vocative is limited to names (general or proper) of persons, and even then it has a distinctive form (stem without any ending) in the singular only. The mark /ˆ/ is used for s. c. "broken pitch" (a glottal stop).

I. The masculine nonpalatal declension:[5]

		I-a	I-b	I-c
nom. sg.		vylk-s 'wolf'	smîkl-ys 'laughter'	ol-s 'beer, ale'
gen.	"	-a	-a	-a/(-s)
dat.	"	-am	-am	-am
acc.	"	-u	-u	-u
loc.	"	-â	-â	-â
nom. pl.		vylk-y	smîkl-y	ol-y
gen.	"	-u	-u	-u
dat.	"	-ym	-ym	-ym
acc.	"	-us	-us	-us
loc.	"	-ûs	-ûs	-ûs

Pattern I-a includes Baltic and Latvian nonpalatal a-stems: *vylks* 'wolf,' *tāvs* 'father,' *koîns* 'hill,' *maiss* 'sack, bag,' etc. Note the Central Latgalian reflexes, nom. pl. *-y*,[6] dat. pl. *-ym*, for the Baltic *-ai*, *-aims*.

Pattern I-b includes nonpalatal a-stem words that end in a consonant cluster unpronounceable before the nom. sg. *-s*. Before this ending *-y-* is inserted. The rest of the pattern is similar to I-a. Examples: *orklys* 'plow,' *voskys* 'wax,' *pūsmys* 'phase,' *osnys* 'sprout,' etc. However, words with Latv. *-Crs* are usually treated as belonging to the pattern II-e, cf. Low Latv. *zviedrs*, Kōrsovan *zvīdris* 'Swede.'

Pattern I-c includes Baltic and Latvian u-stems. In some stock phrases[7] the older ending *-s* is retained in the genitive singular but normally a newer alternative *-a* is used, which makes this pattern indistinguishable from I-a. Even such forms as *Jezus Krystus* 'Jesus Christ,' which have retained this form in the nominative singular use a regular *-a* in the genitive singular (*Jeza Krysta*)—as if they belonged to a subpattern of I-b. Here is the complete Kōrsovan list of the old u-stems: *gods* 'year,' *lads* 'ice,' *mads* 'honey,' *ols* 'beer, ale,' *vyds* 'middle, center.'

II. The masculine palatalized declension:

	II-a	II-b	II-c	II-d	II-e
nom. sg.	mež-š	vec′-s′	ceļ-s′	klēp′-s′	vepr′-is′
gen. "	-a	več -a	-a	klēp -a	vepr -a
dat. "	-am	več -am	-am	klēp -am	vepr -am
acc. "	-u/-y	vec′-i	-i/(-u)	klēp′-i	vepr′-i
loc. "	-â/-ŷ	vec′-î	-î/(-â)	klēp′-î	vepr′-î
nom. pl.	mež-y	več -y	ceļ-i/-y	klēp -y	vepr -y
gen. "	-u	-u	-u	-u	-u
dat. "	-ym	-ym	-im/-ym	-ym	-ym
acc. "	-us	-us	-us	-us	-us
loc. "	-ûs	-ûs	-ûs	-ûs	-ûs

Pattern II-a has Baltic and Latvian a-stems ending in a palatal spirant. New endings are acc. sg. -*y* and loc. sg. -*ŷ*, which are trying to displace the older set of -*u* and -*â*. Examples: *mežs* 'forest,' *pleš* 'bald spot,' *zvōdžs* 'saw,' *kačš* 'cat,' etc.

Pattern II-b includes Baltic and Latvian ja-stems ending in a dental spirant or stop. Full palatalization (Č-grade) occurs before all grave vowels in suffixes. The dat. sg. -*am* is a common Latgalian ja-stem feature (cf. Li. adjectival declension of masc. -*is*). The accusative and locative singular take common Latvian ja-stem endings. In plural the a-stem set of endings are used—a common Latvian feature. Examples: *vec′s′* 'old man,' *dadz′s′* 'thistle,' *kōs′s′* 'hook,' *vêz′s′* 'crayfish,' *latvīt′s′* 'Latvian,' *brîd′s′* 'deer,' etc.

Pattern II-c contains Baltic and Latvian a- and ja-stems ending in -*ļ*- or -*ņ*-: *ceļs′* 'road' (Standard Latgalian *ceļš*) and also 'knee' (S. Ltg. *ceļs′*), *kumeļs′* (S. Ltg. *kumeļš*) 'colt,' *sōļs′* 'salt' *Jōņs′* 'John,' etc.; Standard Latgalian diminutives with -*eņš* become -*eņs′*, cf. *bērneņs′* 'little child.' Here also belong former Baltic n-stems: *akmiņs′* 'stone,' *rudiņs′* 'autumn,' *suņs′* 'hound, dog,' (*j*)*yudiņs′* 'water,' etc. In this pattern a-stems change nom. sg. -*š* to -*s′*, which is a common Latgalian ending for ja-stems. The nominative and dative plural endings contain a vowel of an indeterminate quality somewhere between /i/ and /y/.

Pattern II-d has Baltic and Latvian ja-stems ending with a labial or -*r*-: *guļb′s′* 'swan,' *klēp′s′* 'lap, armful,' *Jum′s′* 'harvest god,' *grōv′s′* 'ditch,' *luktur's'* 'lantern,' etc. This pattern has exact parallels with II-b, except that here a complete depalatalization occurs in the forms which have full palatalization in II-b.

Pattern II-e contains Baltic and Latvian ja-stems ending in a consonant cluster unpronounceable before nom. sg. *-s'*. An *-i-* is inserted before *-s'*. Examples with only *-C'lis'* and *-C'r'is'* are at hand:[8] *krūplis'* 'cripple,' *zaglis'* 'thief,' *vepris'* 'castrated boar,' etc. Except for the nominative singular, the rest of the pattern is similar to either II-c or II-d.

III. The feminine nonpalatal declension:

nom. sg.	sol-a 'island, village'	nom. pl.		Sol-ys
gen	" -ys	gen.	"	-u
dat.	" -ai	dat.	"	-om
acc.	" -u	acc.	"	-ys
loc.	" -â	loc.	"	-oîs

This declension has only one pattern, in which belong all Baltic and Latvian ā-stems:[9] *līpa* 'linden,' *mōsa* 'sister,' *sola* 'island,' *vōrna* 'crow,' etc. Latvian *-as* replaced by Central (and South) Latgalian *-ys*. Latgalian loc. pl. *-ôs* in Kōrsova (and a few other subdialects to the south) becomes *-oîs*.

IV. The feminine palatalized declension:

	IV-a	IV-b	IV-c	IV-d
nom. sg.	mōt'-æ	kūrp'-æ	nōs'-s'	as'-s'
gen. "	-is'	-is'	-s'	-s'
dat. "	-æi	-æi	-æi	-æi
acc. "	-i	-i	-i	-i
loc. "	-î	-î	-î	-î
nom. pl.	mōt'-is'	kūrp'-is'	nōs'-s'	as'-s'
gen. "	-u	kūrp-u	nōš-u	os-u
dat. "	-om'	kūrp'-om'/æm'	nōs'-im'	as'-im'
acc. "	-is'	-is'	-s'	-s'
loc. "	-oîs'	-oîs'	-îs'	-îs'/(-oîs')

Pattern IV-a includes Latvian and Latgalian e-stems: *mōtæ* 'mother,' *vacæ* 'grandma,' *zinæ* 'message, news,' *silæ* 'trough,' etc. In this pattern *-C'-* is retained in stem endings also before a grave suffix vowel. In dative and locative plural endings a slight palatalization is perceivable, although these two endings seem to have been transferred here from the nonpalatal declension (the normal central Latgalian endings are *-æm'* and *-æs'*). Latvian *-es* is replaced by Central and South Latgalian *-is,'* and *-ê* by *-î*.

Pattern IV-b includes Latvian and Latgalian ē-stems ending in a labial or *-r-*: *dúbæ* 'pit,' *kūrpæ* 'shoe,' *zæmæ* 'soil, earth,' *skudræ* 'ant,' etc. Normally there is a depalatalization before a grave vowel, but in the locative plural *-C'-* may also be retained.

Pattern IV-c still carries rather stable Latgalian reflexes of Baltic i-stem declension. The dat. sg. *-æi* is a recent Central and South Latgalian analogy to ē-stem ending. Innovations from the pattern IV-a may enter sporadically the genitive, dative, and locative plural. An interesting phenomenon is the instability of some ē-stem words as to which pattern to follow, cf. Latg. *bite* 'bee,' *reikste* 'switch, rod,' *plaukste/-a* 'palm of the hand, *sēne* 'mushroom' in Kōrsovan may become *bit's', reikst's', plaukst's', sēns'*.

Pattern IV-d has only those few Latvian i-stems that do not palatalize before the gen. pl. *-u*. The complete Kōrsovan list is: *ac's'*, gen. pl. *ocu* 'eye'; *as's'*, gen. pl. *osu* 'axle, 2 meters'; *vut's'*, gen. pl. *vutu* 'louse'; *zūs's'*, gen. pl. *zūsu* 'goose.'

The Kōrsovan trends and features in reforming the noun declensions may well remind one of similar patternings in the Slavic languages. A direct influence of Russian, however, must remain only a speculation. Perhaps it is safer to say that the rise and retention of the C'-series in Latgalian (and in some subdialects of High Lithuanian) *may* be attributed to the stimulus provided by the speech of the neighboring Slavs, but once Latgalian had raised the C'-series to the phonemic status, it became a very frequently utilized and important feature. With this in view, some sub-dialects were almost bound to explore the possibilities of its further utilization beyond the range set by the common Latgalian morpho-phonemics. Involvement of other features in the process followed, and as a result, the Kōrsovan readjustment of the noun declensions has started and continues independently of any identifiable outside influences.

The trends described here are not the only ones evident in the Latgalian speech area. Although the Kōrsovan peculiarities are shared by a few other subdialects, there are still many others that have attempted different innovations or have retained a stable state.[10]

Howard University

NOTES

1. Examples: *kas* 'who, what,' *kas'*! 'rake!,' *kaš* 'he rakes'; *sauc* 'he calls,' *sauc'* 'you call,' *saucu* 'I call,' *sauč, u* 'I called,' etc. The historical sources of the Č-grade in Latgalian are about the same as in the rest of the East Baltic dialects. The main source of the Latgalian C'-grade is the loss of an end syllable containing Baltic *ej/ij*, cf. OP. *bousei*: Ltg. *byûs'* 'will be'; Li. *dagŷs*: Ltg. *dadz's'* 'thistle'; Li. *akis*, gen. sg. *akiēs*, nom. pl. *ākys*: Ltg. *ac's'* (all three forms) 'eye.' Subphonemic palatalizations occur also before any front vowel, but they are not marked in the transcriptions used in this paper.
2. For descriptions and examples see Lelis, *The Place of Latgalian among the Baltic Dialects* (Dissertation, Harvard University, 1961), pp. 85–130.
3. Examples: *bizæ*, gen. pl. *bižu* 'plait (of hair),' but: *pīræ*, gen. pl. *pīru* 'forehead'; past 3rd common *svîdæ*, 1st sg. *svîžu* 'throw,' but: *kôpæ, kôpu* 'climb,' *glôbæ, glôbu* 'rescue,' *styumæ, styumu* 'push,' *krōvæ, krōvu* 'pile, stack,' etc. See also Lelis, *op. cit.,* pp. 121–122.
4. See *ibid.,* pp. 92–94 and 96–97.
5. These paradigms can be compared directly to Standard Latvian or Lithuanian. Grammars for Standard Latgalian are prescriptive, dated and unavailable. See their list in M. Bukšs, *Latgaļu literaturas vēsture* (Munich; Latgaļu izdevnīceiba, 1957), pp. 735–736.
6. The quality of Ltg. /y/ is similar to the Slavic /ɨ/.
7. Cf. *glózæ ols* 'a glass of beer,' *vîna gods* 'of the same age,' *iz vyds* 'in the center,' *iz lads* 'on ice' (but: *lada gobols* 'piece of ice'), etc.
8. The rather frequent Low Latvian cluster-*kšķis* is not found in Latgalian, cf. Low Latv. *vîkšķis* 'bundle' *îkšķis* 'thumb' become Ltg. *veîkšš, eîks's'*.
9. Latvian palatalized ā-stems are treated in Kōrsovan as ē-stems: Latv. *gaļa* 'flesh, meat,' *ziņa* 'message,' etc. become Kōrs. *gaļæ, ziņæ*.
10. For samples of declensional patterns in some other Latgalian subdialects see M. Rudzīte, *Latviešu dialektoloģija* (Rīga, Latvijas valsts izdevnieciba, 1964), pp. 330–341.

SOME REMARKS ON THE GERMAN SIDE OF THE ELBING VOCABULARY[1]

JAMES W. MARCHAND

The study of the sounds of Old Prussian has more than intrinsic puzzle-working importance, and even importance beyond the position of Old Prussian in the reconstruction of Proto-Baltic. For we have here another of those interesting examples of a language attested only through speakers of another language, and methods developed and tested in the field of Old Prussian will have validity elsewhere, just as those tested elsewhere will have validity for Old Prussian. We are extremely fortunate in the case of Old Prussian to have accompanying texts in the language of the people who wrote them. But it is unfortunately true of Old Prussian, as it is of so many languages, that those best equipped to deal with some of the basic problems have not bothered with them.[2] One is reminded of the case of Early Yiddish, generally left for the Semiticist to deal with, and the Freising documents in Old Church Slavonic.

It is a truism that where there is contact of languages such as we have in the case of Old Prussian, both systems must be taken into consideration. Disregard for this necessity has always led to disaster, as, for example, in the case of the ill-fated attempts to attribute a sound shift to Gothic by treating Romance names from Germanic as if they were phonetic transcriptions.[3]

It should be a maxim of the philological method that other similar situations should be taken into account in the development of the methodology for any particular case, and that recourse should be had at every step of the way to a more general theory than that developed to fit any particular case.[4] I hope to be able to point in the direction of supplying both these lacks; I am a German specialist and have worked in precisely those dialects of German which are most important for Old Prussian, namely the so-called colonial dialects. I have been active in developing methods for studying the sounds and phonemes of Gothic and the other Germanic languages, where we are in a somewhat analogous situation.

In general, the methods so far used in determining the pronunciation of Old Prussian may be grouped as follows: (1) etymology, (2) loan words, (3) place names, (4) internal alternations, (5) general phonetic tendencies, (6) general linguistic tendencies, (7) the scribal technique of the German writer. Without going into great detail, I should like to comment on each of these.

ETYMOLOGY

Probably the best argument against the use of etymological evidence is a *reductio ad absurdum*: the assumption that a language contains a certain phone because the proto-language contained it is obviously absurd.[5] In the case of Old Prussian, we have the added fact that use of the etymological criterion would destroy the value of Old Prussian for the reconstruction of Proto-Baltic because of the circularity entailed. Etymological evidence must thus be weighted as very weak.

LOAN WORDS

The evidence of loan words has always been seen as quite strong, but it is just as obviously weak as that of etymology. One has but to inspect the German loans in the Elbing Vocabulary and place them beside their German counterparts to see the unreliability of loan words: e.g., 292 *klette*, OP *clattoy* 'weed'; 359 *leffel*, OP *lapinis* 'spoon'; 428 *stechmess'* OP *stakamecczer'* 'butcher-knife'; 473 *Schroter*, OP *scrutele* 'tailor'; 429 *ros*, OP *russis* 'horse.' In order to explain these discrepancies, one has recourse to Gothic loans, often from nonexistent Gothic words (e.g., the Gothic **lapins* invoked by Trautmann, *Denkmäler*, p. 368), to Middle High German, German dialects, Lithuanian intermediaries, etc. Although it is interesting to speculate on such things, we can only use loan word evidence directly if we know the time of the borrowing and the language and/or dialect from which the borrowing took place.[6]

NAMES

Names represent but a subclass of loan words and the same arguments apply to them.[7] They have the further misfortune that they are subject to extraordinary changes. Thus the material collected by Trautmann and Gerullis must be used with extreme caution, if at all, in determining the phonemes of Old Prussian.

INTERNAL ALTERNATIONS

These can be quite important, since there can be no doubt that they offer firsthand information as to the pronunciation of the language. One must keep in mind, however, that morphophonemic alternations offer information only as to the pronunciation of the language at the time that the alternation arose, and thus form only a subclass of comparative evidence (by internal reconstruction). Thus the 'alternation' 'a'/'o' in the Old Prussian kinship terms, for example (e.g., *pomatre* 'stepmother,' but *passons* 'stepson'), if it be not simply a graphic alternation, may indicate a type of accentuation, but that accentuation may no longer be that of the Old Prussian we have attested.

GENERAL PHONETIC TENDENCIES

Such tendencies are commonly given a great deal of attention, especially in more recent work. The search for 'universals' and for 'symmetry' has had a salutary effect on historical and comparative work, but the very fact that one labels them 'tendencies' shows that they cannot be relied upon. That is, if one did not have asymmetric systems, one could not speak of symmetric systems. It is further true that empirical universals are always subject to correction when more data are gathered. Thus, Jakobson once affirmed that length and stress could not be phonemic in the same language, only to be contradicted by later evidence.[8] Or think of the many scholars who were unwilling to believe in three degrees of vocalic length until it was shown to exist in Estonian. We cannot rely on tendencies.

GENERAL LINGUISTIC TENDENCIES

In his work on the phonemes of the Old Prussian Enchiridion, Schmalstieg has made use of the criterion of coexistent phonemic systems to explain certain features of that text.[9] I am not prepared to say that Schmalstieg is wrong; in fact, I am convinced that he must be to a great extent right, and it is obvious that any language will have such systems and subsystems. It is precisely this generality that makes the use of such a method dangerous; an invulnerable statement (i.e., one which cannot conceivably be contradicted) is scarcely a statement.[10] This remark must apply to all statements which begin with an opener such as "It seems quite likely that . . ." (to be read: "It may well be true that . . ." or "The following assumption allows me to make a number of other assumptions"). This does not mean that I wish to delete all enabling or operational statements; they must be used with extreme care and labeled for what they are.

All this seems to be rather negative and to tend to say that we cannot determine the sounds and phonemes of Old Prussian. To be sure, it is obvious that we cannot. I believe, however, that we can make a closer approximation than we have so far, not by casting aside the evidence mentioned above, but by carefully categorizing it and weighing it, and by deciding beforehand what to do when we encounter cases in which different types of evidence contradict one another.

The final type of evidence has, it seems to me, been neglected in previous work, the evidence of transcription technique. As Schmalstieg points out in his latest work on Old Prussian, there has been too much a tendency to regard our Old Prussian documents as if they were phonetic transcriptions, without regard to the peculiarities of the scribes who wrote them.[11] I intend to devote the rest of my paper to a study of the German side of the Elbing vocabulary, with the intent of pointing out some of the interesting peculiarities of his dialect and scribal practice.

The Elbing vocabulary presents the usual kind of conceptual dictionary found in medieval Latin and German manuscripts.[12] Its only unusual features are those which bespeak the Prussian condition, e.g., words for 'sled,' 'fire-hole,' etc. It is most certainly not, as Berneker and, following him, Trautmann would have us believe, drawn up for legal purposes. One wonders what legal purposes 5 *sebengest'ne* 'Pleiades,' 38 *stopassche* 'powdery ashes,' 612 *vulbem* 'stink-tree,' for example, might have served. The vocabulary contains the following sections (labeling mine), marked by capital letters and/or lines: 1 God and the heavens, 2 time and weather, 3 earth, 4 fire, 5 air, 6 water, 7 man and his parts, 8 family and relations, 9 house, 10 farming, 11 wagon and sled, 12 mill, 13 breads, 14 kitchen and utensils, 15 potables, 16 government & soldiery, 17 saddler, 18 weaver, 19 tailor, 20 shoemaker, 21 smith, 22 bathing, 23 fish, 24 woods, 25 animals, 26 domestic animals, 27 milk, 28 hunter, 29 birds, 30 crawling things, 31 *orbis mundi*. These rubrics are important, since they often give the clue as to the meaning of the German word; e.g., 683 *beer* means 'domesticated boar (*verris*),' and not 'bear,' since it appears among the domesticated animals.[13]   Since the meaning of the word is so important in the determination of the sounds and phonemes of the dialect of the scribe, it should be pointed out here that there are many archaic and unusual words in the vocabulary which still need to be cleared up and that pains-taking work will be needed before we can be sure in this matter. In fact, where the Baltic etyma are certain, the Old Prussian often aids in the determination of the meaning of the German word.

WRITING AND SPELLING

The manuscript is written in a typical fifteenth century bastarda (or more correctly hybrida) and exhibits the usual suspensions and abbreviations of that hand.[14]   Perhaps the most important of its features for the present discussion is the common problem of all medieval German hands, namely the difficulty of telling the difference between 't' and 'c.' Among the features which must be labeled simply 'spelling' is the common Middle German use of `e´, both superposed and written within the line, to indicate length or perhaps, since length may not (as is common among the colonial dialects) have been phonemic in the dialect of the scribe, simply as an orthographic habit.[15]   'y' and 'i' are used interchangeably, often within the same word.   One fairly important point to notice is that 'z' is used to indicate what was presumably /s/, as is common in the documents of the Teutonic Knights: 436 *ezel (Esel)* 'ass,' 546 *senze (Sense)* 'scythe,' 134 *bloze (Blase)* 'bladder,' 87 *nasezule (*Nasensäule)* 'nostril,' since Trautmann and Berneker were led to misunderstand the word 346 *zeeb* because they read the 'z' as indicating /ts/.[16]   As Ziesemer correctly pointed out, the word is undoubtedly to be connected to German *Sieb* 'sieve.' Since we have no etymology for the word *baytan* in the Old Prussian, we have no way of knowing whether this word escaped from the rubric just below it or is the name of a type of cake made of *Sieb* 'coarse flour.'

THE DIALECT

The dialect is undoubtedly simply *Ordensdeutsch,* as Ziesemer already saw, that is, the mixture of East Middle German as a basis with Upper and Low German which became common in the *Ordensland* and which we would expect of a document written in Marienburg at this time.   Just a glance at the *Grosses Zinsbuch* of the Teutonic Knights shows numerous forms corresponding exactly to those in the vocabulary: *smer, putter, rocken, brotspis, rinken, beslayn* (for *beschlagen*), *hocken, drefus* (for *Dreifuss*), *jor, kethe, lenman, obend, oel, pfol, schene, sytenfleisch, smede, soller, czoppe, feuerschene, azanarium* (for *asinarium*), *batstobe, bier (bir, byer), erweis, -weze (Wiese), herße (Hirse), hoer (Haar)* etc. Braune thought that the original of the German must have been Silesian or Upper Saxon,[17] but there is no reason to assume such a *Vorlage*. The interest of the Order in the Prussian language and in the education of Prussians is well known,[18] and there is no reason to assume that the vocabulary in its present form is not the result of that interest.

As a typical Middle German dialect, our document confuses *i* and *e* of whatever provenience:[19] 3 *hemel* (Himmel) 'sky,' 6 *sebengest'ne (Siebengestirn)* 'Pleiades,' 246 *schene* (MHG *schîne*) 'plow iron,' 215 *fenst'leit* (MHG *fensterlit*) 'shutter,' 307 *slete (Schlitten)* 'sled.' We find numerous examples of free variation of 'i/y/e/ei/ey/ee/ẽ' without apparent difference, sometimes within the same word, e.g., *smyt (Schmied)* 'smith,' *smede (Schmiede)* 'smithy.'[20]

Also typical of a Middle German dialect, *a* and *o* of whatever origin are confused: 12 *jor (Jahr)* 'year,' 23 *sonnobent (Sonnabend)* 'Saturday,' 69 *hoer (Haar)* 'hair,' 82 *wimpro* (MHG *wintbrâ*) 'eyebrow,' 161 *blo* (MHG blâ) 'bruise.' This is also true for short *o*, a fact which is often overlooked (except by Pauli): 146 *vussale (Fusssohle)* 'sole,' 182 *stiftacht'* (Stieftochter) 'stepdaughter,' 482 *sacken (Socken)* 'socks.'[21] Even the reverse spellings of original long *a* as 'a,' demanded by Braune,[22] are not lacking, in spite of his having ignored them: 763 *hane (Hahn)* 'rooster,' 225 *ase* (dial. *âse*) 'kitchen bench.' Since this is true, it would seem impossible to use the evidence of this document in the question of Proto-Baltic *ā̃* and *ṍ*.

'u' and 'o' are also not well distinguished, especially in the vicinity of nasals or liquids: 9 *wulken (Wolken)* 'clouds,' 205 *suller* (dial. *söller*) 'attic,' 220 *stobe (Stube)* 'heated room,' 240 *vorch (Furche)* 'furrow,' 274 *stuppel (Stoppel)* 'stubble,' 284 *gromot* (dial. *Grummet*) 'second haying,' 312 *commot (Kummet)* 'yoke.' Thus we would expect to see the same confusion in the Old Prussian side of the document, and Stang's surprise ("Im Preussischen fällt das häufige *o* für *u* vor Nasal im Auslaut auf")[23] and his attempts to explain the phenomenon are based simply on a misunderstanding of scribal practice.

One could continue through a long list of such places where ignorance of the language and practices of the scribe have led Old Prussian scholars astray. It was not my intent to give an exhaustive survey of the German side of the vocabulary. Such a description can only be accomplished after long and arduous study of both sides, with forward and reverse indices of the German as well as the Old Prussian, and with a careful sifting of the evidence as to the meaning of the various words. I have also had to avoid going into vocalic sequences not found in the German such as 'oa,' 'iu,' 'iey,' 'eá,' treated extensively by Mr. Burwell. Suffice it to say that I find the notion that many of these stem from attempts to render palatalization or labialization intriguing.[24]

I hope to have shown in this paper that much groundwork needs to be done before we have a workable phonetic/phonemic interpretation of the Elbing Vocabulary. The same can be said, of course, for the catechisms and the Enchiridion. If we are to make progress in this field, it will have to be on the basis of painstaking and careful work, requiring both a Balticist and a specialist in the German dialects concerned.[25] If my paper has done something to show the way, I shall be grateful.

Cornell University

NOTES

1. The title submitted for the conference was "The Sounds and Phonemes of Old Prussian." I had intended to concern myself mainly with theory and to present some views of Old Prussian phonemics. The paper of Mr. Burwell on "The Vocalic Phonemes of the Old Prussian Elbing Vocabulary" covered many of the views I had intended to present, so that I decided to change my paper and to cover the same ground, so that our differences in method might appear in a clearer light. This paper is, then, a complement to his excellent presentation. I wish to thank him and Professor Schmalstieg for their comments.

2. I do not mean that there has been a total neglect of the German of the vocabulary, but the work of Pauli, Braune, Ziesemer and others has been of too fragmentary a nature to be of service in the basic problems involved in the determination of the technique of the scribe.

3. See my review of Otto Höfler's *Die zweite Lautverschiebung bei Ostgermanen und Westgermanen* in *Indogermanische Forschungen* 65 (1960), pp. 205–210.

4. Cf. M. R. Cohen and E. Nagel, *An Introduction to Logic and Scientific Method* (New York, 1934), p. 397: "Scientific explanation consists in subsuming under some rule or law which expresses an invariant character of a group of events, the particular event it is said to explain. Laws themselves may be explained, and in the same manner, by showing that they are consequences of more comprehensive theories."

5. On the lack of validity of the etymological approach, cf. E. P. Hamp, "Gothic *ai·* and *au* again," *Language* 34 (1958), p. 359 ff.

6. It is interesting, of course, to speculate on the situation which could have caused Old Prussian to borrow German (?) /e/ as /a/ (?), as seen in the above examples.

7. For a general survey of the problem of onomastic evidence, see James W.

Marchand, "Names of Germanic Origin in Latin and Romance Sources in the Study of Germanic Phonology," *Names* 7 (1959), pp. 167-181.

8. Cf. A. Martinet, *Description phonologique du parler francoprovençal d'Hauteville* (*Revue de linguistique romane* 15), p. 1; *Travaux du cercle linguistique de Prague*, 4, p. 117 f., p. 234, 1, p. 42; R. M. S. Heffner, *Harvard Studies and Notes*, 17 (1935), p. 104.

9. William R. Schmalstieg, "The Phonemes of the Old Prussian Enchiridion," *Word* 20 (1964), pp. 211-221, *passim*.

10. On the necessity that a scientific statement be contradictable under at least some conditions, cf. Carl G. Hempel, *Aspects of Scientific Explanation* (New York, 1965), pp. 9 ff. and *passim*; R. Carnap, "Testability and Meaning," and H. Reichenbach, "The Verifiability Theory of Meaning," in H. Feigl and M. Brodback, *Readings in the Philosophy of Science* (New York, 1953).

11. Review of Christian S. Stang, *Vergleichende Grammatik der baltischen Sprachen* (Oslo, 1966), *Language* 44 (1968), pp. 388-398. One can only applaud Schmalstieg's frank assessment of the situation.

12. Cf. W. Ziesemer, "Zum deutschen Text des Elbinger Vocabulars," *Beiträge zur geschichte der Deutschen Sprache und Literatur* 44 (1919-20), pp. 138-146. As Ziesemer points out, it would be useful to find a close *Vorlage*, since this would aid in determining the meaning of our text. The glossary published by Sachse, *Archiv für die neueren Sprachen*, 47, pp. 401-448, offers a typical (expanded) example of medieval German and Latin glossaries.

13. The value of the rubrics has long been seen, cf. the controversy reported by Ziesemer, *op. cit.*, 142 f.

14. The manuscript is described in the facsimile editions and in Trautmann, *Denkmäler*. See A. Bezzenberger and W. Simon, *Das Elbinger deutsch-preussische Vokabular, 17 Tafeln in Lichtdruck* (Königsberg, 1897), and V. Mažiulis, *Prūsų kalbos paminklai* (Vilnius, 1966).

I have unfortunately had only a short time to inspect the facsimile, so that I cannot concern myself more closely with it here. The hand is quite similar to that of the *Grosses Zinsbuch*, for example. See the facsimiles in P. G. Thielen, *Das Grosse Zinsbuch des deutschen Ritterordens* (1414-1438) (Marburg, 1958). For information on the resolution of abbreviations, A. Cappelli, *Dizionario di Abbreviature latine ed italiane*, 6th ed. (Milan, 1961), is indispensable.

15. V. Moser, *Frühneuhochdeutsche Grammatik*, 1, 1 (Heidelberg, 1929), par. 9. On this ′e′ as merely a scribal peculiarity, cf. Ziesemer, p. 144.

16. Ziesemer, p. 144 f. Berneker even wanted to connect the word with Russian *cep* 'chain.'

17. Braune corrected his previous opinion in an editorial footnote to Ziesemer, *op. cit.*, p. 141.

18. Cf. K. Helm and W. Ziesemer, *Die Literatur des deutschen Ritterordens* (Giessen, 1951), p. 26 ff. We know, for example, that William of Modena translated the the schoolbook *Donatus* (undoubtedly the *ars minor*) into Old Prussian in 1228 (cf. Helm-Ziesemer, p. 27).

19. On the dialect of the Teutonic Knights: A. Weller, *Die Sprache in den ältesten deutschen Urkunden des Deutschen Ordens* (Breslau, 1911). For a general survey: W. Mitzka, *Grundzüge nordostdeutsche Sprachgeschichte*, 2d ed. (Marburg, 1959). A masterful study of an East Middle German dialect is P. von Polenz, *Die Altenburgische Sprachlandschaft* (Tübingen, 1954). It is interesting to note that Fraenkel, *Die baltischen Sprachen* (Heidelberg, 1950), p. 24 thinks that our document "ist auch für das Niederdeutsche von Wichtigkeit."

20. It is this fact which has led to the confused notion on the part of Ziesemer that MHG *î* occasionally appears as /ai/ in the dialect of the Teutonic Knights, whereas *û* is never diphthongized, cf. Mitzka, p. 147, footnote 145. 'ey' is simply a graphic representation of (?) /e/ which may derive from MHG *î*. Thus, for example, *Weg* 'path' appears as 799 *weyk*, *Scheide* 'scabbard,' on the other hand, as 425 *schede*.

21. On /a/ from original short /o/, cf. R. Grosse, "Namenforschung und Sprachgeschichte im Meissnischen," *Deutsch-Slawische Forschungen zur Namenkunde und Siedlungsgeschichte* No. 5 (Halle, 1957), p. 75. Grosse speaks of a "Schub nach Hinten" in East Middle German, having the following effect: $i > e$, $e > ę$, $ę > ą$, $a > ǫ$, $o > u$, with the notable exception being $o > å$.

22. W. Braune, *Beiträge zur vergleichenden Sprachforschung* 8 (1876), p. 93, footnote: "In allen Fällen wird altes *â* regelrecht durch *o* vertreten . . . Eine falsche Auffassung des Lautes ist also hier nicht zu finden, sie würde aber vorliegen, wenn der Verfasser etwa statt des richtigen *o* in diesen Fällen *einmal* (italics mine) *a* schriebe." One must assume that Braune would now agree with Pauli that the scribe did not clearly distinguish *a* and *o*.

23. Stang, *op. cit.*, p. 36.

24. Speakers of languages not having palatals and opposing nonpalatals frequently hear the nonpalatals as labialized. Thus the *k* in Russian *komnata* or Icelandic *koma* is frequently heard by Americans as *kw*, and is in fact occasionally so pronounced.

25. In the near future Professor Schmalstieg and I plan to collaborate on a thoroughgoing analysis of the Old Prussian language.

STRESS PLACEMENT AND ACCENT CLASSES IN THE LITHUANIAN NOUN

DAVID F. ROBINSON

The accent classes of the noun in Standard Lithuanian have generally been based on a mixture of diachronic and synchronic considerations. In the system most widely used in handbooks, classes 1 and 2 are often described as "originally stem-stressed," and classes 3 and 4 as "originally end-stressed."[1] Of these, however, only class 1 now has fixed stem stress, while the other three classes exhibit various kinds of mobility. The validity of the classification system is generally recognized, but some linguists, e.g., de Saussure, have termed class 3 "mobile" because it is regarded as the continuation of the Proto-Indo-European mobile paradigm (oxytonal except for the "strong" cases), while class 2 is not, because it is a continuation of the PIE fixed-stress paradigm upon which de Saussure's law has operated.[2]

While the importance of Lithuanian accentological evidence to Indo-European comparative linguistics cannot be denied, nor its importance in the Balto-Slavic controversy, the separate problem of the Lithuanian accentual system viewed synchronically has received comparatively little attention.[3] This paper is an attempt to account for the mobility encountered in the Lithuanian nominal accent classes without reference to the known or presumed history of the language. We believe, however, that such an approach can shed light on historical problems which have so far evaded solution.

In the discussion below, morphophonemic representations will be in parentheses; vocalic length in such representations will be indicated by a macron, morpheme boundary (between stem and desinence) by +, palatalized consonants by an apostrophe after the consonant, stress by ictus before the stressed vowel, and acute intonation by ´ above the appropriate vowel. The ictus *after* morpheme boundary will indicate that the desinence is to be stressed wherever possible. The symbol / means 'in the following environment,' thus: au/j+___ may be read 'the desinence will be *au* if the stem ends in *j*.'

All nouns will be considered to be composed of stem and desinence (no attempt is made to account for a thematic vowel). The inflectional paradigms are referred to, for convenience, in the traditional way: (vír+o), for instance, will indicate the complete paradigm for *výras* which takes o-stem endings.

The inflectional paradigms are as follows (only desinences are given):

sg.	o-stem	io-stem	a-stem	e-stem	i-stem (masc.)
nom.	as	īs[5] (is, if unstressed)	a	ē[6]	is
voc.	æ; au/j+___; (optional: i/C'+___)[4]	ī (i, if unstressed)	a	æ	iæ
gen.	ō̃[6]	jō	ōs	ēs	iæs
dat.	ui	jui	ai	æi	jui
acc.	a	ī	ā	æ̃	ī
ins.	u	ju	a	æ	imi, ju
loc.	æ; ujæ/j+___	ī̃jæ	ōjæ	ē̃jæ	ī̃jæ

pl.					
nom. voc.	ai	jai	ōs	ēs	īs
gen.	ū	jū	ū	jū	ū[8]
dat.	ams	jams	ōms	ēms	ims
acc.	us	jus	as	æs	is
ins.	ais	jais	ōmis	ēmis	imis
loc.	uasæ	juasæ	ōsæ	ēsæ	īsæ

du.					
nom. voc. acc.	u	ju	i	i	ju
dat. ins.[7]	am	jam	ōm	ēm	im

sg.	i-stem (fem.)	u-stem	iu-stem	n-stem	r-stem[10]
nom.	is	us	jus	(n→∅)a[9]	(ær→∅)ē;ua
voc.	iæ	au	jau	iæ	iæ

gen.	iæs	aus	jaus	s	s
dat.	jai	ui	jui	jui	jai
acc.	ī	ū	jū	ī	ī
ins.	imi, ja	umi	jumi	ju	ja
loc.	ījæ	ujæ	jujæ	ījæ	ījæ

pl.

nom. voc.	īs	ūs	jai	īs, s	īs, s
gen.	ū[8]	ū	jū	ū	ū
dat.	ims	ums	jams	ims	ims
acc.	is	us	jus	is	is
ins.	imis	umis	jais	imis	imis
loc.	īsæ	uasæ	juasæ	īsæ	īsæ

du.

nom. voc. acc.	i	u	ju	ju	i
dat. ins.	im	um	jam	im	im

We assume for Lithuanian an underlying system such that any stem syllable may be stressed or have acute intonation, but not both ictus and acute in one stem. The desinence may (or may not) have ictus, but never acute (at this stage). There is a restriction on the occurrence of the ictus, such that no more than one is permitted in a word (i.e., ictus in both stem and desinence is precluded), although it is possible to have an acute in the stem and ictus in the desinence. Our treatment of the characteristics of the four accent classes is given below and compared with the more traditional approach. We do not advocate changing the membership of any of the classes, but rather will give reasons for retaining the membership as at present.

Disyllabic nouns are those whose stems have only one syllable; poly-syllabic nouns will refer to all others, as is customary.

Disyllabic nouns of class 1 have fixed stress and acute stem. Our representation will show for *brólis* (1), for example, (ból+*io*). Poly-syllables of this class also have fixed stress, and have acute intonation on the penult, e.g., *vežėjas* (væžėj+*o*), or else ictus or acute on any pre-penultimate syllable, e.g., *mókytojas* (mókītōj+*o*), *pāsaka* ('pasak+*a*).

Disyllabic nouns of class 2 are "originally" stem-stressed, and have nonacute intonation, i.e., stems have circumflex (rising) if the stressed syllable is long, and simply stress if the stressed syllable is short. In our representation, no ictus will be shown for disyllables, since the lack of an acute will suffice to distinguish this class from class 1, e.g., *rãštas* (rašt+*o*), *bìtè* (bit+*e*). Alternation of stress, for both disyllables and polysyllables, takes place only between ultima and penult. In polysyllables, only the penult will have ictus and no acute may appear. Examples: *mokyklà* (mōk'īkl+*a*),[11] *broliùkas* (brōl''uk+*o*). Most case forms are stem-stressed, exceptions being the nominative singular in *a*, the instrumental and locative singular when monosyllabic, and the accusative plural. Our findings are that all case forms exhibit stem stress, except those containing only one short vowel, which may be preceded by *j* and/or followed by *s*. Such desinences will be termed "short"; all other desinences will be termed "long." Short desinences may not include a long vowel or *m*. In sum, a desinence of the form (j)$\breve{\text{V}}$(s) is short; all others are long. Class 2, then, is composed of nouns with nonacute penults and unstressed desinences in the morphophonemic representation. Nouns of this class, and only such nouns, are subject to the following rule of stress assignment: "if the desinence is short (except nom. sg.), stress the desinence."[12]

Disyllabic nouns of class 3 are "originally" end-stressed, having acute intonation on the stem when the stem is stressed. Polysyllables may have acute or ictus on the initial syllable only; stress alternation must be between initial and final syllables.[13] Examples: *kálnas* (káln+'*o*), *galvà* (gálv+'*a*), *sūnùs* (sū̃n+'*u*), *dóbilas* (dóbil+'*o*), *vègèlè* (végēl+'*e*). Nouns of this class have end stress generally, except for dative and accusative singular, accusative plural, and certain others which vary with the stem class. Our findings are that case forms generally exhibit end stress, but that class 3 nouns are subject to the following rule, in addition to the general rules discussed below: "if the desinence is short (except nom. sg.), stress the stem." In the morphophonemic representation, the desinence is stressed.

Class 4 contains only disyllables. Like class 2, class 4 is characterized by stress alternation only between ultima and penult. Most cases have end stress, exceptions being dative and accusative singular, vocative singular of o-stem and a-stem, genitive singular of o-stem and io-stem, nominative singular of o-stem, and nominative plural of most stems. But since the cases with stem stress in class 4 are also the same cases with stem stress in all other classes, and do not include any cases which are end-stressed in any other class, we have taken them as the basis for our general morphophonemic stress-placement rules, applicable to all nouns in the language. We regard as of class 4 those nouns with unstressed stems and ictus on the desinence, e.g., *nãmus* (nam+'*o*), *dantis* (dant+'*i* [masc.]).

The following chart summarizes the criteria for membership in the four accent classes:

		desinence stressed:	
		no	yes
(a) if disyllabic:			
stem has acute; or,	yes	1	3
(b) if polysyllabic:			
last syllable of stem has			
acute, or other stem	no	2	4
syllable has acute or ictus.			

The first 10 general morphophonemic rules apply to classes 2, 3, and 4. We regard class 1 as outside the system of stress movement (although rules 1 through 6 and rules 9 and 10 apply vacuously, rules 7 and 8 cannot apply to class 1).

1. "Stress stem if nom. sg. ends in -as."
2. "Stress stem if gen. sg. ends in -o."

The first rule applies to o-stems, the second also to io-stems. I am not able to account for these rules historically, unless the class 4 o-stem is a new type in Lithuanian, analogous to the Russian stem-stressed singular and end-stressed plural paradigm, as in *more* or *učiteľ*. In Lithuanian, of course, this would be an independent innovation, and would have spread from class 4 to the entire nominal system.

3. "Stress stem if dat. sg."
4. "Stress stem if acc. sg."

Historically, these two rules reflect the Proto-Indo-European mobile paradigm, in which these cases were "strong," i.e., root-stressed. In Lithuanian, the applicability of the rules is universal in nouns.

5. "Stress stem if voc. sg. is -V̆."

This reflects the root-stress normal in Proto-Indo-European. In Lithuanian, however, the vocative singular in a long vowel or diphthong may be end-stressed.

6. "Stress stem if nom. pl. ends in -s."
   Only the -(j)ai ending is excluded.

7. "Stress ending if loc sg. is -æ."

8. "Stress ending if nom. sg. is -a."

Rules 1 through 8 are general restrictions overruling stress placement in classes 2, 3, and 4, and also overruling the special rules applicable to short desinences in classes 2 and 3. None of these eight rules are ordered with respect to each other, but they must apply after the special rules for accent classes 2 and 3, and before rules 9 through 12.

9. "If desinence is stressed, move stress as far right as possible."

This will produce, for example, loc. pl. *languosè* from (láng+ ´uasæ) (class 3) and ins. pl. *dantimìs* from (dant+ ´imis) (class 4).

10. "Stressed dative in -m(s) takes acute; all other stressed long vowels or stressed diphthongs in desinences take circumflex."

Rule 10 applies to end-stressed dative plural and dual, and also to indefinite adjectives (not covered in this paper) whose dative singular may end in -m. In a description including indefinite adjectives, rule 3 above would have to be modified to read "Stress stem if dat. sg. ends in -i."

11. "Stressed low vowels not under acute in stem are lengthened and take circumflex."

Rule 11 applies to *a* and *æ* in stems.[14]

12. "Erase morpheme boundary."

This rule reflects the fact that the remaining two rules apply regardless of morpheme boundary, but that all rules from 1 through 11 apply in environments specified as stem or desinence.

13. "*tj→č*; *dj→ǯ*´."
14. "Palatalize any consonant before a palatalized consonant or a front vowel; Cj and C'j become C'."

If the above analysis is correct, Standard Lithuanian has an accent-class system including fixed barytones (1), mobile barytones (2), fixed oxytones (4), and mobile oxytones (3). The conditions under which mobility occurs are statable in phonological terms (with the nominative singular a notable but consistent exception). The instances where stress departs from these stipulations are also consistent and constitute general rules for the whole of the nominal system.

Much importance has been attached to earlier forms of the stress pattern of *duktē* 'daughter' by many linguists, where a Lithuanian acc. sg. **dukt'erį* is presumed on comparative grounds to have antedated the sixteenth-century and modern form *dùkteri̧*.[15] Our view is that a polysyllabic noun whose accusative singular form had nonacute penultimate stress (such as is found in accent class 2), but whose other forms included examples with desinential stress (on the pattern of class 3) would violate the Lithuanian pattern. The word *duktē̃* is now of class 3, where peripheral stress is expected. Since its stem is (duktær) without acute, the only possibility for it without its remaining an anomalous type was for it to take on the characteristics of any other polysyllable with neither acute stem nor nonpenultimate ictus in the stem, but with stressed desinences, namely those of class 3. We assume that the Lithuanian pattern morphologically forced a change of stress in all stem-stressed forms.

The accentual possibilities for polysyllables of each accent class are as follows (morphophonemic representation):

Class 1

$(\underline{\ })$ __ __́ + __

$(\mathord{'}\acute{\ })$ $\mathord{'}\acute{\ }$ __ + __

Class 2

$(\underline{\ })$ __ᐟ__ + __

Class 3

$(\underline{\ })$ __ __ + ᐟ__

or:

$(\acute{\ })$ __́ __ + ᐟ__

Most __ __́ + ᐟ__ have become __ __́ + __ (class 1), but see footnote 13.

Class 4 (not attested)

__ᐟ__ + ᐟ__

This would be the type for *duktē̃, *dukteri̧*, but it seems never to have developed. One ictus must be deleted, forcing either class 3 (attested) or class 2 for nouns of this type.

The declension of *duktē̃* offers no accentual problems, except for the gen. sg. *duktēr̃s* (duktær+ˈs). Since *s* cannot itself be stressed, a special rule, not given above, must be assumed, whereby the genitive singular of consonantal stems is stressed as if the morpheme division were (dukt+ˈærs), i.e., the desinence is treated as long, and therefore the stress is not retracted as would ordinarily be required for short desinences in class 3.

Ohio State University

NOTES

1. This is the four-class system of K. Būga found in A. Senn, *Handbuch der litauischen Sprache* 1 (Heidelberg, 1966), pp. 102–103; L. Dambriūnas, A. Klimas, W. R. Schmalstieg, *Introduction to Modern Lithuanian* (Brooklyn, 1966), pp. 369–375; J. Balčikonis *et al., Dabartinės lietuvių kalbos žodynas* (Vilnius, 1954), pp. xi–xii.

2. F. de Saussure, "Accentuation lituanienne" (1896), reprinted in his *Recueil des Publications Scientifiques* (Geneva, 1922), *cf.* C. S. Stang, *Slavonic Accentuation* (Oslo, 1957), p. 60, and *idem, Vergleichende Grammatik der Baltischen Sprachen* (Oslo, 1966), p. 288, n. 2.

3. But see W. R. Schmalstieg, "Baltic Nominal Systems," *Word* 17 (1961), esp. pp. 164–67.

4. For fuller discussion see Senn, *op. cit.,* p. 106, 111–12.

5. For a historical solution to this problem, and a review of the literature on the subject, see W. R. Schmalstieg, "Lithuanian Nouns in '-ys'," *Annali Istituto Universitario Orientale, Napoli,* 3 (1966), pp. 79–88.

6. Since *e* and *o* (except in loan words) are always long in Lithuanian, the macron is redundant, but is included for clarity. The macron will be omitted when the acute is present over *e* or *o*.

7. In all stem classes, other dual case forms are supplied from the plural.

8. The genitive plural of i-stems is not always formed with palatalization of the stem-final consonant. We are here assuming such forms as *dantų* as derived from stems without palatalization, and such as *ligónių* as having stem-final consonants palatalized.

9. *Cf.* Senn, *op. cit.,* p. 138–39; *šuõ* would have the stem (šun).

10. There are only two nouns in this stem class, *duktė* (duktær) and *sesuõ* (sæsær).

11. The rule providing for final stress in the nominative singular is discussed below.

12. Other discrepancies, here and in classes 3 and 4, are accounted for by general morphophonemic rules given below.

13. Senn, *op. cit.,* p. 103, p. 129, discusses certain unproductive type-3 poly-syllables with acute penult. In such words, alternation takes place between ultima and penult.

14. *Cf.* Senn, *op. cit.,* p. 70.

15. Notably F. de Saussure, *op. cit.,* p. 533; J. Kuryłowicz, *l'Accentuation des langues indo-européennes* (Wrocław-Kraków, 1958), Ch. 3, esp. pp. 169–74.

THE OLD PRUSSIAN VERB

WILLIAM R. SCHMALSTIEG

The purpose of this paper is to give a relatively credible analysis of the Old Prussian verbal system.[1] But in doing this I will not count heavily on the evidence of Old Prussian spelling. It seems obvious that the different ways of writing a single word have no significance at all. One would not think this worth mentioning except for the fact that so much Baltic scholarship is predicated on a belief in the accuracy of the spelling of the Old Prussian texts. So I must take a stand against this belief. The German scribes noting down Old Prussian were just not trained phoneticians and there is no reason to believe that they felt that consistency of spelling was a necessary goal in the transcription of Old Prussian. The important thing for Abel Will, at least, was that the Old Prussians be able to understand the word of God. It is a part of the basic ethnocentrism of linguists to believe that everybody is as interested in language and language transcriptions as are linguists. But this is obviously not so. Most people seem to have a very casual interest in their language and it suffices merely to examine the letter of an illiterate person to realize that consistent spelling is not a universally maintained cultural value. In general I would echo Gerullis' (1924) negative comments about the accuracy of the Old Prussian texts; likewise see the papers by Michael Burwell and James Marchand in this volume.

Possibly this paper is a masterful example of self-deception; it may well be madness which would lead anybody to believe that he could make anything out of Old Prussian orthography. On the basis of comparative evidence, however, I propose the following Old Prussian vocalic system:

$$\breve{\bar{\imath}} \qquad \breve{\bar{u}}$$
$$\breve{\bar{e}} \qquad \breve{\bar{a}} \, (< \breve{\bar{a}}, \breve{\bar{o}})$$

One may admit that the system as given above was the underlying or basic system for Old Prussian, but that there also existed an innovating system in which the following changes were taking place: (the arrow goes in the direction from conservative to the innovating) /ē/>/ī/, /ī/>/ei/, /ū/>/ou/ or /au/. On the other hand, these differences between the conservative and innovating systems may only reflect orthographic anomalies. In the transcription vocalic length is unmarked if there is any doubt about it. For an earlier view, see Schmalstieg (1964).

I also assume palatalization of consonants by front vowels; this palatalization, being automatic, is not marked in my morphophonemic transcription of the verbal forms. The palatalization is sometimes marked in the Old Prussian orthography and sometimes left unmarked, cf., e.g., *giēidi* 'waits' (where the palatalization of the /g/ is marked by the following *i*) vs. *gēide* 'id.' (where the palatalization of the /g/ is not marked).

Historically an etymological */j/ coalesced with a preceding consonant to produce a palatalized or palatal consonant. Such a palatalized consonant or /j/ in all probability fronted a following vowel so that an /ā̆/ may possibly have merged with /ē̆/. In any case an etymological (or morphophonemic) /a/ was frequently written with *i* or *e* following a palatalized consonant. The word *giēidi (gēide)* undoubtedly reflects a morphophonemic /geida/, cf. Li. *geídžia* 'desires.' Note that in the morphophonemic transcription I do not mark the palatalization of the /g/, as that is automatic before front vowels. On the other hand, the palatalization of the /d/ is marked, as it contrasts with an unpalatized /d/ which also occurs before /ā̆, ū̆/.

There are also numerous cases where an etymological /ā̆/ is written as *u* or *o* following a velar or labial consonant. For example, we find *kurwan* 'ox' (cf. Li. *kárvė* 'cow'), *kuwijds* 'which' (beside *kawijds* 'id.'). All cases of *u* for etymological /ā̆/ will be normalized to /a/ or /ā/ in the morphophonemic transcription.

One further comment must be made about the orthography. Although in most cases the macron did indeed denote an etymologically long vowel, it did not in cases where it was used either over the first or the second element of a diphthong. Thus the macron on the *e* in *perēit* 'comes' and *gēide* 'waits' merely denotes the stress on the initial element of the diphthong (i.e., it reflects the Common Baltic circumflex), cf. Li. *eĩti* 'to go' and *geĩdžia.* The macron on the *u* in *pogaūt* 'to receive' denotes the stress on the second element of the diphthong and reflects the Common Baltic acute (cf. Li. *gáuti* 'to get'). Naturally the stressed vowel in the diphthong is probably phonetically longer than it would be in a diphthong without stress, but it is not phonemically longer. In other cases, e.g., *perweddā* 'lead,' the *ā* does not denote a long vowel; it merely denotes stress on the *a*. One may suspect that the German, hearing the stressed vowel of Old Prussian, automatically considered it long. Compare the comments of Rysiewicz (1938: 140–147).

We note that the orthographic sequence *-ai* in word-final position frequently alternates with *-a*. Thus, for example, we find the *$\bar{a}$-stem forms *aucktimmisikai* 'authority,' *mensai* 'meat' (also written *mensā*), *īdai* 'food' (cf. Li. *ėda* 'id.'), *crixtisnai* 'baptism' (also written *crixtisna*), *schlusnikai* 'maid-servant.' Among the verbs we find such forms as the 3rd pr. *pogaunai* 'receives' (also written *pogauna*), 3rd pr. *podingai* 'pleases,' *swintinai* 'keeps holy,' (also written *swintina*), etc. Since there is great vacillation between orthographic *e* and *a*, also such doublet forms as *powaidinne*, *powaidinnei* 'instructs' are also to be placed in this category. This is probably merely orthographic vacillation, but the forms ending in orthographic *-i* may reflect the addition of a particle /-ai/ which is known in Lithuanian. Zinkevičius (1966: 431) says that in Lithuanian dialects this particle may be added to pronouns, numerals, adjectives, and certain verbal forms. For example, from *àš* 'I' we find *ašaĩ*, from *dù* 'two' we find *dùjai* from *báltas* 'white' we have the definite form *báltasai*, and from *sùka* 'turns' we find *sùkai*. Since all such forms could be explained as merely orthographic variants, we will not write the word-final /-i/ in the transcription, except in the case of the future tense discussed below.

The personal endings of the Old Prussian verb are to be normalized according to the following pattern.

The first person singular ending is *-ā* derived from an etymological *-ō*. We see this ending in /krikstijā/ *crixtia* 'I baptize.' This particular form might, of course, also be a third person present, because we frequently find third person present forms used for first person singular in Old Prussian, cf. *madli* 'I pray,' *schlūsi* 'I serve,' etc. In the 'to be' verb we find chiefly *asmai*, although we also find *asmau* (1X) and *asmu* (2x). This form shows a contamination of the original athematic ending */-mi/ plus the thematic ending /-ā/ derived from */-ō/. The orthographic variants with *-mau* and *-mu* merely reflect the labialization of the consonant and have nothing to do with the vowel quality. This ending is to be reconstructed as *-mā*. One can see a similar vacillation in the (MDS) *stesma* 'to the' vs. *stesmu*, and in general such vacillation is found after all labials and velars.

On comparative Baltic grounds I would reconstruct the Old Prussian primary second singular ending as /-si/. According to Stang's statistics (1942: 227) we find the ending written as *-sei* (10X), *-sai* (8X), *-si* (8X), *-se* (7X). I cannot agree with Stang (1942: 227) that the writing of *-sai* indicates that an ending *-/sai/ ever existed. Compare similar orthographic variations in many other parts of speech, e.g., *ainawīdai, ainawijdei, ainaweydi,* 'likewise,' *kanxtai, kanxtei* 'proper,' *kaige, kaigi* 'as,' MGS *stēise, steisei, stēisi* 'of the' GS *twaisai, twaisei, twaise* 'of your.'

The secondary second singular ending is *-s* as we see in the various second singular imperatives which end in *-s*, e.g., /vedais/ *wedais* 'lead.'

The third person ending for athematic verbs is *-t*. All other verbs have a zero third ending. The third person functions with either singular or plural subjects.

The only attested first person plural ending in Old Prussian is reflected by the orthographic sequence *-mai*. This may reflect an etymological ending /-ma/ which arose as a contamination of the dual ending *-/va/ plus the plural ending *-/me/. Note that the Latvian dialect first person plural reflexive ending /-mās/ and the Lithuanian dialect ending /-muos/ both seem to reflect an original ending *-/ma/. There is no solid evidence for a Baltic first person plural ending *-mai* corresponding to a Greek middle first person plural ending *-mai*, since the Greek ending itself is apparently an innovation and does not reflect an Indo-European *mai*. An ending /-ma/ would also have its cognate in the Serbo-Croatian and Ukrainian first person plural ending *-mo*. Only if one supposes that the particle /-ai/ were added to an ending *-/ma/, could one reconstruct an Old Prussian first person plural ending /-mai/.

In addition, one should not overlook the possibility that orthographic *-mai* represents /-me/. We find that orthographic *-tai* represents /-te/, so there would be then some reason to suppose that *-mai* could represent /-me/. Of all these possibilities, however, the most likely is that the first person plural ending is /-ma/ and it will be rendered as such in the morphophonemic transcription.

Although the orthographic sequence *-ti* is the most commonly found second person plural ending, the orthographic variants *-tai, -tei, -te* are also found. I suspect that all of these are to be normalized as -/te/ on the pattern of standard Lithuanian.

I therefore reconstruct the personal endings of the Old Prussian verb as (1st sg.) -(*m*)*ā*, (2nd sg.) -*s*(*i*), (3) -0 or -*t*, (1st pl.) -*ma* (or -*me*), (2nd pl.) -*tę*.

THE FUTURE TENSE

As Specht has shown (1928), the so-called Old Prussian optative in -*sai*, etc. is only the particle -*ai* added to the future stem, i.e., the infinitive stem plus /s/. No such particle is known apparently elsewhere in Old Prussian, but the particle is known in Lithuanian dialects, as we have seen above.

Both Endzelīns (1944: 175) and Stang (1942: 267–268) object to Specht's explanation, but I am of the opinion that the latter's reasoning is correct. Endzelīns himself (1951: 965) points out that the future tense can be used in Latvian to give a command. Specht (1928: 177) gives an example from a Lithuanian dialect version of the creation story: *Ir pasake Dzievas: bus šviesu ir stojosi šviesu* 'and God said: let there be light and there was light.'

Therefore the third person future form may appear with final /-ai/ in the transcription (if the particle is added), or without it, if there is no particle.

THE IMPERATIVE

The forms which require comment are the following. The verb /dāt/ 'to give' has the 2nd sg. imp. /dais/ and the 2nd pl. imp. /daite/. These forms seem to derive from */dād-ais/ and */dād-aite/ respectively. When the feeling for the root */dād-/ was lost (as in the 2nd sg. pr. /dāsi/, 3rd pr. /dāst/) the initial syllable */dā-/ in */dād-ais, dād-aite/ seemed to be without function and in this manner the imperatives in question were simplified to /dais, daite/. Quite probably the influence of the Slavic languages is to be noted here, cf. Polish *daj, dajcie*.

The 2nd sg. imp. /at-trais/, 2nd pl. imp. /at-traite/ 'answer!' are to be compared to Li. *te-žinaī* 'may he know,' as far as formation is concerned. The imperative formant -*ai*- is added directly to the vocalic stem; thus **zinā̆ + ai* passes to *žinai* just as **-tra + ai* passes to -*trai*-.

The imperative formant for verbs with a present stem in /ī/ seems to be /ī/. Thus we encounter, e.g., /en-graudīs/ *engraudīs* 'have mercy.' This /ī/ like the etymological */oi/ is an old optative marker (see Brugmann 1933: 554–555 and Meillet 1965: 332). On the other hand, the final syllable of such words as 2nd sg. imp. *isrankeis* 'save' and the penultimate syllable of the 2nd pl. imp. *klausieiti* 'hear' could be interpreted either as having an underlying /ai/ or /ī/. The orthography, as usual, is quite ambiguous.

To judge by such forms as 2nd pl. imp. *laikūtei* /laikāte/ 'consider, hold' and 2nd pl. imp. *enlāikuti* /en-laikāte/ 'continue on' there must have been an imperative in /ā/ for verbs with an /ā/-stem present. In all probability, however, these forms are not imperatives, but second person plural present forms used with imperative meanings. (See also Stang, 1966: 437–440.)

This analysis is predicated on a belief that the Old Prussian verbal system did not differ very much from that of the extant Baltic languages. Thus I do not quote any forms as conjunctives (as does Trautmann, 1910, e.g., p. 413 s. *quoitē*), nor do I believe that there is any optative ending with a formative /sei/ or /sai/; forms which Stang (1966: 440) quotes as permissives are only futures. The only true optative in Old Prussian is the one with the formative /lai/ which is probably cognate with the Lithuanian and Latvian permissive *lai* (see Endzelīns, 1944: 189) and Stang (1966: 441).

The classification system used for the Old Prussian verb here is essentially the same as that commonly used for standard Lithuanian (cf. Senn, 1966: 255). Thus I find four conjugations in Old Prussian; the principle of division is according to the final morpheme of the third person. The first conjugation is characterized by third person final /-a/; the second conjugation is characterized by third person final /-ī/ or /-ei/. It is difficult to know whether this ending, which is reflected by a short /-i/ in East Baltic, but which corresponds to /-ī/ in Slavic, derives from */ī/ or */ei/. I proposed elsewhere (Schmalstieg, 1959) that it derives from */ei/, but the Old Prussian orthographic sequence *ei* could reflect either etymological */ī/ or */ei/. It might also be pointed out that the orthographic *ē* which functions as the present stem vowel frequently in this conjugation may also reflect phonemic /ī/, i.e., it may be a way of writing the /ei/ of the innovating system which derives from /ī/ of the conservative system. In the same way the orthographic *ī* found in the infinitive stem of second conjugation verbs denotes /ē/ of the conservative system. Elsewhere etymological /ē/ is frequently represented by orthographic *ī*, cf., e.g., *īst* /ēst/ 'to eat,' acc. sg. fem. *gīdan* 'shame' and Li. *gė́da* 'id.', etc. The third conjugation is characterized by the third person final morpheme /ā/. The fourth conjugation is the athematic conjugation. In general the classification of the Old Prussian verb is determined by the corresponding classification of its Lithuanian cognate. As is well known, of course, there are many verbs in Lithuanian which could belong to any one of several conjugations; in addition there is no very good assurance that a verb belonging to one conjugation in Lithuanian would necessarily belong to a cognate conjugation in Old Prussian. Nevertheless, this method of organization of the Old Prussian verbal system seems preferable to one based solely on the orthographic evidence of Old Prussian.

The verbs are given below in their respective conjugations. Within each conjugation they are alphabetized according to the first phoneme of the root. The assumed transcription is given first and this is followed by the orthographic representation or representations in the attested texts.

There is probably some kind of glide between the past active participle ending and a preceding stem ending in a vowel. Whether this glide is [v] or [j] does not seem to be clear. In any case an appropriate glide, between brackets, is given in the transcription.

I. First conjugation: (etymological *e/o-verbs; Baltic thematic vowel /a/):
   a. Root type infinitive, present stem same as infinitive stem.
   b. Infinitive in -ē-, present stem without /ē/, either unpalatalized or palatalized, but with thematic /a/ conjugation.
   c. Root type infinitive, present stem ending in /n/.
   d. Root type infinitive, nasal infix in present stem.
   e. Root type infinitive, present stem ending in /j/.
   f. Root type infinitive, present stem ending in a palatalized consonant.
   g. Secondary verb with suffix /in/.
   h. Secondary verb with suffix /ī/.
   i. Secondary verb with suffix /au/.

II. Second conjugation: Present stem in /ī/ and an infinitive stem in /ē/.
III. Third conjugation:
   a. Present stem in /ā/ and infinitive stem in /ī/.
   b. Present stem in /ā/ and infinitive stem in /ā/.
IV. Fourth conjugation:
   Old athematic verbs.
V, VI, VIII. Various anomalous types.

I should like to reiterate that undoubtedly there are many orthographic sequences which could be interpreted in any number of different ways. As a result I would not defend too strongly this system of classification (or any other, for that matter) or the assignment of any particular verb to any particular class.

I. FIRST CONJUGATION:

Ia. Root type infinitive, present stem same as infinitive stem.

   1. Pst. act. prt. nom. pl. masc. /em-baduses/ plus reflexive /si/ embaddusisi 'stuck in'

   2. 3rd pr. /pa-dinga/ podingai 'pleases'; perhaps it is to be phonemicized /pa-tinka/ and to be classed in conjugation Id, cf. Li. pa-tìkti 'to please.'

3. Inf. /gérbt/ gerbt, gḗrbt 'to say'
    2nd sg. imp. /gerbais/ gerbais, gerbaisa
    2nd pl. imp. /gerbaite/ gerbaiti.

4. Inf. /prei-gérbt/preigḗrbt 'to teach.'

5. Sup. /gimtun/ gemton 'to be born'
    Pst. act. prt. nom. sg. masc./gimuns/ gemmons, gemmans,
    Pst. act. prt. acc. sg. masc. /ainan-gimusin/ ainangimmusin.

6. Pst. act. prt. nom. sg. masc. /en-gimuns/ engemmons 'inborn.'

7. Pst. act. prt. nom. sg. masc. /nauna-gimuns/ naunagemmons 'new born'
    Pst. psv. prt. acc. sg. masc. /nauna-gimtan/ naunagimton.

8. Pst. act. prt. nom. sg. masc. /gubuns/ gubas 'gone.'

9. Pst. act. prt. nom. sg. masc. /per-gubuns/ pergubons, pergūbons, pergūbans
    'come.'

10. Pst. act. prt. nom. sg. masc. /unsai-gúbuns/ unsey gobuns, unsei gūbans,
    unsaigūbons, unseigubons 'ascended.'

11. Inf. /ímt/ ῑmt 'to take'
    Pst. act. prt. nom. sg. masc. /imusis/immusis
    Pst. pass. prt. nom. sg. fem. /imtá/ imtā
    1st sg. pr. /imā/ imma
    1st pl. pr. /imama/ immimai
    2nd pl. pr. /imate/ immati
    2nd sg. imp. /imais/ imais, immais, ymays
    2nd pl. imp. /imaite/ ymaity, jmmaitty, ymayti, ymmayti, immaiti, imaiti
    3rd pst. /imēts/ or /ēmēts/ immats, ymmeits, ymmeyts, ymmits, jmmitz
    3rd pst. /imā/ imma
    3rd sg. opt. /imlai/ imlai.

12. 3rd pr. /ap-ima/ ebimmai 'includes.'

13. Inf. /en-imt/ enimt 'to accept'
    Sup. /en-imtun/ enimton
    Pst. pass. prt. nom. sg. masc. /en-imts/ enimts, animts
    Pst. act. prt. nom. sq. masc. /en-imuns/ enimmans
    1st pl. pr. /en-imama sin/ enimmimaisin.

14. 2nd sg. imp. /kirtais/ or /kertais/ kyrteis 'strike.'

15. Pst. pass. prt. nom. sg. masc. /au-klepts/ or /au-klipts/auklipts 'hidden,' cf. Gk.
    kléptein and Goth. *hlifan* 'to steal.'

16. Inf. /krūt/ krut 'to fall.'

17. 2nd pl. imp. /kurtaite/ kurteiti 'err.'

18. 3rd pr. /lēza/ līse 'crawls'
    Pst. act. prt. nom. sg. masc. /-lēzuns/ semmailisons, semmai līsuns, semmay
    lysons, sammay lesuns 'descended.'

19. Inf. /limtvei/ limtwei, limtwey, lembtwey 'to break'
    3rd pst. /limāts/ līmauts, limatz, lymuczt. Note vacillation in orthography
    between *a* and *u* following labial.

20. Pst. pass. prt. nom. sg. masc. /pa-mests/ pomests 'subjected'
    Pst. pass. prt. nom. sg. neut. /pa-mestan/ pomeston.

21. 1st pl. pr. /paikama/ paikemmai 'we deceive.' This verbal stem may well
    belong in conjugation 1f.

22. 1st pl. pr. /au-paikáma/ aupaickēmai 'we drive away.'

23. 3rd pr. /pa-paiká/ popaikā 'deceives.'

24. Pst. act. prt. masc. nom. pl. /au-paluses/ aupallusis 'find, found'
    3rd pr. /aú-pala/ aupallai, aūpallai.

25. Inf. /pīst/ pijst 'to bring'
    Pst. act. prt. masc. nom. sg. /pīduns/ pūdauns
    3rd pr. /pīda/ pīdai; also used with past meaning
    1st pr. /pīdama/ pidimai, pīdimai.

26. Pst. pass. prt. nom. sg. masc. /per-pīsts/ perpists 'brought'
    3rd pr. /per-pīda/ perpīdai
    3rd pst. /per-pīdā/ perpīdai.

27. Inf. /prei-pīst/ preipīst 'to bring.'

28. Sup. /is-prastun/ issprestun 'to understand,' or perhaps this verb belongs
    in class Ic, cf. Li. *su-pràsti* 'to understand.'

29. 1st pl. pr. /pa-prastama/ poprestemmai 'we feel,' but this verb may have the
    Baltic *-st-* suffix, see Endzelīns (1944, 166).

30. Inf. /rénktvei/ rānctwei, rancktwey, ranktwey, 'to steal'
    Pst. act. prt. nom. sg. masc. /renkuns/ ranguns, cf. Li. *rinkti, reñka.*

31. 3rd pr. /san-rénka/ senrīnka 'gathers.

32. Inf. /per-réist/ perrēist 'to bind up.'

33. Pst. pass. prt. nom. sg. masc. /san-rists/ senrists 'connected'
    Cf. Li. *rišti* 'to tie, to bind.'

34. 3rd opt. /au-skendlai/ auskiēndlai 'may drown, may sink.'

35. Pst. act. prt. nom. sg. masc. /stenuns/ stīnons, styienuns, stenuns 'suffered.'

36. 3rd pr. /en-terpa/ enterpo 'is useful,' see Endzelīns (1944: 165).

37. 3rd pr. /tlāka/ tlāku 'threshes,' but see Leskien (1963: 33–34) for a better
    explanation of this word.

38. Inf. /trept/ trapt 'to step to.'

39. 3rd pr. /er-trepa/ ertreppa 'transgresses.'

40. 1st pl. pr. /per-vakama/ perweckammai 'we despise.'

41. Inf. /vest/ west 'to lead'
    Inf. /vestvei/ westwey, westwei
    2nd sg. imp. /vedais/ wedais, wedeys, weddeis
    3rd pst. /vedē/ weddē.[1]

42. 3rd pr. /per-vedá/ perweddā 'lead.' Note the macron on a vowel which is

surely etymologically short, cf. Li. *vēda* 'he leads,' see Rysiewicz, (1938: 139).

43. Pst. act. prt. nom. sg. masc. /pra-veduns/ prawedduns 'led through.'

44. Pst. pass. prt. nom. sg. masc. /pra-vilts/ prawilts 'betrayed'
3rd pst. /pra-vilā/ prowela.

Ib. Infinitive stem in etymological /ē/, thematic vowel /a/ in present stem. In the examples cited it is impossible to determine whether the present stem originally had a stem-final etymological /j/ or not.

1. Inf. /bilēt/ bīllīt, billit, 'to say'
Inf. /bilētvei/ billitwei, billītweī
Pst. act. prt. nom. sg. masc. /bileuns/ billīuns
Pst. pass. prt. nom. sg. neut. /biletan/ billiton, billīton, billīcon
1st sg. pr. /bilā/ billi; or perhaps 3rd pr. form with 1st sg. pr. meaning
3rd. pr. /bilá/ billā, billa, bille, billē, billi
1st pl. pr. /biláma/ billēmai.

The past forms listed by Trautmann (1910: 312) are to be equated with the corresponding present form given above or else they presuppose a different infinitive (Stang, 1942: 201) /biltvei/. In the latter case the forms are to be as follows:
3rd pst. /bilā/ billa, byla, bela, billē, although this last form may be derived from *bilētvei*; the form *billai* which seems to translate a first person singular present is actually a third person past. The alternative past is /bilāts/ billāts, belats, bylaczt, bilats.

2. Sup. /per-bilētun/ perbillīton 'to deny.'

3. Pres. act. prt. dat. sg. fem. /ni en-bilantai/ nianbillintai 'immature,'
literally 'not speaking'
Pres. act. prt. gen. sg. masc. /nien-bilantes/ niaubillīntis
It seems quite possible that verbs with the stem /bilē-/ might be placed in the II conjugation instead of Ib.

4. Inf. /gīvēt/ giwīt 'to live,' cf. Bulg. *živéja* 'I live'
2nd sg. pr. /gīvasi/ giwassi, gīwasi
3rd. pr. /gīva/ giwa, gīwu (used with 2nd sg. meaning; note vacillation between *a* and *u* after labial), giwe, see Stang, (1966: 452).
1st pl. pr. /gīvama/ giwammai, giwemmai
Gerundive? /gīvantei/ giwāntei

5. Modal auxiliary /kai/ quoi 'will, shall, would' is probably a shortened form of (inf.) */kaitēt/ 'to wish, to want' used with any person or number subject. Compare the development of Bulg. *šte*. Cf. also in Simon Grunau's Vocabulary ny koytu 'won't you.'

6. 3rd pr. /kaitá/ quoitē, quoitā 'will.' This verb is to be compared with Li. *káitėti* 'to care; to be lacking, to be wanting,' Latv. *kaitēt* 'to harm.' The semantic relationship is similar to the several senses of the English word *want*.
1st pl. pr. /kaitáma/ quoitāmai
2nd pl. pr. /kaitáte/ quoitēti
2nd sg. opt. /kaitēlaisi/ quoitīlaisi

3rd opt. /kaitēlai/ quoitijlai, quoitilai, quotīlai

3rd opt. /kaitēlaite/ quoitijlaiti, quoitīlaiti, cf. ankaitītai which apparently contains the same root.

7. Pst. act. prt. nom. sg. masc. /pa-kaitēuns/ poquoitīuns 'desired'
Pst. pass. prt. nom. sg. neut. /pa-kaitētan/ poquotīton
Pst. pass. prt. nom sg. masc. /pa-kaitēts/ poquoitēts; the orthography may denote that the stem perhaps should be read /kaitˊ/ with a palatalized stem-final /t/.

8. Inf. /stalēt/ stallit 'to stand'
Pst. act. prt. /stalēuns/ stalliuns
3rd. pr. /stalá/ stallā, stalle, stallē, stalli
1st pl. pr. /staláma/ stallēmai
2nd pl. pr. /staláte/ stallēti; this verb also may well belong in the II conjugation rather than in Ib, or perhaps the orthographic evidence is to be interpreted that the final /l/ of /stal/ is palatalized.

9. 3rd pr. /-stalá/ empriki stallē, emprīkistallaē 'opposes.'

10. Inf. /is-stalēt/ isstallīt 'to carry out.'

11. 3rd pr. /per-stalá/perstallē, perstalle 'oversee.'

Ic. Root type infinitive, present stem ending in /n/.

1. Pst. act. prt. nom. sg. masc. /gau[v]uns/ or /ga[v]uns/ gauuns 'gotten.'

2. Pst. act. prt. nom. sg. masc. /au-gau[v]uns/ or au-ga[v]uns/ augauuns 'acquired'
1st pl. pr. /au-gaunama/ augaunimai.

3. 3rd pr. /en-gauna/ engaunai, engaunei ,'receive.'

4. Inf. /pa-gaút/ pogaūt 'to receive'
Pst. act. prt. nom. sg. masc. /pa-gau[v]uns/ or /pa-ga[v]uns/ pogauuns
Pst. pass. prt. nom. sg. masc. /pa-gauts/ pogauts, pagauts; note vacillation of spelling with o and a after labial.
Pst. pass. prt. acc. sg. fem. /pa-gautan/pogauton
Pst. pass. prt. nom. pl. masc. /pa-gautai/ pogautei
3rd pr. /pa-gauna/ pogaunai, pogauni, pogāunaī
1st pl. pr. /pa-gaunama/ pogaunimai.

5. Gerundive /stānantei/ stānintei, staninti 'standing.'

6. Inf. /pa-stāt/ postāt 'to become'
Inf. /pa-stātvei/ postātwei
Pst. act. prt. nom. sg. masc. /pa-stāuns/ postāuns
3rd pr. /pa stūna/ postanai, postānai
1st pl. pr. /pa-stānama/ postanimai
3rd pst. /pa-stā/ postai, postāi
2nd sg. fut. /pa-stāsi/ postāsei

Id. Root type infinitive, nasal infix in present stem.

1. 3rd pr. /pa-línka/ polīnka, polijnku 'remains'; note spelling vacillation between a and u after velar consonant, see Stang (1966; 452, n. 2).

2. 3rd pst. /is-migē/ ismigē 'fell asleep.'

3. Pst. act. prt. nom. sg. masc. /en-miguns/ enmigguns 'asleep.'

4. Pr. act. prt. nom. sg. masc. /sendan[t]s/ sindats, syndens 'sitting'
   Pst. act. prt. nom. sg. masc. /sēduns/ sīdons, sīdans.

Ie. Root type infinitive, present stem in /j/

1. Inf. /au-laut/ aulāut, 'to die'
   Pst. act. prt. nom. sg. masc. /au-lau[v]uns/ or /au-la[v]uns/
   aulawns, aulauns, aulauuns
   Pst. act. prt. acc. pl. masc. /au-lau[v]usins/ or /au-lavusins/ aulauūsins
   aulaunsins, aulausins, aulauwussens
   Pst. act. prt. nom. sg. fem. /au-lausi/ or /au-lavusī/ aulausē. Perhaps the /1/
   in this word is soft and the softness was just not marked under the
   influence of Polish orthography (see Mažiulis, 1966: 55).

2. Pst. pass. prt. acc. sg., gender unclear, /pa-leitan/ palletan 'poured.'

3. Pst. pass. prt. acc. sg., gender unclear, /pra-leitan/ pralieiton, prolieiton,
   proleiton, praliten 'shed, poured out.'

4. Pst. act. prt. nom. sg. masc. /is-līuns/ islīuns 'poured out.'

5. Inf. /pāt/ poūt 'to drink'
   Inf. /pātvei/ poutwei
   Sup. /pātun/ pūton, poūton
   2nd pl. imp. /pā[j]aite/ poieiti, pogeitty, pugeitty, puieyti, puietti
   2nd sg. imp. /pā[j]ais/ pogeys; it may be difficult to imagine an /ā/ rendered
   by orthographic u, but such vacillation does occur elsewhere, cf. kawijds
   vs. kuwijds 'which,' supuni 'wife' in the Third Catechism vs. supana 'bride'
   in Simon Grunau's Vocabulary. One can note also that the Lithuanian name
   of Abel Will's parish is Pabečiai, but in German it is known variously as
   Pobeten, Pobethen, or even Pubeten (see Mažiulis [1966: 30–40] and footnote 212).

If. Root type infinitive, present stem ending in a palatalized consonant derived from
   consonant plus */j/.

1. Pst. pass. prt. nom. sg. masc. /er-dérkts/ erdērkts 'poisoned.'

2. 3rd pst. /draudē/ driāudai 'forbade'
   2nd pl. imp. /draudaite/ draudieiti.

3. 1st pl. pr. /galbama/ galbimai 'we help'
   3rd fut. /galbsai/ galbsai, galbse.

4. Pst. pass. prt. nom. sg. neut. /pa-galbtan/ pogalbton, pogalbtou 'helped.'

5. Inf. /gantvei/ guntwei 'to drive'
   1st pl. pr. /ganama/ gunnimai.

6. 3rd pr. /géida/ gēide, giēidi 'wait.'

7. 3rd pr. /san-geida/ sengijdi 'attains.'

8. Inf. /girtvei/ girtwei 'to praise'
   1st pl. pr. /girama/ girrimai.

9. Pst. pass. prt. nom. sg. masc. /en-kāpts/ enkopts, encops, enquoptzt 'buried'; cf. Li. *kōpti bùlves* 'to earth potatoes.'

10. 3rd pr. /kneipá/ kniēipe 'obtains.'

11. 3rd pr. /kuntá/ kūnti 'takes care of.'

12. Inf. /pa-kúnst/ pokūnst, pakūnst 'to protect'
    Pst. act. prt. nom. sg. masc. /pa-kuntuns/. pokūntuns, pokūntons, (ni) pokūntuns
    3rd pr. /pa-kúnta/ pokūnti
    3rd fut. /pa-kúnsai/ pokūnsi
    2nd sg. imp. /pa-kuntáis/ pokuntieis.

13. 3rd pst. /kūrē/ kūra 'created'; or is this really a 3rd pr. form to be phonemicized as /kūrā/? See Endzelīns (1944: 178).

14. Pst. pass. prt. nom. sg. neut. /pa-kvelptan/ poquelbton 'kneeling'

15. 3rd pr. /er-láṅga/ erlāngi 'lift up.'

16. 3rd pr. /maźa/ massi, also used as 1st and 2nd pr. form
    1st pl. pr. /maźama/ massimai
    3rd opt. /maźalai/ musīlai; this form may be phonemicized /mazēlai/ in which case the verb would belong in conjugation Ib. Note the vacillation between the spelling of the stem with *a* and *u* after the labial consonant. This verb is, however, probably a borrowing from Slavic.

17. 1st pl. pr. /mentáma/ mentimai 'we lie.'

18. 1st pl. pr. /ap-mentáma/ ep-mentimai 'we deceive.'

19. Pr. act. prt. acc. sg. fem. /rīpantan/ rīpintin, rīpintinton 'following'
    2nd pl. imp. /rīpaite/ rīpaiti, but see Endzelīns (1944: 106).

20. 1st pl. pr. /san-rīpama/ serrīpimai 'we experience.'

21. 1st pl. pr. /au-spáṅdama/ auschpāndimai 'we entice away, alienate,' probably borrowed from German *spannen,* cf. Trautmann (1910: 308).

22. 3rd fut. /teíks/ teīks 'put, leave, give.'

23. Inf. /ténstvei/ tiēnstwei 'to attract'
    2nd pl. imp. /tenśaite/ tenseiti.

24. 3rd pst. /per-traúkē/ pertraūki 'covered.'

25. 3rd pr. /triṅa/ trinie 'threatens.'

26. Pst. pass. prt. acc. sg. masc. /per-trenktan/ pertrincktan 'obdurate,' cf. Li. *treñkti* 'to clash.'

27. 3rd pr. /varǵá/ warge mien 'it bothers me.'

28. Pst. act. prt. nom. sg. masc. /at-vēruns/ etwiriuns 'opened' act. prt. used with pass. meaning.
    3rd pr. /at-véra/ etwēre
    2nd sg. imp. /at-veŕais/ etwerreis.

29. Inf. /at-vérpt/ etwiērpt, etwiērpt, etpwērpt, 'to forgive'

Pst. act. prt. nom. sg. masc. /at-vérpuns/ etwiērpons
Pst. pass. prt. acc. sg. gender unclear, /at-verptan/ etwierpton
1st sg. pr. /at-verpā́/ etwerpe; possibly a third person present used for first
person singular present
3rd pr. /at-vérpa/ etwiērpei
1st pl. pr. /at-vérpama/ etwērpimai, etwerpymay, atwerpimay
2nd sg. imp. /at-verpais/ etwerpeis, atwerpeis.

30. Inf. /pa-vérpt/ po-wiērpt 'to abandon'
    Pst. act. prt. nom. sg. masc. /pa-verpuns/ powiērpuns
    2nd pl. imp. /pa-vérpaite/ powiērptei.

31. 1st pl. pr. /vertama/ wertemmai 'we swear.'

Ig. Secondary verb with suffix /in/.

1. Pst. act. prt. nom. sg. masc. /auginuns/ auginnons 'raised, brought up.'

2. Pst. pass. prt. nom. sg. masc. /pa-augints/ poaugints 'brought up.'
   2nd pl. imp. /pa-auginaite/ poauginneiti

3. Inf. /pa-ba[j]int/ pobaiint 'to punish.'

4. Pst. act. prt. nom. sg. masc. /pa-banginuns/ pobanginnons 'moved.'

5. Pst. act. prt. nom. sg. masc. /at-baudinuns/ etbaudinnons 'awakened'
   Pst. psv. prt. nom. sg. masc. /at-baudints/ etbaudints.

6. Inf. /bebint/ bebbint 'to mock'
   1st pl. pr. /bebinama/ bebinnimai.

7. 1st pl. /brevinama/ brewinnimai 'we benefit.'

8. Pst. pass. prt. nom. sg. masc. /pa-brandints/ pobrendints 'laden.'

9. 2nd pl. imp. /buvinaite/ buwinanti 'live.'

10. Inf. /ap-deivātint/ epdeiwūtint 'to bless.'

11. 3rd pr. /dēlina/ dīlinai 'accomplishes.'

12. 3rd pr. /pa-drūktina/ podrūktinai 'confirm'; used with 1st sg. pr. meaning.

13. Inf. /pa-gadint/ pogadint 'to destroy.'

14. Inf. /galintvei/ gallintwey, gallintwei 'to kill.'

15. Pst. pass. prt. acc. sg. masc. /ainan-gamintan/ ainangeminton 'only begotten,'
    cf. Li. *gamìnti* 'to produce.'

16. Inf. /pa-gatavint/ pogattawint 'to prepare'
    Pst. pass. prt. nom. sg. masc. /pa-gatavints/ pogattawints, (ni)pogattawints
    3rd opt /pa-gatavinlai/ pogattewinlai.

17. 3rd pr. /gīvina/ gewinna 'work.' Cf. Li. *gývas* 'alive.'

18. Inf. /glandint/ glandint 'to comfort.'

19. Inf. /jaukint/ iaukint 'to train.'

20. Inf. /kakint/ kackínt, kakīnt 'to attain'
    2nd sg. imp. /kakinais/ kackinnais.

21. Inf. /en-kasint/ enkausint. Cf. Russian *kosnut'sja* 'to touch.'

22. Pst. pass. prt. nom. sg. masc. /en-kérmenints/ enkermenints, enkērmenints 'incorporated.'

23. 3rd pr. /er-kīnina/ erkīnina 'sets free.'

24. Sup. /kitavidintun sin/ kitawidintunsin 'to prevent.'

25. 3rd pr. /klumstina/ klumstinai 'knocks'
    2nd pl. imp. /klumstinaite/ klumstinaitai.

26. Inf. /kumpint/ kumpint 'to disturb'
    3rd pr. /kúmpina/ kūmpinna.

27. Pst. act. prt. nom. sg. masc./laipinuns/ laipinnans, laipinnons 'commanded'
    1st sg. pst. /laipinā/ laipinna, lapynna; or perhaps /laipina/ 3rd pr. used as
    1st sg. pst.

28. Pst. pass. prt. nom. sg. masc. /en-laipints/ enlaipints 'ordered'
    3rd pr. /en-laipina/ enlaipinne.

29. Pst. act. prt. nom. sg. masc. /pa-laipinuns/ polaipinnons 'ordered.'
    Pst. pass. part. acc. sg. masc. /pa-laipintan/ polaipinton
    1st sg. pr. /pa-laipinā/ polaipinna; or perhaps 3rd pr. used as 1st sg. pr.,
    cf. above.

30. 2nd pl. imp. /laustinaite/ laustineiti 'humble (yourself).'

31. Pst. act. prt. nom. sg. masc. /lazínuns/ lassīnnuns 'put'; cf. Slavic *ložiti*
    3rd pst. /lazinā/ lasinna.

32. Inf. /līgint/ līgint 'to judge'
    Inf. /līgintvei/ leiginwey
    Sup. /līgintan/ līginton, leygenton.

33. Inf. /is-maitint/ ismaitint 'to lose'
    Pst. pass. prt. acc. sg. masc. /is-maitintan/ ismaitinton.

34. Inf. /mākint/ mukint 'to teach'
    Pst. act. prt. nom. sg. masc. /mākinuns/ mukinnons
    Pst. pass. prt. nom. sg. masc. /mākints/ mukints
    3rd pr. /mākina/ mukinna
    1 pl. pr. /mākinama/ mukinnimai
    2nd pl. imp. /mākinaite/ mukinaiti, mukineyti, mukinaity
    3rd fut. /mākinsai sin/ mukinsusin.

35. Inf. /is-mākint/ ismukint 'to learn.'

36. Pst. pass. prt. nom. sg. masc. /pa-mākints/ pomukints 'instructed.'

37. Inf. /minintvei/ menentwey 'to mention.'

38. 2nd pl. imp. /er-pilnīnaite/ erpilninaiti 'fill.'

39. Inf. /en-perint/ empijrint 'to gather'; used instead of pst. pass. prt.

40. 3rd pr. /is-rankina/ isrankinna 'saves.'

41. 3rd pr. /sādina/ saddinna, sedinna; cf. Li. *sodìnti* 'to plant.'

42. Pst. act. prt. nom. sg. masc. /en-sādinuns/ ensaddinnons 'instituted.'
    Pst. pass. prt. nom. sg. masc. /en-sādints/ ensadints
    Pst. pass. prt. nom. sg. neut. /en-sādintan/ ensadinton.

43. 3rd pr. /sātvina/ sātuinei 'satisfy' (used with meaning of 2nd sg. pr.).
    Cf. Li. *sótinti* 'to satisfy.'

44. Pst. act. prt. nom. sg. masc. /au-skandinuns/ auskandinnons
    Pst. pass. prt. nom. sg. masc. /au-skandints/ auskandints.

45. Pst. act. prt. nom. sg. masc. /skīstinuns/ skijstinnons 'purified'
    Pst. pass. prt. nom. sg. masc. /skīstints/ (ni)skijstints 'made (im)pure.'

46. Inf. /sklaitint/ sklaitint 'to put asunder.'

47. Pst. pass. prt. nom. sg. masc. /is-sklaitints/ isklaitints 'excluded.'

48. Inf. /spartint/ 'to strengthen'
    3rd pr. /spartina/ spartina, schpartina, spartinno.

49. Inf. /pa-spartint/ pospartint 'to strengthen.'

50. 1st pl. pr. /prei-statinama/ preistattinnimai 'we present.'

51. Inf. /súndintwei/ sūndintwti 'to punish.'

52. Inf. /svintint/ swintint 'to keep holy'
    Inf. /svintintvei/ swintintwey, swyntintwey
    Pst. act. prt. nom. sg. masc. /svintinuns/ swintinons, swintinninuns
    Pst. pass. part. nom. sg. masc. /svintints/ swintints, swyntits
    3rd /svintina/ swintina, swintinai.

53. Pst. act. prt. nom. sg. masc. /taukinuns/ taukinnons 'promised'
    1rst sg. pr. /taukinā/ tankinne; possible 3 pr. used with meaning of 1sg. pr.

54. Pst. act. prt. nom. sg. masc. /pa-taukinuns/ potaukinnons 'promised'
    Pst. pass. prt. acc. sg. masc. or fem. /pa-taukintan/ potaukinton.

55. Inf. /teisint/ teisint 'to honor.'

56. Pst. act. prt. nom. sg. masc. /per-tenginuns/ pertengginnons 'sent'
    Pst. pass. prt. acc. sg. masc. /per-tengintan/ pertengninton.

57. Inf. /tikint/ tickint, teckint 'to make'
    1st pl. pr. /tikinama/ tickinnimai, teckinnimai
    2nd pl. imp. /tikinaite/ tickinnaiti.

58. Pst. act. prt. nom. sg. masc. /pa-tikinuns/ po-tickinnuns 'made.'

59. 3 pr. /túlnina/ tūlninai 'increases' (used with meaning of 2nd sg. pr.)
    2nd pr. imp. /túlninaite/ tūlninaiti.

60. Inf. /ūlint/ ūlint 'to fight.'

61. 3rd pr. /vaidina (sin)/ waidinna 'show,' waidinnasin.

62. Pst. act. prt. nom. sg. masc. /en-vaidinuns/ enwaidinnons 'signified.'

63. Inf. /pa-vaidint/ powaidint 'to instruct'
    3rd pr. /pa-vaidina/ powaidinne, powaidinnei
    2nd pl. imp. /pa-vaidinaite/ powaidinneiti.

64. Inf. /valnint/ walnint, walnennint 'to improve.'

65. Inf. /vangint/ wangint 'to complete.'

66. Inf. /vartint/ wartint 'to turn'
    3rd pr. /vartina sin/ wartinna sin.

67. Inf. /zmānint/ ʋmūnint 'to honor'
    Inf. /zmānintvei/ smunintwey, somonentwey
    2nd sg. imp. /zmāninais/ smuninais.

68. 3rd pr. /er-zváigzdina/ erschwāigstinai 'enlightens'
    Pst. act. prt. nom. sg. masc. /er-zvaigzdinuns/ erschwāistiuns.

69. 3rd pr. /pa-zváigzdina/ poswāigstinai 'cause to shine.'

Ih. Secondary verb with suffix /ī/.

1. 3rd fut. /dalīs/ dellieis '(will) share'; Cf. Li. *dalýti* 'to divide.'

2. Inf. /krikstītvei/ crixtitwi 'to baptize'
   Pst. pass. prt. nom. sg. masc. /krikstīts/ crixtits, crixteits
   1sg. pr. /krikstijā/ crixtia (perhaps this is a 3rd pr. used with 1st sg. pr. meaning)
   2nd pl. imp. /krikstīte/ crixtity, crixtidi, crixtiti, crixteiti.

Ii. Secondary verb with suffix /au/

1. Inf. /dínkaut/ dīnkaut 'to thank'
   1st sg. pr. /dínkaujā/ dīnckama, dīnkama, (Trautmann: 276), but perhaps this is a 3rd pr. used with a 1sg. pr. meaning
   1st pl. pr. /dínkaujama/ dīnkaumai, dinkauimai
   2nd pl. imp /dínkaujaite/ dinkauti
   3rd pst. /dínkavāts/ dinkowats, dinkowatz, dīnkauts, dinkauts, dinkautzt, dinkauczt.

2. Inf. /san-geidaut/ sengidaut 'to attain.'

3. Inf. /gerdaut/ gerdant 'to say'
   1st sg. pr. /gerdaujā/ gerdawi (perhaps this is a 3rd pr. used with the meaning of 1st sg. pr.)
   3rd fut. /gerdaus/ gerdaus (probably for 2nd sg. fut. /gerdausi/ with meaning of 2nd fut.)

4. 3rd fut. /en-gerdaus/ engerdaus 'will say' (probably for 2sg. fut. /engerdausi/ with meaning of 2nd fut).

5. 3rd pr. /pa-gerdauja/ pogerdawie 'preach.'

6. 3rd pr. /prei-gerdauja/ preigerdawi 'promises.'

7. Inf. /grēkaut/ grikaut 'to confess.'

8. Inf. /neikaut/ neikaut 'to go into.'

9. Sup. /pastautun/ pastauton 'to fast.'

10. Inf. /pa-pekaut/ popeckūt, popeckut, popekūt 'to protect'
    3rd pr. /pa-pekauja/ popeckuwi.

11. 3rd pr. /rikauja/ rikawie, rickawie (used with meaning of 2nd sg.) 'rule'
    2nd pl. imp. /rikaujaite/ rikauite.

12. Inf. /surgaut/ surgaut 'to be anxious.'

13. 3rd pr. /per-surgauja/ persurgaui 'takes care of.'

14. 3rd pr. /verauja/ wēraui 'protects.'

15. Pst. pass. prt. nom. sg. masc. /ap-vinauts/ (ni) ebwinūts 'irreproachable'
    Pst. pass. prt. nom. sg. fem. /ap-vinauta/ (ni) ebwinūtei.

16. Inf. /at-vinaut/ etwinūt 'forgive, excuse.'

17. Pst. pass. prt. acc. sg. masc. /ni-vinautan/ niwinūton 'innocent.'

18. 3rd pr. /vúkauja/ or /vákauja/ wūkawi 'demands,' cf. wackītwei (II22).

19. Pst. act. prt. nom. sg. masc. /per-vukauns/ or /per-vakauns/ perwūkauns
    'called.'

II. Second conjugation: present stem in /ī/ and infinitive stem in /ē/.

1. 3rd pr. /budī/ budē 'watch over.'

2. Pst. act. prt. nom. sg. masc. /dergēuns/ dergēuns 'hated'
   3rd pst. /dergē/.

3. Inf. /druvēt/ druwīt 'to believe'
   Pr. act. prt. acc. sg. fem. /druvintan/ (ni) druwīntin
   1st sg. pr. /druvá/ druwē, druwe, drowe, drowy (perhaps this is a 3rd pr.
   form used with a 1st sg. pr. meaning)
   2nd sg. pr. /druvīsi/ druwēse
   3rd pr. /druvī/ druwē, drowe, druwe
   1st pl. pr. /druvíma/ druwēmai
   1st pl. pr. /druvīte/ druwētei.

4. 3rd pr. /grēkī si/ grīkisi 'sins'
   1st pl. pr. /grēkīma/ grīkımai.

5. Pst. act. prt. nom. sg. masc. /kabēuns/ kabīuns 'hang, hung.'

6. Pst. pass. prt. nom. pl. masc. /en-kaitētai/ankaitītai, enkaitītai 'tempted,' or
   perhaps this is conjugated like quoifē and belongs in class Ib.

7. Inf. /kirdēt/ kirdīt 'to hear'
   Inf. /kirdētvei/ kirdītvei
   1st pl. pr. /kírdima/ kīrdimai
   2nd pl. imp. /kirdīte/ kīrdeiti, kirdiiti.

8. Inf. /pa-laipsētvei/ pallaipsītwei, pallapsitwei, pallapsittwey, pallapsitwey
   'to covet'
   3rd pr. /pa-laipsī/ pallapse.

9. 3rd pr. /per-lánkī/ perlānkei, perlānki 'belongs to.'

10. Inf. /laukēt/ laukīt 'to search out'
    2nd pl. imp. /laukīte/ laukijti. Cf. Li. laukéti 'to wait a little bit.'

11. 3rd pr. /kaima-lūkī/ kāimaluke 'visits.' Cf. Li. lūkéti 'to wait a bit.'

12. Inf. /milḗt/ milijt 'to love'
    Pst. act. prt. nom. sg. masc. /milḗ[j] uns/ milijuns
    Pst. psv. prt. voc. pl. masc. /milḗtai/ milijtai
    3rd pr. /milī́/ milḗ, mile
    2nd sg. imp. /milī́s/ mijlis; cf. in Simon Grunau's Vocabulary pomeleis 'lick'
    (see Trautmann, 1910: 405)
    2nd pl. imp. /milī́te/ milijti.

13. Pst. act. prt. nom. sg. masc. /er-nertḗuns/ ernertīuns, ernertiuns 'angered'
    1st pl. pr. /er-nertī́ma/ ernertimai.

14. Pst. act. prt. nom. sg. masc. /peldḗuns/ peldīuns 'acquired, gained.'
    Cf. Li. *peldḕti* 'to repent, to spare.'

15. Inf. /segḗt/ seggī́t, segī́t, seggit, siggī́t, siggit 'to do'
    Pst. act. prt. nom. sg. masc. /segḗuns/ seggīuns, seggīūns
    1st sg. pr. /segā́/ segge or perhaps this is a 3rd pr. used with the meaning of
    a 1st sg. pr.
    2nd sg. pr. /segī́si/ seggḗsei
    3rd pr. /segī́/ segge, segḗ, seggḗ
    1st pl. pr. /segī́ma/ seggḗmai
    2nd pl. pr. /segī́te/ seggī́tei, seggḗti
    2nd. pl. imp. /segī́te/ seggī́tei, seggī́ta, segeitty, segeyti.

16. Inf. /au-šaudḗt/ auschaudijt 'to trust'
    Inf. /au-šaudḗtvei/ auschaudītwei
    3rd pr. /au-šaudī́/ auschaudḗ.

17. Inf. /pa-skā́lḗt/ poskulit 'to exhort'
    Sup. /pa-skā́lḗtun/ paskulīton
    3rd pr. /pa-skā́lī́/ paskulḗ, paskollḗ, paskulḗwie (used as 1st sg. pr.)
    2nd sg. imp. /pa-skā́lī́s/ poskuleis.

18. Pst. act. prt. nom. sg. masc. /per-tenḗuns/ pertennīuns 'neglected.'

19. Inf. /turḗt/ turī́t, turrit 'to have'
    Inf. /turḗtvei/ turrettwey, turryetwey, turrītwei
    The 2nd sg. prs. form /tur/ is apparently some kind of abbreviated form
    used to denote obligation.
    3rd prs. /turī́/ turri, turei, ture (also used with meaning of 1st sg. pr. and
    2nd sg. pr. at times)
    1st pl. pr. /turī́ma/ turrimai
    2nd pl. pr. /turī́te/ turriti
    3rd opt. /turḗlai/ turrīlai
    1st pl. opt. /turḗlaima/ turrīlimai

20. 3rd sg. fut. /tusḗsai/ tussīse 'he will be silent.'

21. 1st pl. pr. /vaidlī́ma/ waidleimai 'we charm.'

22. Inf. /vakḗtvei/ wackītwei 'to call, to attract,'
    cf. wūkawi.

23. 3rd pr. /en-vakī́/ enwackḗ 'calle'
    1st pl. pr. /en-vakī́ma/ enwackḗmai, enwackḗimai.

24. 3rd pr. /prei-vakī/ preiwackē 'calls.'

25. 3rd pst. /vidē/ widdai 'saw'; cf. Slavic *viděti.*

III. Third conjugation: Present stem in /ā/

IIIa. Infinitive in /ī/

1. 3rd pr. /per-bándā/ perbānda 'tempts,' Cf. Li. *bandýti* 'to try.'

2. 2nd sg. imp. /dīrīs/ dereis 'see.'

3. Inf. /en-dīrīt/ endeirīt 'to look upon'
   Inf. /en-dīrītvei/ endyrītwei
   3rd pst. /en-dīrā/ endeirā
   2nd sg. imp. /en-dīrīs/ endirīs
   Since Lithuanian has both the cognate forms *dyréti* and *dýroti* 'to look at,'
   this verb could well belong in the II as well as the III conjugation.

4. 2nd sg. imp. /en-graudīs/ engraudīs 'have mercy.'

5. Pst. act. prt. /klantī[v] uns/ klantīuns, klantīwuns 'cursed'
   1st pl. pr. /klantāma/ kla⁻ ⁺emmai.

6. Inf. /per-klantīt/ perklanfīt 'to damn'
   Pst. act. prt. nom. sg. masc. /per-klantī[v] uns/ perklantīuns
   Pst. pass. prt. nom. sg. masc. /per-klantīts/ perklanfīts, preclantyts
   Pst. pass. prt. nom. sg. masc. /per-klantītan/ perklantīton
   1st pl. pr. /per-klantāma/ perklantemmai.

7. Pst. act. prt. nom. sg. masc. /pra-klantīts/ proklantitz 'damned.'

8. Sup. /klausītun/ klausiton 'to hear'
   Pst. act. prt. /klausīuns/ klausiuns
   1st pl. pr. /klausāma/ klausēmai
   2nd pl. imp. /klausīte/ klausieiti.

9. Pr. pass. prt. nom. sg. masc. (?) /pa-klausīmanas/ poklausīmanas 'heard.'

10. Inf. /er-mērīt/ ermīrit 'to imagine'

11. Inf. /pa-mērīt/ pomīrit 'to consider.'

12. Inf. /is-rankīt/ isrankīt 'to save'
    Pst. act. prt. /is-rankīuns/ isrankīuns
    2nd sg. imp. /is-rankīs/ isrankeis
    3rd opt. /is-rankīlai/ isrāikilai.

13. Pst. pass. prt. nom. sg. masc. /skrīsīts/ skrīsits, scrijsits, scrisits, skresitzt
    'crucified.'

14. Pst. pass. prt. nom. sg. masc. /en-ténsīts/ entēnsīts 'included'
    Pst. pass. prt. nom. pl. masc. /en-tensītai/ entensītei.

15. Pst. act. prt. nom. pl. masc. /ap-zentlīuns/ ebsentliuns 'designated.'

IIIb. Infinitive stem in /ā/.

1. Inf. /bi[j]ātvei/ biātwei 'to fear'
   3rd pr. /bi[j]ā/ biā.

2. Inf. /dvigubāt/ dwibugūt 'to doubt'
   3rd pr. /dvigubā/ dwigubbū.

3. 3rd pr. /pa-glabā/ poglabū 'caressed' (used with meaning of 3rd pst.).

4. 3rd pr. /kalsā/ kaltzā, kelsāi 'to sound; to purport,' translates German *lauten*;
   (see Senn, 1966: 286).

5. Inf. /laikāt/ laikūt 'to fulfill'
   Pst. pass. prt. nom. sg. masc. /laikāts/ laikūts
   3rd pr. /láikā/ lāiku
   1st pl. pr. /láikāma/ lāikumai
   2nd pl. imp. /láikāte/ lāikutei; or is this a 2nd pl. pr. form used with imperative meaning?

6. 3rd pr. /at-láikā sin/ etlāikusin 'refrain.'

7. 1st pl. pr. /en-laikāma/ enlaikūmai 'we hold on'
   2nd pl. imp. /en-láikāte/ enlāikuti; or is this a 2nd pl pr. form used
   with imperative meaning?

8. Inf. /er-laikāt/ erlaikūt 'to preserve'
   Pst. pass. prt. nom. sg. masc. /er-laikāts/ erlaikūts
   Pst. act. prt. nom. sg. masc. /er-laikā[v] uns/ erlaikūuns
   3rd pr. /er-láikā/ erlāiku

9. 3rd pr. /is-láikā/ islāiku, islāika 'preserve'; also used with meaning of 2nd sg.
   pr.

10. Inf. /pa-laikāt/ polaikūt 'to keep'
    Pst. pass. prt. nom. sg. masc. /pa-laikāts/ polaikūts
    3rd pr. /pa-láikā/ polāiku
    1st pl. pr. /pa-láikāma/ polāikumai.

11. Inf. /prei-laikāt/ preilaikūt 'to teach.'

12. Pst. pass. prt. acc sg., gender unclear /maisātan/ maysotan 'mixed.'

13. Sup. /maitātun sin/ maitātun sin 'to nourish oneself'
    3rd pr. /maitā/ maitā.

14. Inf. /pa-maitāt/ pomaitat 'to feed.'

15. Pst. pass. prt. nom. sg. neut. /peisātan/ peisāton, peisaton 'written'
    3rd pr. /peisā/ peisāi, peisai.

16. Pst. act. prt. nom. sg. masc. /pa-peisāuns/ popeisauns 'described'
    Pst. pass. prt. nom. sg. neut. /pa-peisātan/ popeisāton.

17. Inf. /teikāt/ teickut 'to create'
    Pst. act. prt. nom. sg. masc. /teikā[v] uns/ teikūnus, taykowuns
    3rd pst. /teikā/ teikū, teiku.

18. Pst. pass. prt. nom. sg. neut. /en-teikātan/ enteikūton 'established'
    Pst. act. prt. nom. sg. neut. /en-teikā[v] uns/ enteikūuns.

19. Pst. act. prt. nom. sg. neut. /pa-teikā[v] uns/ poteikūuns 'created'

20. Pst. pass. prt. nom. sg. neut. /pa-tikāts/ patickots 'conceived.'

21. Inf. /at-trātvei/ attrātwei 'to answer'
    3rd sg. pr. /at-trā/ ettrāi
    2nd sg. imp. /at-trais/ ettrais
    2nd pl. imp. /at-traite/ attrāiti.

22. Inf. /vaitijāt/ waitiāt, waitiat 'to speak'
    Pr. act. prt. acc. pl. fem. /vaitijantans/ emprijki waitiaintins 'contradictor'
    Sup. /vaitijātun/ waytiaton, waitiatun
    1st pl. pr. /vaitijāma/ waitiāmai.

23. 3rd pr. /en-vaitijā/ enwaitia 'says.'

24. Pst. act. prt. nom. sg. masc. /na-vaitiāuns/ nowaitiāuns 'slandered.'

25. Inf. /zegnāt/ signāt, sīggnat 'to bless'

25a. Pst. act. prt. nom. sg. masc. /ap-zegnāuns/ ebsignāuns 'blessed'
    Pst. psv. prt. nom. sg. masc. /ap-zegnāts/ ebsignāts
    Pst. psv. prt. nom. pl. masc. /ap-zegnātai/ absignātai
    3rd pst. /ap-zegnā/ ebsgnā
    3rd fut. /ap-zegnāsai/ ebsignāsi.

26. Inf. /er-zināt/ ersinnāt/ 'to recognize'
    1st pl. pr. /er-zināma/ ersinnimai
    2nd pl. pr. /er-zināte/ ersinnati.

27. Inf. /pa-zināt/ posinnat 'to recognize'
    Pst. act. prt. nom. sg. masc. /pa-zināts/ posinnāts
    3rd pr. /pa-zinā/ posinna, also used as 1st sg.
    1st pl. pr. /pa-zināma/ posinnimai.

IV. Fourth conjugation: Old athematic verbs.

1. Inf. /būt/ bout, boūt 'to be'
   Sup. /būtun/ būton, boūton, baūton, bouton
   Pr. act. prt. nom. sg. masc. /-sens/ emprijkisins 'present'
   Pr. act. prt. dat. sg. masc. /-sentasmā/ emprīkisentismu
   Pst. act. prt. nom. sg. masc. /bū[v] uns/ boūuns, baūuns
   1st sg. pr. /esmā/ asmai, asmau, asmu
   2nd sg. pr. /esi/ assai, essei, asse, aesse, assei
   3rd pr. /est/ ast, aest, est, asch, hest
   3rd pr. /estits/ astits
   1st pl. pr. /esma/ asmai
   2nd pl. pr. /este/ astai, estei, asti
   3rd prt. /bē/ bē, bēi, be
   3rd fut. /būsai/ bousai, baūsei, boūsei, bousei, boūse, bouse
   2nd sg. imp. /saisai/ seisei
   2nd pl. imp. /saite/ seīti, seiti
   3rd opt. /būlai/ baulai, boūlai.

2. Inf. /dāt/ dāt, dat 'to give'
   Inf. /dātvei/ dātwei, datwei
   Sup. /dātun/ daton, dātun-si
   Pst. act. prt. nom. sg. masc. /dāuns/ dāuns, dauns
   Pst. pass. prt. nom. sg. masc. /dāts/ dāts, dats, daeczt
   Pst. pass. prt. nom. sg. neut. /dātan/ daton
   2nd sg. pr. /dāsi/ dāse
   3rd pr. /dāst/ dāst, dast
   3rd pst. /dā/ dai
   3rd. pst. /dāts/ daits, daitz, dayts
   3rd fut. /dāsai/ dāsai, dase
   2nd sg. imp. /dais/ dais, days
   2nd pl. imp. /dáite/ dāiti, daiti.

3. Inf. /au-dāt sin/ audāt sien 'to happen'
   3rd pr. /au-dāst sin/ audāst sien
   3rd fut. /au-dāsai sin /audasei, audasseisin, audaseysin
   3rd fut. /au-dās sin/ audāsin (35, 23).

4. 3rd pr. /en-dāst sin/ endāst sien 'undertakes.'

5. Pst. act. prt. nom. sg. masc. /pa-dāuns/ podāuns 'given'
   Pst. pass. prt. nom. sg. neut. /pa-dātan/ podāton, podaton
   3rd pr. /pa-dāst/ podāst.

6. Pst. act. prt. nom. sg. masc. /per-dāuns/ perdauns 'sold.'

7. Pst. act. prt. nom. sg. masc. /san-dāuns/ sendāuns 'put together' Perhaps the /ā/ in this word is a misprint for an /ē/ and the word should be classed with IV8 below.

8. Pst. pass. prt. acc. pl. fem. /san-dētans/ senditans 'folded'
   Pst. pass. prt. dat. sg. fem. /san-dētai/ senditmai.

9. 2nd sg. pr. /éisi/ ēisei 'you go'
   3rd pr. /éit/ ēit/
   2nd sg. imp. /jeis/ jeis
   2nd pl. imp. /jeite/ jeithy, jeiti.

10. Inf. /per-éit/ perēit, pereit, 'to come'
    3rd pr. /per-éit/ perēit, pereit
    1st pl. pr. /per-éima/ perēimai
    3rd fut. /per-eisai/ pareysey
    3rd fut. /per-eis/ pereis (7, 5)
    3rd opt. /per-éilai/ perēilai.

11. Inf. /ēst/ īst, ist 'to eat'
    Inf. /ēstvei/ istwei, istwe
    Pst. act. prt. nom. sg. masc. /ēduns/ īduns
    2nd pl. imp. /ēdaite/ īdeiti, idaite, ydieyti, edeitte.

12. Inf. /meigti/ meicte 'to sleep'; cf. Old Li. *miegti* 'sleeps.'

13. 3rd pr. /virst/ wirst, wijrst, wīrst, werst 'becomes,'
    i.e. translates German *wird*
    1st pl. pr. /vírstma/ wīrstmai
    2nd pl. pr. /vírste/ wīrstai

3rd fut. /virsai/ wirse, but this verb may have the Baltic -*st*- suffix, see Endzelīns (1944: 166).

V.

Anomalous forms:
The following verb apparently has athematic forms in the singular but the /ī/
conjugation in the plural:

1. Inf. /vaist/ waist 'to know'
   2nd sg. pr. /vaisi/ waisei, waisse
   1st pl. pr. /vaidīma/ waidimai
   2nd pl. pr. /vaidīte/ waiditi.

VI.

The following three verbs are apparently Slavic borrowings with an /ī/ in both the
present and infinitive stems:

1. Inf. /madlīt/ madlit, madlīt 'to pray'
   Inf. /madlītvei/ madlitwei
   Sup. /madlītun/ madliton
   3rd ps. /madlī/ madli used with 1st sp. pr. meaning
   1st pl. pr. /madlīma/ madlimai
   2nd pl. imp. /madlīte/ madliti.

2. Inf. /slūzītvei/ schlūsitwei 'to serve'
   3rd pr. /slūzī/ schlūsi
   1st pl. pr. /slūzīma/ schlūsimai
   2nd pl. pr. /slūzīte/ schlūsiti
   3rd opt. /slūzīlai/ schlūsilai, schlusilai

3. Pst. act. prt. nom. sg. masc. /per-slūzīuns/ perschlūsiuns
   1st pl. pr. /per-slūzīma/ perschlūsimai.

VII.

There seems to be no particular reason for classing the following verbs in one class
or another:

1. Pst. pass. prt. nom. sg. masc. /an-dejants/ andeiānsts 'hindered.'

2. Pst. act. prt. nom. sg. masc. /grīmuns/ grīmons 'sung.'

3. 3rd pr. /pa-leika/ ? polijcki 'bestow'
   Pst. act. prt. nom. sg. masc. /pa-leikuns/ polīkins.   Possibly this verb
   belongs in class Ia.

4. Inf. /pa-láikt/ polāikt 'to remain.'

5. Pst. act. prt. nom. sg. masc. /muravuns/ murrawuns 'grumbled'; borrowing
   from German *murren* (perhaps to be classed in Ii).

6. Pr. act. prt. nom. sg. masc. /skelánts/ skellānts, schkellānts, skellants
Pr. act. prt. nom. pl. masc. /skelántai/ skellāntei, skellāntai.

7. Pst. pass. prt. nom. sg. masc. /at-skī[vʲ]uns/ attskiwuns, etskīuns, etskyuns
'resurrected'
1st pl. pr. /at-skīma/ etskīmai
2nd sg. pr. /at-skīsi/ etskīsai

INDEX

This index is based partially on the vocabulary given in Trautmann. The verbs can be located in the body of the text by their conjugation and number. Thus, for example, *absignātai* III b 25a is the verb no. 25a in conjugation III b.

NOTES

1. Quite probably this form should be transcribed /vedé/. The macron in weddē does not necessarily denote contrastive length here any more than it does in

perweddā. The form /vede/ could then be compared directly with the Slavic third person singular aorist *vede* 'led.' According to Stang (1966: 467) the stress of OP weddē could well reflect an etymological mobile stress and then agree directly with Li. *vēdè*. The etymological mobile stress and long vowel of *vedē* is probably an East Baltic development (see Schmalstieg, 1961 and 1965).

In the articles mentioned above I propose that the preterit of such verbs as Li. *nèšti*, *vèsti*, etc. reflects an old **vedam* < **vedom*, (2nd sg.) **vedes*, (3) **vede(t)*. With the unification of the thematic vowel the 1st sg. **vedam* was replaced by 1st sg. **vedem*. There existed beside the conjugation **vedem*, *vedes*, **vede(t)* a conjugation **pirkam* (standing for underlying **pirkām*, since long diphthongs were phonologically impossible), **pirkās*, **pirkā(t)*. In Common East Baltic the primary endings (1st sg.) *-u*, (2nd sg.) *-i* replaced the secondary endings, giving **veḋau* (for underlying **vedeu*), **vedei* and *pirkau*, *pirkai*. The lengthening of the final vowel of **vede(t)* follows the proportion: *pirkau*, *pirkai* are to **pirkā* as **vedeu vedei* are to x and x = **vedē*.

REFERENCES

Brugmann, Karl. 1933. *Kurze vergleichende Grammatik der indogermanischen Sprachen*. Berlin and Leipzig.

Endzelīns, J. 1944. *Altpreussische Grammatik*. Rīga.

Endzelīns, J. 1948. *Baltu valodu skaņas un formas*. Rīga.

Endzelīns, J. 1951. *Latviešu valodas gramatika*. Rīga.

Gerullis, Georg. 1924. "Zur Beurteilung des altpreussischen Enchiridions," *Streitberg Festgabe*. Leipzig, pp. 96–104.

Leskien, A. 1963. *Die Declination im Slavisch-litauischen und Germanischen*. Leipzig. (Reprint of original 1876 edition.)

Mažiulis, V., 1966. *Prūsų kalbos paminklai*. Vilnius.

Meillet, A., 1965. *Le slave commun*. Paris, Librairie Honoré Champion.

Rysiewicz, Zygmunt. 1938. "L'accentazione del 'antico prussiano," *Studi baltici* 7, pp. 88–147.

Schmalstieg, William R. 1959. "Slavic stative verbs in *-ī-*," *International Journal of Slavic Linguistics and Poetics* 1, (2), pp. 177–183.

Schmalstieg, William R. 1961. "The Lithuanian preterit in *-ė*," *Lingua* 10, pp. 93–97.

Schmalstieg, William R. 1964. "The Phonemes of the Old Prussian Enchiridion," *Word* 20, pp. 211–221.

Schmalstieg, William R. 1965. "Again the Lithuanian preterit in '*-ė*'," *Annali Istituto Universitario Orientale Napoli*, sez. ling. 6, pp. 123–126.

Schmalstieg, William R. 1968. "Labialization in Old Prussian," *Studies in Slavic Linguistics and Poetics in honor of Boris O. Unbegaun*. New York.

Schmid, Wolfgang P. 1963. *Studien zum baltischen und indogermanischen Verbum*. Wiesbaden.

Skardžius, Pranas. 1943. *Lietuvių kalbos žodžių daryba*. Vilnius.

Specht, F. 1928. "Zu den altpreussischen Verbalformen auf *-ai*, *-ei*, *-sai-sei*," *Zeitschrift für Vergleichende Sprachforschung* 55, pp. 161–184.

Stang, Christian S. 1942. *Das slavische und baltische Verbum*. Oslo.

Stang, Christian S. 1957. *Slavonic accentuation*. Oslo.

Stang, Christian S. 1966. *Vergleichende Grammatik der Baltischen Sprachen*. Oslo.

Trautmann, Reinhold, 1910. *Die altpreussischen Sprachdenkmäler*. Göttingen.
Ulvydas, K. et al., 1956. *Lietuvių kalbos žodynas*. Vilnius.
Zinkevičius, Z. 1966. *Lietuvių dialektologija*. Vilnius.

The Pennsylvania State University

OLD PRUSSIAN ADVERBS IN -*n*

OLGA C. SHOPAY

There are five basic monuments in Old Prussian, all translated from German. Of these, two are vocabularies, and three are translations of Catechisms labelled I, II, and III. Although the translators of Catechisms I and II remain anonymous, it is assumed that they were translated in a manner similar to Catechism III. More commonly known as the Enchiridion, Catechism III was translated by Pastor Abel Will in 1561.

This article is based on Will's translation and concerns forms ending in -*n*, which, according to Trautmann,[1] function as adverbs of manner. Trautmann seems to have based his analysis of Old Prussian grammar on the grammar of German; thus, he determined the parts of speech in Old Prussian according to their function in German sentences. However, on the basis of the data collected, it is most probable that these forms in -*n*, characteristic of the Enchiridion alone, are wrong forms used in place of the well-attested -*ai* form of the adverbs and are actually the accusative cases of the corresponding adjectival forms.

On the basis of comparative linguistics and Trautmann's analysis, it seems that Old Prussian adverbs of manner derived from adjectives ordinarily end in -*ai*. This -*ai* ending is well attested in the Baltic languages and corresponds to Li. -*ai*, Latv. -*i*, and OCS -*ě*.[2] Thus, the ending of OP *labbai* corresponds to Li. *labai*, Latv. *labi*, and OCS *dobrě*.

As for those forms that end in -*ei* rather than -*ai* Trautmann suggests that -*ei* occurs after a palatalized consonant.[3] In Old Prussian, phonetic [a] may have been in complementary distribution with [e], the former

Reprinted from Olga C. Shopay, "Old Prussian Adverbs in -*n*," *The Slavic and East European Journal*, Vol. XI, No. 3 (© 1967 by the Regents of the University of Wisconsin), pp. 296–301.

occurring after unpalatalized consonants and the latter after palatalized consonants.[4] In many instances, however, -ei may be just a simple scribal rendering of /ai/, e.g., ainawīdai vs. ainawijdei.

According to Trautmann, adverbs ending in -u, which are derived from adjectives with the suffix -iskas, have the same origin as those in -ai.[5] If this is true, then forms ending in -isku may be regarded as belonging to the well-attested group ending in -ai, that is, -isku may be a variant of -iskai. Two reasons are considered here. One, it has been suggested that immediately following unpalatalized labial and velar consonants there was apparently a tendency for back and central vowels to be raised, rounded, and backed even more. In word final position, this allophonic rounding and backing was so clear that Abel Will frequently rendered the diphthong /ai/ by orthographic -u.[6] Two, in the entire Enchiridion there are 42 occurrences of adverbs ending in -iskai and -isku. Of these, only 14 end in -isku; the remaining 28—in -iskai. Thus -isku is merely an orthographic rendering of -iskai, for we find such doublets as deineniskai vs. deinenisku, etniwingiskai vs. etniwingisku, laimiskai vs. laimisku, perarwiskai vs. perarwisku. In addition to these, empolijgu may have been written for *empolijgai.

Among the other possible endings for adverbs derived from adjectives arc those in -a, -e, and -i. Although Trautmann suggests -a < IE -od, -e < IE-i, and -i < IE -i,[7] it is perhaps best to regard these as orthographic mistakes for -ai. Thus there are such occurrences as ainaweydi (ainawīdai, ainawijdei); angsteina (angstainai); arw̄i (arwiskai); reide (reidei).

The only other forms regarded by Trautmann as adverbs of manner end in -n.[8] Adverbs in -n, however, are practically unknown in Baltic, except for adverbs of motion derived from illatives and adverbial expressions of time or place. No adverbs in Old Prussian use the accusative case in -n except those of time or place. In the Enchiridion there are no occurrences of illatives, but there are occurrences of the accusative case functioning as an adverb of time or place, e.g.: schindeinan 'today,' schen nacktin 'tonight,' deinan bhe nacktien 'day and night,' endangon 'in heaven.'[9] These forms are clearly adverbs of time and place and are the only true adverbs used in the accusative case in Old Prussian. They are not considered in this article, because they are not adverbs of manner and are not derived from adjectives, but are clearly nouns in the accusative case, the use of which is well attested in the Baltic languages, cf. Li. šiañdien 'today.'

Below I have listed all the occurrences of adverbial -n (according to Trautmann) and those of the corresponding -ai forms. For reasons already mentioned, I have included in the -ai group those forms in -ei, -isku, -a, -e, and -i, if they occur. The German translation of each example is given

with the Old Prussian and numbers in parentheses refer to pages in Trautmann.

1. (a) *ainawydan*:

as	tennēismu	subsai	asmai	bhe	entennēismu	rīkin	po
ich	sein	eygen	seye	und	in seinem	Reych	unter

tenesmu	giwīt	bhe	stesmu	schlusilai	en	prabuskai	tickrōmiskan
jm	lebe		jm	diene	in	ewiger	Gerechtigkeit

niwinūtiskau	bhe	deiwūtiskan	*ainawydan*	kaigi	tāns	ast	etskīans
Unschuld	und	Seligkeyt	*Gleich*	wie	er	ist	aufferstanden

esse	gallan	giwa	bhe	rickawie	en	prabutskan	(31).
vom	Tode	Lebet	und	Regieret	in	Ewigkeyt	(30).

(b) *ainawīdai*: prastan Crixtisnan enkopts ēnstan gallan kai *ainawīdai* kāigi Christus
ast esse stans Gallans etbaudints (43); durch die Tauffe begraben in den Todt Das
gleich wie Christus ist von den Todten aufferwecket (42).

(c) *ainawīdai*: Beggi stas wijrs ast steisei Gennas gallū *Ainawīdai* kai Christus sta
gallu ast steison perōniskan (65); Denn der Man ist des Weibs Heupt *Gleich* wie auch
Christus das Heupt ist der Gemeine (64).

(d) *ainawīdai*: bhe stans gurīnans malnijkikans *ainawīdai* titet kai stans urans (71);
unnd die armen Kindlein *gleich* so wol als die Alten (70).

(e) *ainawijdei*: stas Swints Nosēilis ast mien prastan Euangelion perwūkauns sen
swaians Dāians erschwāistiuns en tikrōmiskan Druwien Swintinons bhe erlaikūuns
Ainawijdei kāidi tans stan postippin Christiāniskan nosemmien preiwackē (33); der
Heylige Geyst hat mich durchs Euangelion beruffen mit seinen Gaben erleuchtet im
rechten Glauben geheyliget und erhalten *Gleich* wie er die gantze Christenheyt auff
Erden berufft (32).

2. (a) *deininiskan*: bhe mes kīrdimai dijgi schklāits *deininiskan* is Deiwas wirdan
serrīpimai (71); Denn wir hörens auch sonst *täglich* auss Gottes Wort erfarens (70).

(b) *deineniskai*: sen wissan prewerīngiskan bhe maitāsnan schiēise kermenes bhe
gīwas Laimiskai bhe *deineniskai* persurgaui (31); mit aller Notturfft und Narung diss
Leibes unnd Lebens Reychlich und *Täglich* versorget (30).

(c) *deinenisku*: bhe wissamans druwīngins *deinenisku* wissans grīkans laimintiskai
etwiērpei (33); unnd allen Glaubigen *teglich* alle sünde reichlich vergibt (32).

(d) *deinenisku*: Bhe etkūmps *deinenisku* etskīmai bhe winna perēimai (43); Unnd
widerumb *teglich* herausskommen und aufferstehen (42).

(e) *deininisku*: beggi mes *deininisku* tūlan grīkimai (37); Denn wir *teglich* viel
sündigen (36).

3. *enwāngiskan*: bhe *enwāngiskan* stan potaukinton weldīsnan en Dengan sen
wissans Swintickens engaunai (81); und *entlich* das verheissen Erbtheyl im Himel mit
allen Heyligen entpfahe (80).

4. *ginnewīngiskan*: mes kīrdimai is schismu Ebangelion kāigi *ginnewīngiskan* sien
stas Soūns Deiwas noūson mijls rikijs Jhesus Christus prīki stans malnijkikans
waidinnasin sēnku (71); Wir hören auss diesem Euangelio wie *freundtlich* sich der
Son Gottes unser lieber HErr JESUS CHRISTUS gegen den Kindlein stellet damit
(70).

5. *isspresennien*: Bhe kas stesmu wirdan druwe tans turri kan stai billē bhe kāigi
stai kaltzā *Isspresennien* Etwerpsennien stēisai Grīkan (49); Und wer denselbigen

Wortten gleubet der hat was sie sagen und wie sie lauten *Nemlich* Vergebung der Sünden (48).

6. *kērmeneniskan*: Pastauton bhe *kērmeneniskan* sien pogattawint ast aina kanxta iswinadu kanxtinsna (49); Fasten und *Leiblich* sich bereyten ist wol eine feine eusserliche zucht (48).

7. (a) *kittawidin*: bhe kai stesmu ni massi *kittawidin* pogalbton boūt ter kai tans prastan Crixtisnan is Deiwan naunagimton (71); unnd das jhm nicht *anders* geholffen werden möge denn das es durch die Tauffe auss Gott Newgeboren (70).

(b) *kittewidiskai*: Stas Wissemusīngis Tāws noūson Rikijas Jesu Christi kas tien N. *kittewidiskai* prastan undan bhe stan Swintan Noseilien gemmans (79); Der Allmechtig Gott unnd Vater unsers Herrn Jesu Christi der dich N. *anderweit* durchs Wasser und den heiligen Geist geborn (78).

(c) *kittewidei*: Kas adder *kittewidei* mukinna bhe giwa (35); Wer aber *anders* lehret und lebet (34).

8. (a) *labban*: kai tebbe *labban* ēit (25); (no translation).

(b) *labban*: Kai tebbei *labban* ēit (59); Das dirs *wol*-gehe (58).

(c) *labbai*: Deiwas rīks pereit *labbai* essetennan subbai ir bhe noūson madlan (35); Gottes Reich kombt *wol* on unser Gebet von jhm selbs (34).

(d) *labbai*: Deiwas labbīngs etnīwings quāits audāst sien *labbai* schlāit noūsen madlan (35); Gottes guter gnediger Wille geschicht *wol* ohn unser Gebet (34).

(e) *labbai*: beggi mes deininisku tūlan grīkimai bhe *labbai* wissaweidin sūndan per schlūsimai (37); Denn wir teglich viel sündigen unnd *wol* eitel straff verdienen (36).

(f) *labbai*: (kawids ni *labbai* musīngin massi bouton) (47); (welches doch nicht *wol* solt möglich sein) (46).

(g) *labbai*: adder enkaitītai ast stans wīrst ans Klausīwings *labbai* waist sen toūls bilijsnans prei glandint (47); und angefochten sind die wird ein Beichtvater *wol* wissen mit mehr Sprüchen zu trösten (46).

(h) *labbai*: Adder stas ast tickars wertīngs bhe *labbai* pogattawints (49); Aber der ist recht wirdig und *wol* geschickt (48).

(i) *labbai*: kas swaiāsmu supsei buttan *labbai* perstallē (55); der seinem eigen Hause *wol* fürstehe (54).

(j) *labbai*: Stans Uraisans quai *labbai* perstalle (55); Die Eltesten die *wol* fürstehen (54).

(k) *labbai*: Tīt wīrst *labbai* stalliuns enstan buttan (61); So wird es *wol* im hause ston (60).

9. *mijlan*: Schlāit stans en smūnin lāikumai bhe stēimans schlūsimai poklusmai *mijlan* bhe teisīngi lāikumai (25); Sondern sie in Ehren halten und jhn dienen gehorsam sein und alle *lieb* und trew erzeygen (24).

10. *muisieson*: Kadden adder ains sien ni aupallai tīt pobrendints sen stawīdsmu adder *muisieson* grīkans (45); Wenn aber jemandt sich nicht befindet beschweret mit solcher oder *grössern* sünden (44).

11. *nitickran*: quei as *nitickran* seggīuns asmai (53); wo ich *unrecht* gethan habe (52).

12. *poklusmingiskan*: Mes madlimai tien gantzei *poklusmingiskan* (81); Wir bitten dich gantz *gehorsamlich* (80).

13. *postippan*: Waisse tu adder *postippan* niainan (47); Weyssestu aber *gar* keine (46).

14. (a) *skijstan*: Quei stas wirds Deiwas kaltzīwingiskai bhe *skijstan* mukints wīrst (35); Wo das Wort Gottes lauter unnd *rein* gelert wirdt (34).

(b) *skīstai*: mes tennēiwillen son paggan *skīstai* bhe teisingi giwammai (25); wir umb seinen willen *keusch* und züchtig leben (24).

15. *tūlan*: mes deininisku *tūlan* grīkimai (37); wir teglich *viel* sündigen (36).

16. (a) *ukalāngewingiskān*: Kaigi ains Butta staws stansubban swaiāsmu seimīnan *ukalāngewingiskān* preilaikūt turri (47); Wie ein Haussvatter dasselbige seinem Gesinde *einfeltigklich* fürhalten soll (46).

(b) *uckalāngwingiskai*: kāigi ains butte tawas stansubban swaiāsmu seimīnan no *uckalāngwingiskai* prei laikūt turri (29); Wie ein Haussvater denselbigen seinem Gesinde auff das *einfeltigest* fürhalten solle (28).

(c) *ucka lāngiwingiskai*: kāigi ains Butta Tawas stan subban swaiāsmu Seiminan *ucka lāngiwingiskai* preilaikūt turri (33); Wie ein Haussvater dasselbige seinem Gesinde *auffs einfeltigst* fürhalten solle (32).

(d) *uckcelāngewingiskai*: kāigi stan subban ains Buttantāws swaiāsmu seimijnan *uckcelāngewingiskai* turri preilaikūt (39); Wie dasselbige ein Haussvater seinem Gesinde sol *einfeltiglich* fürhalten (38).

The first example illustrates that in principle the German word can be placed directly below the Old Prussian word which it translates. In general, this is true for all the above examples.

On the basis of these examples and throughout the entire Enchiridion, it can be assumed that Abel Will based the syntax of Old Prussian on that of German. It is most probable that when making his translation, Abel Will used an unreliable method, for in almost no two languages is the syntax exactly identical throughout. Working side by side with his Old Prussian informant, Abel Will probably asked him the translation of each word.[10] As a result of this word-for-word translation, there was probably some confusion on the part of his Old Prussian informant. As is evident from the examples cited, in each instance the word form in German, if considered separately, could be either an adverb or an adjective. The use depends on the context and is determined by its function in the sentence. Since Will used a word-for-word translation, and since all of the German words cited can function either as adverbs or adjectives, it is reasonable to assume that his Old Prussian informant was uncertain as to the use of these forms. Since the -*n* forms correspond well to the accusative case of the adjectives, I assume that the Old Prussian informant, confused in some instances, used the adjective in the accusative case, Nesselmann's *kein anderes Mittel.*[11] It is important to note that if Catechisms I and II were translated in a similar manner, then the occurrence of -*n* as an adverb must be an error made by Will's Old Prussian informant, for no adverbs of manner in -*n* appear in Catechisms I and II, whereas the -*ai* forms are well attested in all three Catechisms.

The -*ai* forms occur more frequently, for there are 106 of them versus 17 in -*n*. These 17, cited in the examples, appear in 16 words; each word has one occurrence, but *labbas* has two. Six of the sixteen words cited occur in both the -*ai* and -*n* forms; in all instances the -*ai* form is predominant. Those that have occurrences in -*n* and not -*ai* occur as adverbs only once in the text. Since the *-ai* forms occur more frequently than those in *-n*, and since *-n* occurs only in the Enchiridion, it is most probable that *-n* is a mistake for the well-attested *-ai* form.

In all three Catechisms, nine of these sixteen words show well-attested accusative case forms in *-n* which correspond well to Trautmann's adverbial form in *-n*. The accusative case is used more frequently in all instances, but particularly in those words that have no occurrence of *-ai*. This, together with the predominant use of the accusative case, is perhaps the best evidence for regarding the *-n* forms of the adverbs as accusatives, for each of these forms is used only once as an adverb in *-n*, but, for example, *mijlan* occurs seven and *nitickran* four times as an accusative.

According to Trautmann, the adverb in *-an* < IE *-om* corresponds to OCS *malo, dobro,* Latin *multum, primum,* and Skt. *citrám.*[12] Old Prussian *-an* should be represented by final *-ъ* in Slavic, if it is assumed that Pre-Slavic **-on* > *-ъ*. The only way *-an* could possibly be related to Slavic *-o* is if *-on* > *-o* as a result of the action of the law of open syllables.[13]

The *-o* of the Slavic adverb is commonly related to its corresponding short form neuter adjective in *-o* and the neuter adjective in *-a* in Baltic. Thus one may say that the Lithuanian neuter adjective *gēra* is related to Slavic *malo.* However, if one assumes that the *-o* of *malo* has its origin in *-om* and is related to *-an* in Old Prussian, as Trautmann does,[14] then the only way *malo* could be related to *gēra* is if the *-a* of *gēra* came from a nasal. But this does not seem to be the case, for in Lithuanian we should then have **-ą* and not *-a*.

In conclusion, it seems reasonable to discount 16 words in a poorly translated sixteenth-century document as the evidence for the establishment of a Common Baltic morphological category—in this case the category of adverbs of manner in *-n.*

Ohio State University

NOTES

1. R. Trautmann, *Die altpreussischen Sprachdenkmäler* (Göttingen, 1910), p. 250.
2. J. Endzelīns, *Altpreussische Grammatik* (Rīga, 1944), p. 138.
3. Trautmann, *op. cit.* p. 249.
4. W. Schmalstieg, "The Phonemes of the Old Prussian Enchiridion," *Word* XX (1964), p. 212.
5. Trautmann, *op. cit.* p. 249.
6. Schmalstieg, *op. cit.* pp. 217–218.

7. Trautmann, *op. cit.* p. 250.

8. *Ibid.*

9. Trautmann, *op. cit.* pp. 206–207.

10. O. Shopay and W. Schmalstieg, "Old Prussian *labban* 'well' and 'good'?" *General Linguistics* VI (1966), p. 73.

11. Trautmann, *op. cit.* p. 207.

12. Trautmann, *op. cit.* pp. 249–250.

13. W. Schmalstieg, "Slavic *o-* and *ā-* Stem Accusatives," *Word* XXI (1965), pp. 238–243.

14. Trautmann, *op. cit.* p. 16.

REMARKS ON BALTIC VERB INFLEXION

CALVERT WATKINS

The following remarks are taken from the Balto-Slavic chapter of my forthcoming book, *Geschichte der indogermanischen Verbalflexion*, which forms part one of volume three of the *Indogermanische Grammatik*, currently being prepared by Professors Kuryłowicz, Cowgill, Ivanov, and myself. As such, these remarks will necessarily contain much that must be predicated on results (dealing with other languages) demonstrated elsewhere, which must here be taken more or less on faith; for this I beg the readers' indulgence.

1. The history of the personal endings in the Baltic languages has been treated *in extenso* by Stang, in his fundamental *Vergleichende Grammatik der baltischen Sprachen*, (pp. 405–421). The immediate prototypes of the Letto-Lithuanian endings, in principle appearing as such before the enclitic reflexive particle -*s(i)*, are:

	thematic		athematic
1st sg.	-*uo*		-*mie*
2nd sg.	-*ie*		-*sie*
3rd p.	(-*a*)		-*ti*
1st du.		(-*a*)-*vā*	
2nd. du.		(-*a*)-*tā*	
1st pl.		(-*a*)-*mē̄*	
2nd pl.		(-*a*)-*tē̄*	

In the absence of the reflexive particle the finals in long vowel are shortened, whence Li. *nešù*, *nešì*, OLi. *duomi*, *duosi*. As everywhere in

Baltic, the third person shows the same form in all numbers. Synchronically stated, the 3rd p. *-a* is the thematic vowel; the ending proper is zero.

2. Old Prussian shows somewhat less clear forms, given the ambiguities inherent in the transmission of this language. We have

thematic	athematic
(-*a*)	-*mai*
(-*a*) (-*si*)	-*sei, -sai, -se*
(-*a*) ~ (-*a*)-*ts*	-*t* ~ -*ti-ts*
-*mai*	
-*ti, -tei, -tai*	

Optional *-ts* in the 3rd p. forms, which are archaisms in the Old Prussian tradition (Stang, 1966: 410), is an enclitic pronoun nom. sg. masc., Balt. **tas.* Such forms reflect an old Indo-European syntactic feature, directly comparable to OHitt. verbal *aki-aš* 'he dies,' *ešzi-at* 'it is,' *pait-aš* 'he went,' nominal *ekunaš-aš* 'he [is] cold.' Similar structures are found in Celtic and Tocharian, and I may add, following Fortunatov, Slavic as well *(veze+t ъ)*.

There is an apparent tendency in Old Prussian to generalize the 3rd p. for all persons of the singular; cf. *as druwē* 'I believe,' 2nd sg. *druwē tu* beside *druwēse tu,* 3rd sg. *druwē,* from the productive *-ēja-* type. Here *-se* in the 2nd sg. has probably been secondarily affixed. W. P. Schmid, (1963: 4 ff), suggests that the commonly accepted explanation of the Old Prussian singular as showing a 3rd sg. form generalized for all persons is incorrect, and that the three persons fell together by regular phonological development. Thus 1st sg. *-a* < **-ō.* Stang formerly took *krixtia* 'I baptize' as a genuine reflex of 1st sg. **-iō* (1963: 176, 225 n.2), but neither this view nor that of Schmid is noted in *Vergleichende Grammatik.* Vaillant (1966: 3.8) likewise assumes 1st sg. **-ō* > OP *-a.* While possible in the 1st sg., it remains necessary to assume that thematic 2nd sg. *giwassi* has been built on 3rd sg. *giwa*; it cannot show the 2nd sg. **-i,* which Schmid assumes for Old Prussian. For this reason I am inclined to take the traditional view that the singular forms are all basically 3rd sg. forms. But that OP *a* is the regular reflex of IE and Balt. *ō seems clear from the equation OCS *dastъ*: OLi. *duosti*: OP *dast,* despite Stang (1966).

3. Of the athematic endings, 3rd sg. *-t(i)* of Letto-Lithuanian and Old Prussian clearly maintains the Indo-European primary athematic ending **-ti.*

Athematic 1st sg. Letto-Li. -*mie* corresponds to OP -*mai,* and doubtless reflects Balt. *-*mai*; for the phonology cf. Stang (1966: 52–68). This ending is an independent creation paralleling that of Gk. -*mai* and Toch. B -*mai*; it represents a contamination of the old perfect ending 1st sg. *-*ai* (cf. OCS *věd-ě*) with the old athematic 1st sg. *-*mi* (cf. OCS *da-mъ*). As Stang points out (1966: 315 and 406), this view of Endzelīn's is confirmed by the fact that a large percentage of the old Lithuanian athematic verbs are stative-intransitives going back to Balto-Slavic and Indo-European perfects.

For Letto-Li. 2nd sg. -*sie* Old Prussian shows both -*sai* and -*sei* (-*se,* -*si*). Parallelism would induce us a priori to assume a Balt. *-*sai* like *-*mai,* built on the old athematic 2nd sg. *-*si* with the final -*ai*; or even conceivably a crossing of *- *i* and the *-*tai* in Lat. -*is-tī.* Stang prefers to suppose Balt. -*sei,* but the Old Prussian variant -*sei* can show the combined influence of the 3rd sg. final -*ei* and the 2nd pl. -*tei* beside 1st pl. -*mai.*

Both East and West Baltic have innovated in the form of the 1st and 2nd pl. Letto-Li. -*mē,* -*tē* have a long vowel in the reflexive after 1st and 2nd sg., cf. Kuryłowicz, 1952: 208. The assumption of an original short vowel is further confirmed by the frequent dialectal and colloquial literary Lithuanian loss of the final vowel, giving endings -*m* -*t.* In the first plural both Lithuanian and Latvian dialects show also forms with back vowel: Li. -*ma,* refl. -*mo-si,* Latv. -*ma,*-*mā-s.* Allowing for the secondary character of the long vowel, these forms permit us to postulate basic endings -*ma* < *-*mo,* -*te,* which agree not only with cognate languages like Celtic *-*mo,* *-*te,* but with Old Prussian -*mai,* -*tei* as well. The latter have affixed an -*i* to the original final (cf. Stang, 1966: 417), which assimilated them to other members of the paradigm. Li. *-*me* may either reflect an inherited apophonic doublet of *-*mo,* like Gk. -*me(n),* or imitate the 2nd pl.

4. In the thematic type, 1st sg. -*uo* goes back to IE -*ō,* as in Gk., Lat. -*ō.* This ending itself is a contraction of earlier *-*o-ǫo,* with the "thematic vowel" -*o-* followed by the *-*ǫo* underlying the 1st sg. perfect ending, Gk. -*a.*

5. For the thematic 2nd sg. -*ie* Stang (1966: 407) (cf. Stang, 1956: 1. 137ff.) makes the important observation that the oldest Lithuanian form is -*ai,* preserved in archaic forms with a fused reflexive particle like 2nd sg. *mekstai-si* beside 1st sg. *mekstuo-siu, rupinai-s* beside *rupinuo-siu.* It is thus this -*ai* which is metathesized to -*ie-s,* -*i.* On the origin of this ending see below. I can find no motivation for Schmalstieg's derivation of this ending (as -*i* abstracted from athematic -*si*) in *Lingua* (1961: 10. 372–373).

6. In the thematic 3rd sg. East and West Baltic agree in the basic ending *-a*. Beside the normal endings of OP *giwa* 'lives,' *waidinna* 'they show' archaic *imma-ts* 'took' (present in form, the preterite in *ymm(a)i-ts)*, we have occasional forms in *-ai, -e(i)*: *powaidinne(i)* 'means,' *eb-immai* 'grasps.' These forms are best taken with Stang as originally proper to presents in 3rd sg. *-ǎ̄ja* (and *-inǎ̄ja), -ḗja*, with apocope to *-ǎi, -ĕi* (> *-ĕ̌*). But they have clearly spread beyond their original bounds.

The ending *-a* has almost universally been assumed to show the Indo-European thematic vowel, followed by the secondary 3rd sg. ending *-t*: a pre-Baltic *-at*. The form does not agree with any cognate language; it is presumed to be derived from *-et* via the generalization of the Baltic vowel *-a-* < *-o-* everywhere in the thematic paradigm (cf. Stang, 1966: 407).

Yet it is not sufficient to say merely that the *o*-variant of the thematic vowels was generalized. We know the critical position in the paradigm of the 3rd sg., and expect a priori that if a generalization does take place, it will be in favor of the variant found in the 3rd sg., i.e. *e* rather than *o*. This is the case in all the instances known to me of such a generalization in Indo-European languages: the vowel is *e*. Compare Armenian *beremkʻ* after *berē*, Slavic *vezemъ* after *vezetъ*, Hittite *daškiwani* after *daškizzi*. I may add that Gothic 2nd and 3rd sg. middle *-aza, -ada* have not generalized the *o*-grade beside Gk. *-e[s]o -eto*; they are built on an inherited 3rd sg. middle *-a* of Pre-Germanic, equatable with Hitt. 3rd sg. mid. *-a* < IE *-o*. Thus *-aza*←3rd sg. *-a* + *-za*. The renewal of the ending in Germanic, *-a* →*ada*, is directly comparable to that of Hittite *-a* → *-atta* and Vedic *-a[t]* → *-ata*, and it is doubtless in the light of this morphological transformation that the traditional phonological irregularity of the final vowel of Germanic *-da* < IE *-to* is to be explained.

Schmalstieg's explanation of the generalization of *-a-* as a consequence of the neutralization of the *e:a* opposition after palatalized consonants (1964: 20.35–39; 1966: 7.57) remains hypothetical because of the question of the chronology of palatalization in Balto-Slavic, the divergent results in Baltic and Slavic, and the unmotivated generalization from the yod-presents.

Lithuanian *vēža* after *vēžame* is thus somewhat odder than traditionally assumed. We must rather take 3rd sg. *vēža* as the basic member of the paradigm, and its ending *-a* original. The 2nd pl. *vēžate* after *vēža* is entirely regular, and in complete accord with both our general notions of paradigmatic change, and with attested changes in Baltic: OP 1st pl. *giwammai lāikumai turrimai* after 3rd p. *giwa lāiku turri*, (cf. Endzelīns, 1944: §222). The problem is to explain the *-a* of *vēža* as an old form.

7. It can be shown that the (West) Tocharian thematic paradigm *ākau āśt(o) āśäm* goes back to a basic set of endings *-ō *-eta *-e*, from earlier *-o-ə̯o *-e-tə̯o *-e*. The endings proper *-ə̯o *-tə̯o zero* are added to the thematic vowel in the *e*-grade; the change *e* > *o* before ə₂ is an automatic IE phonological rule.

In the Hittite thematic mediopassive and *ḫi*-conjugation, the basic endings are *-aḫḫa -atta -a.* They go back to an *-o-ə̯o -o-tə̯o -o,* and are thus formed exactly like the Tocharian endings, save that the thematic vowel has the *o*-grade.

Beside this type of paradigm, it can be shown that there existed a thematic paradigm with *zero*-ending also in the 2nd sg. The basic form was *-o-ə̯o *-e *-e*; with the generalization of *-i* in the 2nd sg. (by polarization), we have the thematic paradigm *-ō -ei -e* underlying that of Greek, Celtic, and Slavic.

The pattern that emerges is clear; and there is a set missing:

$$
\begin{array}{ll}
\text{-}o\text{ə̯}o & \text{-}o\text{ə̯}o \\
\text{-}et\text{ə}o & \text{-}ot\text{ə}o \\
\text{-}e & \text{-}o
\end{array}
$$

$$
\begin{array}{l}
\text{-}o\text{ə̯}o \\
\text{-}e(i) \\
\text{-}e
\end{array}
$$

I suggest the missing set is specifically

$$
\begin{array}{l}
\text{-}o\text{ə}o \\
\text{-}o(i) \\
\text{-}o,
\end{array}
$$

and that this paradigm is the direct antecedent of the oldest Baltic thematic present, as established by Stang:

$$
\begin{array}{ll}
\text{-}\bar{o} & \textit{neš-úo(-s)} \\
\text{-}ai & \textit{neš-ie(-s)} \\
\text{-}a & \textit{nēš-a(-s)}
\end{array}
$$

The postulated thematic 3rd sg. *-o,* i.e., the *o*-grade vowel and *zero* ending, is not isolated in Indo-European languages. Not only is it attested (in the middle function) in the Hittite type 3rd sg. *ney-a* (cf. Skt. *nayati, nayate*),

it is significantly found in Greek as well, and in the active function, in the
-o of the archaic compositional type Hom. *phugo-ptólemos, hamarto-wepês,*
the apophonic counterpart of *arkhê-kakos.*

The preservation of both apophonic forms of the ending, **-e(i) ~ *-o(i),*
in the single dialect area of Balto-Slavic, is perfectly in line with the
preservation of both in Greek, *arkhe- ~ phugo-.* Compare also 3rd pl.
*-ent in *ēen* but **-ont* in Aeol. *eon.* Hitt. 2nd sg. ipv. *-ški < *-ske* but *-iya,*
mid. *-iya-hḥuti < *-io;* and in the nominal system, OLat. gen. sg. *nominus
~ nominis < *-os ~ *-es.*

It will be noted that this reconstruction of the Baltic thematic paradigm
is in complete accord with the theoretical views, if not the details of the
reconstruction, of V. N. Toporov in his important contribution "*K voprosu
ob èvolucii slav. i balt. glagola*" [1961: 5, 35–70 (dated 1957) cf. especially
pp. 59–63 on the Baltic inflexion]. Toporov reconstructs a set of endings
-ō -(ē)i -zero, which is as it were "athematic thematic," since the thematic
vowel is incorporated in the 1st and 2nd sg. It was Stang who made
possible the correct restoration of the 2nd sg. (Balt. *-ai*), which permits its
integration into a symmetrical structure *-ō -ai -a* exactly paralleling *-ō -ei -e.*

Harvard University

REFERENCES

Endzelīns, J. 1944. *Altpreussiche Grammatik.* Latvju Grāmata, Riga.
Kuryłowicz, Jerzy 1958. L'accentuation des langues indo-européennes[2] (Polska
     Akademia Nauk. Komitet Językoznawczy 17) Wrocław-Kraków.
Schmalstieg, William. 1961. "Primitive East Baltic **-uo-, *-ie-* and the 2nd Sg.
     Ending," *Lingua* 10, pp. 369–374.
Schmalstieg, William. 1964, "A Balto-Slavic structural parallelism," *Word* 20, pp. 35–
     39.
Schmalstieg, William. 1966. "Neutralization of /a/ and /e/ in Hittite and Baltic,"
     Annali Istituto Orientale di Napoli, Sezione Linguistica, p. 57.
Schmid, Wolfgang P. 1963. *Studien zum baltischen und indogermanischen Verbum.*
     Harrassowitz, Wiesbaden.
Stang, Christian S. 1942. *Das slavische und baltische Verbum* (Skrifter utgitt av Det
     Norske Videnskaps-Akademi i Oslo II. Hist.-Filos. Klasse. No. 1) Oslo.
Stang, Christian S. 1956. "Ein Beitrag zum Problem vom Diphthong *ie* im
     Litauischen," *Die Welt der Slaven* 1, pp. 136–139.
Stang, Christian S. 1966, *Vergleichende Grammatik der baltischen Sprachen.*
     Universitetsforlaget, Oslo.
Toporov, V. N. 1961. "K voprosu ob èvolucii slavjanskogo i baltijskogo glagola,"
     Voprosy Slavjanskogo Jazykoznanija No. 5, pp. 35–70.
Vaillant, André 1966. *Grammaire comparée des langues slaves* Tome 3, Le verbe,
     Klincksieck, Paris.

BASE SHAPES OF LATVIAN MORPHEMES

VALDIS J. ZEPS

In postulating base shapes, one typically tries to arrive at a morphophonemic formulation that will provide maximum uniformity in, at least, stems, e.g., the forms *tin* 'he winds' and *tît* 'to wind' can safely be reconstituted to *ˆtin + a and *ˆtin + ti, in each case showing the same underlying stem shape *ˆtin. The phonetic *tin* and *tît* are subsequently developed from underlying representations by the application of morphophonemic rules.[1] Only in cases of clear suppletion, e.g., *eju* 'I go' and *gāju* 'I went,' no effort need be made to find an underlying unity to all surface manifestations. Typically, allomorphs such as dæg-, dæk-, deg-, dek- and dedz- of the verb for 'to burn,' as in *dæg, dekšu, dæktu, degu,* and *dedz,* are all derived by morphophonemic rules from an underlying *dæg.

The allomorphs of *dæg, just listed, belong to a single paradigm. If one attempts to extend the principle of maximum uniformity to all stems of a derivational complex, morphophonemics rapidly assumes the appearance of etymology:

Root *ˆsk-1-
šķeļ 'he splits,' full-grade vocalism, *j*-theme, *a*-present, ϕ-person
šķila 'split long,' zero-grade front vocalism, *aa*-theme, ϕ-case
skals 'taper, splint,' full grade back vocalism, *a*-theme, *s*-case
skaîda 'he chops,' full-grade back vocalism, *d*-iterative, *i*-theme, *aa*-present,
    ϕ-person.

It should be pointed out that the above analysis is meant to be synchronic. There are historically related stems that can no longer be analyzed in terms of each other, e.g., *sêdêt* 'to sit,' *suôdrēji* 'soot,' and *lizda* 'nest.' On the other hand, there are synchronic relationships that cannot be supported by straight-line etymologies, e.g.:

Root *`sk̦-nb-

šk̦iebj 'he tilts,' full-grade front vocalism, *j*-theme, *a*-present, ϕ-person.

šk̦ùoba 'he distorts,' full-grade back vocalism, *i*-theme, *aa*-present, ϕ-person

šk̦ibs 'crooked,' zero-grade front vocalism, *a*-theme, *s*-case

The postulated *`sk̦-nb- cannot be historically justified (there is no historical *k̦*, nor does an *n* belong here, cf. German *schief*).

I am not prepared to argue that a componential analysis of the degree just illustrated is now feasible. In fact, for purposes of individual paradigms, more complete lexical shapes, of the order *^skæl-i-, *skil-aa-, *skal-a-, *^skald-ī-, etc., are quite satisfactory. The factoring out of *^sk-l- is a near-etymological enterprise and need not be undertaken in an exposition of synchronic inflectional morphology. At the same time, there is no reason to adopt base shapes that will make synchronic etymology (if there is such) difficult.

Several principles can be formulated to help select the shape of a stem with both inflectional and derivational ends in view.

a. Given representations which are equally functional and equally marked in the individual segments, but where one representation is further removed from the phonetic surface than the other, the representation closer to the phonetic surface is to be preferred: *riēpa* 'tire' can be represented as either *r̄ænp- or *r̄æip-; other things being equal, the latter shape is preferable.

b. Given representations which are equally functional, but which differ in the degree of markedness of individual segments, the less marked representation is to be preferred.[2] In the case of *škeĩt*, both *^šk̦æl-i- and *^skæl-i- will lead to the correct surface forms, but *š* and *k̦* are phonologically more complex than *s* and *k*, and the latter are to be preferred.

c. Given competing base shapes, the one that agrees with derivationally related forms is to be preferred. Thus, in the case of *šk̦iebt*, the base shapes * skæib-, *` skænb-, *` sk̦ænb-, *` sk̦æib-, are all possible. Previous considerations would lead one to prefer *` skæib- (less phonologically complex than either of the forms with *k̦* and closer to the phonetic surface than *` skænb-). For the related *sk̦ùobît*, however, *` sk̦anb- is the only base shape available. Accordingly, *` sk̦ænb- should serve as the base shape for *šk̦iebt*.

Similarly, the form *mežs* 'forest' could have either *mædi + a or *mæzi + a as its underlying stem. Principle (a) would suggest the latter; the existence of a related *medît* 'to hunt, however, decides the selection in favor of the form with a *d*.

For some forms, no viable base shape can be constructed; typically, these are late loans, e.g., *kinō* 'cinema' (with no *k/c* change), but some are clearly native (or early dialect loans), e.g., *bèigas* 'end' (with no *æi/ie* metathesis). Some method of handling such forms is, of course, necessary; a number of mechanisms have been proposed in the past, such as negative marking ("no *k/c* rule"); none have proved quite satisfactory. For the purposes of this paper, I have adopted the term "inert" to cover such instances of negative marking, e.g., *kinō* (*k* inert), read "*k* in *kinō* is not subject to regular morphophonemic changes, specifically the *k/c*-rule."

The remainder of the paper consists of a list of base shapes for a substantial portion of Latvian primary verbs.[3] There are five subclasses to the list; this paper interrupts the list in the middle of the fourth subclass, for reasons of space.

1. FIRST SUBCLASS.

The first subclass subsumes verbs with no inherited ablaut and no mutations of stem-final dentals and velars to palatals and *c/dz*, respectively (except, in the case of the velars, the second person singular present). The verbs are listed in their third person singular present and past forms, and in the infinitive, and are preceded by a starred stem

OBSTRUENT STEMS.

*kæp-, cæp, cepa, cept 'fry, bake'
*mæt-, mæt, meta, mest 'throw'
*sit-, sit, sita, sist 'beat'
*væd-, væd, veda, vest 'lead, carry'
*ˆǣd-, æ̂d, ê̄da, ê̄st 'eat'
*næs-, næs, nesa, nest 'carry, bring'
*ˆsāk-, sâk, sâka, sâkt 'to begin'
*ˆbǣg-, bæ̂g, bêga, bêgt 'to flee'
*ˆaug-, aûg, aûga, aûgt 'grow'
*dæg-, dæg, dega, degt v.i. 'to burn, be on fire'

One additional obstruent stem is usually adduced here, namely *nāk, nāca, nākt* 'to come.' The difficulty here is the *k/c* mutation in the past and the absence of a comparable mutation in the present. One way of thinking about this verb is to say that its past tense belongs to the fourth subclass.

SONORANT STEMS.

The following *n*-stems, all with an *i*-vocalism, are usually adduced here:
*m̄in-, min, mina, mīt 'to tread'
*ˆpin-, pin, pina, pît 'to plait'
*s̄kin-, šķin, šķina, šķît 'to pick legumes'

*^tin-, tin, tina, tît 'to wind'
*⁻trin-, trin, trina, trît 'to rub'

One *m*-stem, usually adduced here, ŋæm, ŋēma, ŋem̂t 'to take' has a long vowel in the past tense; such lengthening is typical of the fourth subclass. A further peculiarity of this verb is the accent switch from ⁻to ^ in the future; this constitutes the sole instance of accentual alternation in a stem in all Latvian morphology.

Stems with the infinitives *ar̂t* 'to plough,' *malt* 'to grind,' and *kalt* 'to forge' are usually classed with the fourth subclass on the basis of their present tense forms; on the basis of their other forms, they could be considered here as well.

VOWEL STEMS.

A number of stems in *æi* and *ii* are usually adduced here. There are, however, some real difficulties in their classification; they will not be discussed here.

2. SECOND SUBCLASS.

The second subclass subsumes verbs with an inherited e/φ ablaut. In all cases, the *e* of the stem must be followed by a sonorant and may, in turn, be followed by an obstruent.

*` kærp-, cæ̀rp, cir̃pa, cir̃pt 'to shear'
*` kært-, cæ̀rt, cir̃ta, cir̃st 'to hack, chop, hew, fell'
*` gæn-, dzæn, dzina, dzìt 'to drive'
*` kræmt-, kræm̂t, krim̃ta, krim̂st 'to gnaw'
*` pærk-, pæ̀rk, pir̃ka, pir̃kt 'to buy'
*` vælk-, væ̀lk, vilka, vilkt 'to pull, draw'
*` tælp-, tæ̀lp, tilpa, tilpt 'to fit into'; more commonly, this verb is encountered with the suffix *st*, which automatically requires a zero grade present: *tìlpst*.

One still sees listed in grammars *` gæm- 'to be born,' and \*` dæl- 'to wane.' Both are obsolete as second subclass verbs, and are used in the fifth subclass only.

The verb *^vær+d- (vær̂du, vira, vir̂t) 'to boil, seethe' has an additional   present tense suffix *d*.

The verb *` lænd+n- (lìen ⟨ ` lænd+n+a, lída ⟨ ` lind+aa, lìst) 'to crawl' has an extra *n* present suffix, and exhibits the *n/i* change in all forms, and in the present, metathesis as well. Note well that the postvocalic *n* cannot be considered an infix, insofar it is needed to account for the length of the forms with an *i* vocalism.

A number of other verbs (*snigt* 'to snow,' etc.) are usually listed here, for historical reasons. They will be discussed in conjunction with the third subclass.

The length in the presents of *` kærp-, \*` kært-, and *` pærk- is regulated by a late rule affecting only low vowels before an *r*.

3. THIRD SUBCLASS.

Most of the verbs of this subclass can be characterized as having a Baltic *n*-infix; a number of other verbs need to be discussed here as well.

The second person singular present of verbs ending in labials or dentals is actualized with a final -*i*. All have falling pitch.

*` kri+n+t-, krìt, krita, krist 'to fall'
*` li+n+p-, lìp, lipa, lipt 'to stick, adhere'
*` ni+n+k-, apnìk, apnika, apnikt 'to become tiresome (to)'
*` mi+n+t-, mìt, mita, mist 'to dwell'
*` ti+n+k-, patìk, patika, patikt 'to be pleasing (to)'
*` iu+n+t-, jùt, juta, just 'to feel'
*` klu+n+p-, klùp, klupa, klupt 'to stumble,'
*` bru+n+k-, brùk, bruka, brukt 'to collapse'

*ˋ dru+n+p-, drùp, drupa, drupt 'to crumble'
*ˋ mu+n+k-, mùk, muka, mukt 'to flee, scamper away'
*ˋ plu+n+k-, plùk, pluka, plukt 'to run (said of color), to fade'
*ˋ ru+n+k-, rùk, ruka, rukt 'to shrivel'
*ˋ spru+n+k-, sprùk, spruka, sprukt 'to get away'
*ˋ su+n+t-, sùt, suta, sust 'to swelter, steam'
*ˋ zu+n+d-, zùd, zuda, zust 'to get lost'
*ˋ pra+n+t-, pruòt, prata, prast 'to know how'
*ˋ ta+n+p-, tuòp, tapa, tapt 'to become'
*ˋ la+n+k-, luòk, laka, lakt 'to lap (drink with one's tongue)'
*ˋ ra+n+d-, ruòd, rada, rast 'to find'
*ˋ ra+n+k-, ruòk, raka, rakt 'to dig'
*ˋ sma+n+k-, smuòk, smaka, smakt 'to suffocate'
*ˋ za+n+g-, zuòg, zaga, zagt 'to steal'

The above verbs have an *-i-*, *-u-*, or *-a-* vocalism; verbs with an *-e-* vocalism raise some problems, largely of a historical nature (most of them are supposed to reflect an older *ei/i* alternation, and are, in traditional grammars, treated as belonging to the second subclass.)

*ˋ bræ+n+d-, brièn, brida, brist 'to wade'
*ˋ tæ+n+k-, tièk, tika, tikt 'to happen, get'

To be noted is the *æ/i* alternation in the stem vocalism, strongly reminiscent of the alternation in *ˋ gæn-, dzæn/dzina; this alternation presents a slight descriptive problem—one would like to have it be conditioned by the same environment as in gæn-, i.e., have the nasal be part of the definition of the environment in which *æ* is replaced by *i*; this, however, is a difficult point of view to hold if *n* is viewed as a present *infix*; rather one would have to think of *n* being part of the basic form and explain the past as the product of two rules (a) *æ* to *i* in the past, (b) *n* to *ϕ* in the past. There is, however, a counterexample in the form *ˋ lænd+n- (see second subclass), and no general *n*-to-*ϕ*-in-the-past rule is practicable.

In *ˋ bræn+d- and *ˋ tæ+n+k-, the *n*-infix is supposedly historically correct, albeit not strictly speaking proven. There is a whole set of other verbs usually classified under a second subclass that are synchronically indistinguishable from at least *ˋ tæ+n+k-.

These verbs are:
lièk, lika, likt 'to put'
mièg, miga, migt 'to fall asleep'
snièg, sniga, snigt 'to snow'
stièg, stiga, stigt 'to become stuck, bogged down'
šķièt, šķita, šķist 'to seem'

One set of workable base forms for the above are *ˋ læ+n+k-, *ˋ mæ+n+g-, *ˋ snæ+n+g-, *ˋ stæ+n+g-, *ˋ skæ+n+t-; this solution, while attractive for stems as presented, loses appeal upon inspection of putative cognates. Verb by verb, the following complications present themselves.

The verb *mīgt* may be synchronically relatable to *maĩgs* (or *maĩgs*) 'tender, gentle' (? < Liv. *maigāz*, So. Est. *maǵas*), as the sequence *maĩgs mìegs* 'gentle sleep' suggests. In that case, *i* seems to be the best suggestion for the third segment. Whether this *i* should be regarded as an infix, is not clear. A base form like *ˋ mæ+i+g-, with an *æ/i* ablaut and a loss of the infix, is certainly workable; at the same time, one may wish to prefer to treat the *ˋ mæig-/mig- alternation in traditional terms, i.e., as *e*-grade vs. *ϕ*-grade.

As to the other verbs, *stigt* is inseparable from *stàigns* 'mucky, boggy,' suggesting an underlying *ˋ stæig-; *šķist* belongs with *skàitīt* 'to count,' certainly historically, probably synchronically as well, suggesting *ˋ *skæit-*; *likt* is usually connected with *laĩks* 'time,' suggesting *ˋ *læik-*; as to *snigt*, the choice between *ˋ snæ+n+g- and *ˋ snæig- will have to be made on some à priori grounds, e.g., *ˋ snæig- is closer to the phonetic surface.

The above considerations, in effect, provide synchronic reasons to leave *ˋ mæig-, *ˋ stæig-, *ˋ skæit-, *ˋ læik-, and *ˋ snæig- in the second subclass, and to adjust rules accordingly.

Three more verbs are usually cited under subclass three:

*ˋ sæi+n-: sièn, sèja, sièt 'to bind'
*ˋ skræi+(n)-: skrièn *or* skrej, skrèja, skrièt 'to run'
*ˋ slæi+n-: slièn, slèja, slièt 'to lean' v.t.

The difficulty with listing them here is, that in other respects they more resemble verbs in -æi-, of the first subclass (not discussed in this paper.) Further special difficulties are created by the optional present tense *aùn* (usually *aùj*) 'to put on footwear.'

4. FOURTH SUBCLASS

The fourth subclass subsumes verbs with a *j*-present tense suffix, so actualized after labials (*glâbju*), causing mutations in dentals (*plẽšu*) and velars (*braùcu*). The base forms shall be presented as ending in *I*, whereby *I* = [-obst, -cons, -grav] .

  a. STEMS IN *p*:
*ˆkāpI-, kâpj, kâpa, kâpt 'to step, climb'
*ˋ kampI-, kaṁpj, kaṁpa, kaṁpt 'to snap, gulp'
*ˋ kanpI-, kuòpj, kuòpa, kuòpt 'to cultivate, take care of'
*ˆkrāpI-, krâpj, krâpa, krâpt 'to deceive'
*ˋ rāpI-, ràpjas, ràpâs, ràptiês 'to crawl'
*ˋ slæpI-, slèpj, slèpa, slèpt 'to hide'
*ˋ stæipI-, stièpj, stièpa, stièpt 'to stretch'
*ˋ tæipI-, tièpjas, tièpâs, tièptiês 'to insist, to whine'
*ˋ tærpI-, tèrpj, tèrpa, tèrpt 'to dress, adorn' v.t.
*ˋ træipI-, trièpj, trièpa, trièpt 'to daub'
*ˋ uærpI-, vèrpj, vèrpa, vèrpt 'to spin'

  b. STEMS IN *b*.
*ˆglābI-, glâbj, glâba, glâbt 'to save, rescue'
*ˆgrābI-, grâbj, grâba, grâbt 'to grab, rake'
*ˋ ǵærbI-, ǵèrbj, ǵèrba, ǵèrbt 'to dress' v.t.
*ˋ knābI-, knàbj, knàba, knàbt 'to peck'
*ˆknæibI-, kniêbj, kniêba, kniêbt 'to pinch'
*ˆræibI-, riêbj, riêba, riêbt 'to disgust'
*ˋ stræbI- (Pres. stem *stræbI-), strebju, strēbu, strèbt 'to slurp.' A long present can be encountered as well.
*ˋ skænbI-, šķièbj, šķièba, šķièbt 'to tilt, twist, distort' Cf. *šķuobĩt*, its frequentative, based on *ˋ skanb-.
*ˋ urbI, uȑbj, uȑba, uȑbt 'to drill'

  c. STEMS IN *t*.
*ˋ iautI-, jaùš, jaùta, jaùst 'to discern'
*ˋ plætI- or *plætI-, pleš, plèta, plèst *or* pleš, plèta, plest, *or* plèš, plèta, plèst, *or* pleš, pleta, plest 'to spread.' The orthographic norm tends to gravitate toward the short vowel forms, especially in the present and the infinitive, in order to avoid homographs with *plẽš, plèst* 'to tear.' The past tense, where no homographs are

possible (past tense of *plêst* is *plêsa*) tends to stay long; still, in literary Latvian, a short past tense *pleta* is beginning to make some inroads, albeit without any dialect base.

* ˋ pūtI- (or ˋ puutI-? cf. *paùts* 'egg, testicle'), pùš, pùta, pùst 'to blow'
* ˋ skait-, skàisas, skaìtâs, skaìstiês 'to become angry'

Clearly connected with *kaîte* 'flaw, ailment,' but synchronic morphophonemics probably cannot provide for a movable *s-*.

* ˋ uærtI-, vèrš, vèrta, vèrst 'to turn, direct'
* ˋ kæntI- (*n* inert), ceñšas, ceñtâs, ceñstiês 'to strive'
* ˋ kæitI- (to match *skaitI-, above) or * ˋ kæntI- (to match the verb just preceding), ciês, ciêta, cist 'to suffer.'

    d. STEMS IN *d*.

* ˆaudI-, aûž, aûda, aûst 'to weave'
* ˋgaudI-, gaùž, gaùda, gaùst 'to lament, tell one's sad story'
* ˋ glaudI-, glaùž, glaùda, glaùst 'to smooth, pet'
* ˆgrūdI- (or * ˆgruudI-? cf. *graûds* 'grain'), grûž, grûda, grûst 'to push'
* ˆkandI-, kuôž, kuôda, kuôst 'to bite'
* ˆlaidI-, laîž, laîda, laîst 'to let'
* ˆandI-, uôž, uôda, uôst 'to smell' v.t., v.i. (Li. *úosti*)
* ˆpaudI-, paûž, paûda, paûst 'to impart a message, tell'
* ˆsædI-, sêžas, sêdâs, sêstiês 'to sit down' (historically connected with *suôdrēji* 'soot.'

There seems to be little reason to postulate a æ/uo (an) alternation synchronically.

I hope that the above list has been properly illustrative of the relative ease and difficulty with which a list of base shapes can be constructed, given a set of morphophonemic rules, and a set of principles to facilitate decisions in ambiguous cases.

University of Wisconsin

NOTES

1. See M. Halle and V. J. Zeps, "Survey of Latvian Morphophonemics," MIT Res. Lab. of Electronics *Quarterly Progress Report* No. 83 (1966), 105–113.
2. For a recent, still not definitive, discussion of markedness see N. Chomsky and M. Halle, *Sound Pattern of English* (New York; 1968), 400–435.
3. Cf. any traditional grammar, e.g., V. Baltiņa-Bērziņa, *Latviešu valodas gramatika* 3d ed. (Latviešu Apgāds, 1946).